Management Risk

Management Risk

The Bottleneck is at the Top of the Bottle

Dimitris N. Chorafas

First published 2004 by
PALGRAVE MACMILLAN
Houndmills, Basingstoke, Hampshire RG21 6XS and
175 Fifth Avenue, New York, N.Y. 10010
Companies and representatives throughout the world

PALGRAVE MACMILLAN is the global academic imprint of the Palgrave
Macmillan division of St. Martin's Press, LLC and of Palgrave Macmillan Ltd.
Macmillan® is a registered trademark in the United States, United Kingdom
and other countries. Palgrave is a registered trademark in the European
Union and other countries.

ISBN 1–4039–2143–1

This book is printed on paper suitable for recycling and made from fully
managed and sustained forest sources.

A catalogue record for this book is available from the British Library.

Library of Congress Cataloging-in-Publication Data
Chorafas, Dimitris N.
  Management risk: the bottleneck is at the top of the bottle/Dimitris N. Chorafas.
    p. cm.
  Includes bibliographical references and index.
  ISBN 1–4039–2143–1 (cloth)
    1. Risk management – United States. 2. Finance. 3. Business ethics – United States.
  4. Executives – United States – Conduct of life. 5. Risk management – Europe.
  6. Business ethics – Europe. 7. Executives – Europe – Conduct of life. I. Title.
  HD61.C546 2004
  658.15′5–dc21   2003056341

10   9   8   7   6   5   4   3   2   1
13 12 11 10 09 08 07 06 05 04

Printed and bound in Great Britain by
Antony Rowe Ltd, Chippenham and Eastbourne

Contents

List of Figures and Tables

Figures

Tables

Preface

Based on an extensive research project in the US, UK, and continental Europe, this book has been written for both professionals and the academic market, particularly senior-level and graduate studies in Business Administration and Management. In the professional market, the book addresses practitioners in business and industry: manufacturing companies, merchandising firms, commercial banks, securities houses, service companies, and consultancies. It is designed for people interested in the benefits provided by sound management, as well as the avoidance of malpractices which lead to investors being misled by the companies' senior management, financial analysts, and public accountants.

The information resulting from this research will be vital to members of the board, chief executive officers (CEOs), chief operating officers (COOs), financial directors, members of Audit Committees, auditors (both internal and external), and lawyers (corporate and partners of law firms), institutional investors, investment advisors, financial analysts, operations managers, consultants, and regulators.

The text outlines the reasons why *management risk* must be examined within the perspective of each company's business challenges. Research results suggest there is a synergy between shareholder value and business ethics. Senior executives who participated in the research and during the meetings underlined:

- Senior management's accountability not only for financial results but also for *reliable financial reporting*
- The benefits as well as the risks associated with *value differentiation* through novel strategic policies
- The reasons why *honesty is the best policy* at the level of the board, the CEO, and senior management
- The risks associated with *near-sighted management*, skills obsolescence, overcentralization, and dubious deals.

Among the critical questions this book addresses are: What can be learned from Enron, Global Crossing, Tyco International, WorldCom, Allied Irish Banks (AIB), the American International Group (AIG), American Express, Merrill Lynch, J.P. Morgan Chase, and a great number of other companies. Was management skill really lacking, or was it that management attention was absent because the board, the CEO, and senior executives had spread themselves too thin dealing with diverse and uncorrelated issues?

Management risk has many origins, and lack of management attention is a central one. As the complexity of business increases, one of the scarcest commodities becomes the time and attention of senior management. Very few business leaders are able to cope with troubles on many fronts. Globalization, innovation, technology, new sophistication of financial instruments, the flood of information, and the amount of risk being assumed has changed the nature of crisis management. Much more powerful tools – and a new code of ethics – are needed to cope with simultaneous fights on several fronts.

* * *

In practically every Group of Ten (G-10) country, and in many others, in the 2000–3 timeframe, the banking system had to contend not only with a deteriorating overall economic situation but also with a persisting bear market on the stock exchanges and substantial loan losses. This caused credit institutions to set up risk provisions in their balance sheets, while insurance companies found themselves obliged to liquidate equities in their portfolios. Although it cannot be inferred from this situation that banks, insurance firms, and other companies had acute liquidity or solvency problems, financial and industrial firms throughout the G-10 landscape and elsewhere have been confronted with serious profitability issues. The better-managed entities took measures to cut costs and reduce their risk exposure, but few used a really sharp knife to cut the salaries of their senior executives, or significantly reduce their stock options.

Whether in cash or through options, *overpay* is one of the manifestations of management risk. The same is true of any remuneration, beyond a basic salary, not related to performance. Overpay has another major negative – inciting senior management to take inordinate risk, and use a high level of leverage, to get a bigger bonus. France Télécom is a prime example. After privatization, its top brass ran up a debt of Euro 70 billion, outstripping the gross domestic product (GDP) of every African country except Egypt and South Africa. The French taxpayers had to pick up more than half of the bill, since the French government owned 56.5 percent of France Télécom.

Mismanagement is a glaring example of management risk, and so is malfeasance. On February 25, 2003, four former Qwest Communications executives were indicted by a grand jury in Denver, CO, on criminal charges stemming from an alleged accounting fraud that investigators said had improperly boosted the US telecom group's revenues. The Securities and Exchange Commission (SEC) also filed a civil complaint against eight executives at Qwest Communications, claiming that they had manipulated another contract to inflate revenues by $100 million. John Ashcroft, the US Attorney General, characterized the investigation of the telecoms group as "active and on-going," suggesting that additional action might follow.

In the 2001–3 timeframe, with Enron, Global Crossing, Adelphia Communications, WorldCom, Tyco and many other well-known companies either going bankrupt or facing serious legal troubles, the SEC, Department of Justice, and Attorney Generals of several states had their hands full. On April 28, 2003, announcing a settlement with ten major Wall Street firms, William Donaldson, the Chairman of SEC, said that he was profoundly saddened and angry, about the conduct alleged in the SEC complaints, adding that: "There is absolutely no place for it in our markets, and it cannot be tolerated."

Heavy penalties, "disgorgement" of fraudulently acquired profits, and the like, are manifestations of management risk. Nor was the nearly $1.4 billion settlement the end of the worries of banks involved in the malpractice referred to in the preceding paragraph. More red ink may still run as, after having settled with the Attorney General and the regulators, Wall Street firms can now expect plaintiff lawyers to start civil suits, including class actions. Eliot Spitzer, the Attorney General of New York State, who brought the charges, remarked during the settlement that malfeasance went well up the corporate food chain. While the CEOs of the financial institutions which reached the settlement may have been spared personal indictment, legal proceedings in the future may well cover further aspects of malfeasance. All entities should therefore get serious about the legal implications of management risk.

* * *

The twelve chapters of this book have been divided into two parts. Part I examines senior management's responsibility towards their shareholders. Starting on a positive tone, Chapter 1 draws the reader's attention to the correlation between management ethics and personal accountability.

Chapter 2 presents the opposite perspective: what constitutes the background of mismanagement and how difficult it is to get rid of a bad CEO whose actions damage the company. Chapter 3 explains some of the means that have been employed to mislead investors, other stakeholders, and regulators. Creative accounting and Earnings Before Interest, Taxes, Depreciation, and Amortization (EBITDA) are the two key issues here.

The damage to investors from financial analysts and others who should have been reliable in their reporting is the theme of Chapter 4. Many of their fraudulent acts led to reputational risk. While the abuse of management pay and executive options is not yet a criminal act, Chapter 5 demonstrates that as this practice spreads and increases in magnitude, legislators and regulators may have to act to bring it under control.

Chapter 6 completes Part I by focusing on the responsibilities of certified public accountants (CPAs, chartered accountants) and of the board of directors. The text presents the reader with a history of audit miscarriages, and concludes with the evolution of legislation regarding financial malfeasance. A basic principle in business is: "if you have nothing to hide, don't hide anything."

The six chapters of Part II concentrate on case studies of highly leveraged companies, their rapid ascent to stardom, and their equally swift crash. Chapters 7 starts with the deals done at Enron which eventually brought down the company, its shareholders, and its employees – but not its senior management, which was pulled out of the wreckage relatively unscathed. The blame for Enron's débâcle does not fall on one single person but on several, as Chapter 8 suggests. Enron's superleveraging started soon after the Commodities Future Modernization Act, on which its top brass capitalized to gear the company sky-high. Then came kickbacks and forays into noncore business, like broadband, which became financially disastrous. Enron was helped by its bankers in superleveraging itself, as well as in some other deals which were on the borderline of legality, as Chapter 9 suggests. Beefing up the value of its stock through a very favorable but unrealistic equity analysis was instrumental in attracting investors. From private individuals to pension funds, those who bought Enron's equity came down with the company.

Chapter 10 draws the reader's attention to the Ponzi games that can be played with derivative financial instruments. As Warren Buffett aptly suggested, derivatives are so complex and based on outcomes so distant that parties on both sides of the same bet can book a notional profit. If that means big trading bonuses today, who cares about future losses which may destroy shareholder value and bring a company to its knees?

Chapter 11 explains how securitization of loans can be done, and gives advice on how a company can protect itself from being taken to the cleaners. Chapter 12 presents examples of companies which should have known better about how to avoid a downturn, or a very expensive settlement with clients. Bad loans, derivatives gambles, and basic mismanagement mean that for credit institutions the going is tough. A common point in all of the case studies in this book is that senior management should be much more alert, able to avoid tunnel vision, and steer away from deals which cost much more than they are worth. Market power is one of the most basic conditions for innovation – but not market power at any price.

* * *

Let me take this opportunity to thank Stephen Rutt and Jacky Kippenberger, for suggesting this project, and seeing it all the way to publication, and to Keith Povey and Barbara Docherty for the editing work. To Eva-Maria Binder goes the credit for compiling the research results, keying the text, and preparing the camera-ready artwork and index.

October 2003
Dimitris N. Chorafas   *Valmer and Vitznau*

Acknowledgments

Many organizations, through their senior executives and system specialists, participated in the research projects that led to the writing of this book and its documentation. The author is grateful to them all. Any opinions, findings, conclusions and recommendations expressed in this material are those of the author.

Part I

Management's Responsibility Towards the Shareholders

1

Senior Management Ethics and Personal Accountability

1 Introduction

Larry Hite had been a successful trader. He had also worked as a bank examiner. It is said that one day, before leaving a credit institution following an audit, he turned to the bank's president and, as a joke, said: "Got you!" The CEO had a heart attack on the spot. A more rigorous audit of the bank's books found that its CEO had embezzled $75,000.[1] An analyst who heard that story asked: "Only?"

Senior management ethics and personal accountability are at stake, whether embezzlement is counted in thousands, millions, or billions of dollars. The Hite story demonstrates in a nutshell the moral basis on which at least some of modern business has been run. Global Crossing, Adelphia Communications, Arthur Andersen, and WorldCom are recent examples. George W. Bush says that a few rotten apples should not be seen as characteristic of all business. That is true, but some rotten apples may spoil the other apples in the basket. "The problems revealed were systemic, not the result of a few bad apples," the December 30, 2001 editorial in *BusinessWeek* said. While only a few CEOs may go to jail for breaking the law, the breakdown "was endemic to both the corporate and financial systems." The same editorial pointed out the conflicts of interest of Wall Street analysts who:

- Sit in on board meetings
- Go on road shows, and
- Mislead individual investors.

Such behavior, *BusinessWeek* aptly suggests, is not synergistic; it is counterproductive to raising capital and investing in the economy. This lack of virtue in the late 1990s and the first few years of the twenty-first century is also reflected in the failure of boards to do their job as shareholder representatives and advocates. Many boards rubber stamped CEO demands for:

- Options
- Personal loans

- Repricing of underwater options
- Creative accounting practices, and
- A loose code of ethics.

Figure 1.1 presents the reasons why market dynamics steadily changed the business frame of reference. But there should always be a system of "traffic lights" with which business processes must comply for their own good.

This is not what happened after the 1980s, as poor leadership at the top executive level and complacent boards of directors, combined to gravely hurt companies. The synergy of lack of leadership and of questionable ethics bred CEO malfeasance and ensured that companies went into a vicious spiral which depressed the markets.

There is a fundamental difference between the junk bonds bubble and the Savings and Loans (S&L) crisis of the late 1980s and the global capital markets meltdown of 2000–3. The latter had its origins in 1990 in Japan, gained momentum with the collapse of the Asian "tigers" in 1997, and hit the big time in America and Europe in 2000:

- Small investors did not get burned by Michael Milken's junk bonds collapse and the Salomon Brothers Treasuries' troubles
- But small investors, pensions funds, and insurance companies were devastated when AT&T (the former staple investment Ma Bell) lost

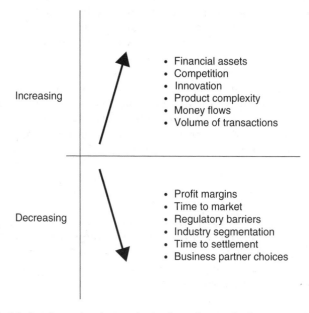

Figure 1.1   Market dynamics change the business frame of reference

$80 billion in capitalization and, from Enron to WorldCom, the market's darlings fell off the cliff.

On November 18, 2002, a financial news report by CNN said that in just one year (2002), corporate scandals had cost investors an estimated $200 billion. Among those who lost a fortune were pension funds: many pensioners paid for CEO malfeasance by losing their nest egg.

2   "Irrational exuberance" and "infectious greed"

In 1996, Alan Greenspan, Chairman of the Federal Reserve (the Fed), captured the spirit of the era in two words: "irrational exuberance." In 2002, he came up with a new slogan "infectious greed." Infectious greed was at the root of corporate governance breakdown and its associated CEO malfeasance. In Greenspan's words this happened not because people were greedier than in earlier times, but because there was "an outsized increase in opportunities" which people tried to capture and exploit to their own benefit.

CEOs are powerful business people, most of the time control their boards, and it is not that easy to get rid of them (see Chapter 2). What happened in the early years of the twenty-first century was a monumental display of failing corporate governance and lowered performance standards. The Chinese word for "crisis" is composed of two characters:

- The symbol for danger, and
- The symbol for opportunity.

The market is the mirror of risks and opportunities. The exuberance of the massive stock market bubble in the 1995–2000 timeframe was a sign of danger that most investors did not wish to recognize, let alone comprehend, probably because they thought that opportunity would be limitless. What followed was that the bubble burst, and its aftermath burned the large majority of investors. The financial world is very different today from the way it was in the late 1990s.

Between the beginning of 1995 and the stock market's peak less than six years later, the capitalization of US companies rose by $12 trillion, with nearly three-quarters of that money lost in the couple of years that followed the crash of 2000. During the boom, the irresistible force of huge opportunities was met by greatly reduced shareholder vigilance. As the Fed chairman Alan Greenspan suggested, lawyers, internal and external auditors, corporate boards, Wall Street security analysts, rating agencies, and large institutional holders of stock for one reason or another all failed in their mission. Part and parcel of this mission should be to detect and blow the whistle on those who breach the level of trust essential to well-functioning markets. Analysts were too complacent about the data they were given by companies. Investors failed to appreciate that only the exceptionally well-managed or strategically positioned companies could handle a sustained nominal earnings growth of 10 percent or more a year.

A CEO who promises year-after-year double-digit increase in profits is, in all probability, one willing to cut corners. Several of them did so. (See the role of creative accounting in Chapter 3 and the misleading of investors in Chapter 4.) When the market rose, investors were willing to believe anything; when it fell, they were prepared to trust nothing, as they found it difficult to recover from the disillusion they had suffered. The result was that business confidence was destroyed. The wrongdoers included:

- Auditors who had become the servants of managers rather than of shareholders
- Brokers promoting their own interests rather than offering dispassionate investment advice to investors
- Bankers who cut deals with dubious investment partners and helped hide their losses
- Directors who were subservient to CEOs rather than to their duty as regulators, and
- Executives who put their short-term enrichment through such things as stock options ahead of their responsibilities to their company and its shareholders.

All these people were tainted by Greenspan's "infectious greed," and showed that ours is not necessarily a moral society. The late Dr. Vittorio Vaccari foresaw this course of events when, in 1990, he described: "The frenzied pace of contemporary living, the fleeting nature of intentions and commitments, the slavery to consumerism, the indulging tolerance of permissiveness, the capricious adoring of fashion, the idolization of the unnecessary, the celebration of vice…, all of these mask a wound of contemporary humanity."[2]

All these, Vaccari suggested, "act like an anesthetic, producing a state of moral numbness. And how rare it is that those who have fallen under the spell…wake up." The awakening came with the 2000–3 crisis, when it was finally discovered that somehow ethics has taken their leave, even if everyone seemed to know that if we built a moral society, then most people would like to be honorable. Propelled by "infectious greed":

- Creative accounting fabricated a make-believe world of incentive payments while bankers, manufacturers and retailers hid their losses
- Overaggressive CEOs and chief financial officers (CFOs) booked sales before getting paid, manipulated the letter of contracts they entered into, and inflated revenues
- Many companies used derivative financial instruments for gearing, as well as to turn losses into profits with the connivance of banks, and
- Every sort of dubious business practice found a home (see section 3).

A long list of companies, including some well-known ones, fell under this spell. Apart from those mentioned in the Introduction there were Xerox, Tyco International, ImClone Systems, Qwest Communications, MobilCom, Rite Aid, and many others. Even certified public accountants (CPAs) such as Arthur Andersen participated in misleading financial reporting.

Rite Aid was no high-tech outfit but a drug retailer, an "Old Economy" company. Yet four of its former top managers – CEO Martin L. Grass, Chief Counsel and Vice-President Franklin C. Brown, Executive Vice-President and Chief Financial Officer Franklin M. Bergonzi, and Executive Vice-President for Pharmacy Services Eric S. Sorkin – faced various combinations of charges in a thirty-seven-count criminal indictment in June 2002 that ranged from conspiracy to defraud to conspiracy to obstruct justice. Though they pleaded non-guilty, each faced up to ten years in prison for allegedly operating an illegal accounting scheme that triggered a $1.6 billion restatement of net income.[3]

There are many reasons to believe that the list of companies in this roster will grow, for a variety of reasons. In late July 2002, for example, the Justice Department opened a criminal investigation into allegations of price-fixing at Mercedes–Benz USA, a subsidiary of Mercedes–Benz Manhattan. This investigation started after a price-fixing lawsuit was filed on behalf of Mercedes' customers by a New Jersey dealer.

At about the same time, in a different type of incident, ConAgra Foods issued a recall of 19 million lb of fresh and frozen ground beef after the Agriculture Department said that it might have been contaminated with the deadly bacteria *E.coli*:

- In normal times, price-fixing and a food recall would not have raised eyebrows, but we are not in normal times
- Everything which points to a malfunctioning of the social and industrial systems should raise concern.

Here is another case. In mid-March 2002, New York State Attorney-General Eliot Spitzer announced the arrest of five people who had fraudulently attempted to obtain expedited death certificates for relatives who they claimed had died in the attack on the World Trade Center on September 11, 2001 (9/11). In fact, none of the alleged deceased had died in the Twin Towers or were even in the vicinity of the World Trade Center on that day. The purpose of obtaining the death certificate was to defraud charities, government agencies, and insurance companies of money intended for the families of victims killed in the terrorist attacks. Fraudulent death certificates and fraudulent financial statements reflect the same "infectious greed" culture. In order to ensure that the experience is not repeated, the SEC imposed a late August 2002 deadline after which CEOs and CFOs must sign affidavits when their companies file financial statements, or report a significant event. Some 1,000 companies have been affected by this directive and nearly

400 could not meet the deadline, which had to be extended, while several foreign companies quoted on the US capital markets used lobbyists to try to get them off the hook (there is more on this below).

3   Stress testing and market confidence

In the aftermath of the $3.8 billion WorldCom fraud (which has since grown beyond $9.0 billion), US president George W. Bush promised a full government investigation of what he called "outrageous" accounting irregularities. The SEC, already under fire over its relatively slow response to the collapse of Enron, said: "The WorldCom disclosures confirm that accounting improprieties of unprecedented magnitude have been committed in the public markets."

Corrupt companies may be only a fraction of the approximately 16,000 publicly owned enterprises in the US, but if the embezzlement of company property goes unpublished and unpunished, this will set a very bad example for the majority of entities which have abided by accepted rules of:

- Corporate governance
- Accounting discipline, and
- Dependable financial reporting.

Because of serious breaches of the unwritten code of corporate ethics, global equity markets were battered in 2000–3. WorldCom was just one in a succession of corporate scandals. After the revelation of accounting irregularities, the stock was suspended as the markets absorbed the news that the No. 2 US long-distance telephone and data services group had improperly booked $3.8 billion in expenses as capitalization.

In order to re-establish market confidence, new regulatory measures must take a number of issues into consideration. One is that white-collar criminals are apt to be better educated and better able to cover their tracks. Their malfeasance typically involves a series of complicated transactions made over a period of time, nothing like a classical bank robbery. Prosecutors find themselves obliged to build accounting expertise within their ranks and rely more on analytical investigations. They are also keen to find business insiders and to identify witnesses – a job that can be complicated, given:

- The pervasive nature of white-collar crime, and
- The sophisticated nature of the derivative financial instruments used.

Another fact of life with which prosecutors now have to live is that fraudulent business executives generally have access to superior lawyers and are able to mount better defenses than the historical subjects of federal probes. Enron's former CEO Kenneth Lay, for example, hired veteran defense lawyer Earl Silbert, the original Watergate prosecutor. Andrew S. Fastow, the former Enron CFO, was first represented by David Boies, who was Al Gore's attorney during the Florida election dispute in 2000 and who represented the US government in its antitrust case against Microsoft. WorldCom's Bernie Ebbers was represented by Reid Weingarten, who won an acquittal for former Teamsters boss Ron Carey on federal perjury charges. The celebrity of lawyers at the CEOs' side in such alleged malfeasance cases is not calculated to reassure the markets.

Such accounting improprieties and misbehavior of chief executive officers inevitably had a negative impact on market psychology. On June 26, 2002, right after the WorldCom news broke, the Dow Jones Industrial Average fell below the 9,000 level for the first time in nine months, and the technology-heavy Nasdaq composite fell back to a level last seen almost four years earlier. Even before its bankruptcy, WorldCom's fall from grace had deepened investors' new-found skepticism of corporate America, providing momentum for:

- Stricter corporate governance
- More rigorous financial reporting, and
- Better oversight by regulators.

The corporate improprieties revealed were not seen as being limited to just a handful of companies, but as a sign of something rotten throughout corporate America. Even those entities with apparently strong business management and transparent balance sheets looked suspect.

Other revelations of fraudulent reporting followed WorldCom. On June 28, 2002, came the news that Xerox had carved out WorldCom-type creative accounting of $2 billion, spread over a five-year period, another bad day on the stock market. News that WorldCom and Xerox had overstated cash flow by several billions sent the already battered shares of the two firms sharply down:

- Improper accounting for expenses joined off-balance sheet debt and revenue manipulation on the list of major investor concerns
- Many offences were a new twist on old accounting practices, but the underlying causes – white-collar fraud – remained the same, and they called for policy responses to restore confidence.

Practically everybody appreciated that market confidence could not be restored as long as new scandals continued to surface. In late July 2002 came the revelation of the "prepays" engineered for Enron by J.P. Morgan Chase and Citigroup to turn losses into profits for fraudulent financial reporting reasons (see Chapter 9). Enron and WorldCom, among others, were an arrow in the heart of a basic bull market assumption that the US:

- Had the highest accounting standards, and
- Was the best-regulated financial reporting platform of the world's financial markets.

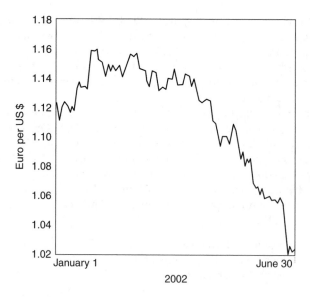

Figure 1.2   Accounting scandals and the dollar, January 1–June 30, 2002

Analysts pointed out a basic principle of economic theory: positive market psychology takes time to build, but it can be destroyed at a stroke as investors discover reasons why they should not trust the market. Two other market distortions were also of particular concern:

- Insufficient monitoring of risk positions of hedge funds, and
- Weak banking supervision in offshore financial centers (OFCs).

As Hans Eichel, the German finance minister, remarked in the *Financial Times*,[4] offshore financial centers are potentially destabilizing because they often have poor supervisory regimes. Many trades taking place in OFCs conceal complex financial transactions, dubious reporting practices, and unwarranted risks. Nor do the nature of these transactions necessarily conform with international standards.

Investors wondered how WorldCom's capitalization could have risen to $115 billion in 1999, making the equity the fifth most widely held stock in the US. Simon Flanner, of Morgan Stanley, estimated that as a result of the June 2002 restatement, WorldCom's operating margin was just 16.8 percent – a fraction of the of the 30 percent + margins it had boasted as recently as 2000 and the 21 percent that it still claimed prior to the disclosure.[5] When similar accounting problems were revealed in the Asia markets, the blame fell on:

- Cronyism
- An inadequate judiciary, and

- A banking system that allowed overinvestment in unprofitable projects.

In the US, the blame fell squarely on corporate executives who had distorted accounts. The disillusionment with the performance of US companies, and their corporate ethics, spread to the dollar which, as shown in Figure 1.2, had slipped within an ace of parity with the Euro by the end of June 2002, though it took another five months to fall below Euro parity – all the way to $1.17 to the Euro on May 20, 2003. US Senator Jon Corzine, a former co-chairman of Goldman Sachs, encapsulated the market's mood: "The litany of abuse and failures of business ethics and repeated undermining of elements of investor confidence...is just unacceptable."[6] Some financial analysts found the courage to express their opinion about who was king in the prevailing market climate: "Cash has now outperformed the S&P 500 for the time period spanning the last 55 months. The 'bull market in cash' continues," Richard Bernstein said.[7]

4   The sense of a bubble

Not only are market bubbles man-made but they burst because people prick them. Accounting has become a way to gear and inflate bubbles, because bankers and traders are so inventive. We have reached a level of sophistication in financial instruments which often escapes the investor's, analyst's, auditor's, or regulator's comprehension. Products are used to:

- Conceal the true financial health of companies, and
- Promote build-up of "irrational exuberance."

Deregulation, globalization, and technology mean that new financial products succeed one another at a rapid pace. Because rapid innovation has escaped prudential risk control, some of these instruments become increasingly more complex. Accounting standards boards (ASBs), whose job is to establish norms, have also fallen far behind, and when they try to catch up the lobbyists erect walls of resistance to obstruct better-focused regulation. This sort of an environment made it very easy for companies to bypass existing rules – even precise norms, when they are available – until the final blow-up of Enron and WorldCom destroyed market confidence. The irony is that just before this happened the factors characterizing a financial bubble had come to the fore. These included:

- Increased use of leverage
- Make-believe liquidity
- A swarm of new issues, and
- Many comparatively inexperienced newcomers in the market.

The careful reader will notice that an exponential price increase is not one of these five bullets, though anecdotal evidence abounds that inflationary pressure is one of the bubble's motors. What makes investors run to enter the market, and builds up the bubble, is an "infectious greed" for abnormal capital gains because of the fear that money is being devalued because of inflation.

The mirage of ever-greater capital gains masks other economic and financial facts. In 1991 and in 2002, for instance, while restructuring slowed the pace of labor costs, profit margins did not improve. Amid weak demand, globalization and low inflation robbed companies of pricing power. In 1991 and in 2002 there were also longer-term problems, including:

- Record consumer indebtedness
- A burgeoning US current account deficit
- A squeeze on state and local governments, and
- Overbuilding in commercial and multifamily construction.

These factors have borne down on the economy. In terms of industrial activity, the problems were compounded by the record indebtedness of telecoms, at unprecedented levels, and the decline of the telecoms supplier industry. In early 2002, the UK saw its biggest single default so far, to the tune of $10.6 billion, by the British–American cable firm NTL.

Organizations comprise of people, and even in bankruptcy people never learn. In mid-November 2002, NTL admitted that its underlying earning for the year had been flattered by up to £45 million ($70 million), following an incorrect allocation of expenses between the company's capital and operating budgets. This type of disclosure was at the heart of the financial malfeasance that brought down WorldCom. In NTL's case, it raised doubts over the company's ability to pull itself out of Chapter 11 bankruptcy protection.

Investors discovered that they had been taking an inordinate amount of risk, while they believed that they could trust the market and that nothing abnormal could happen to them. They also came to appreciate that in the corporate world some things are not unambiguously black or white – that there is a great difference between:

- *Normal risks*, attached to traditional, widely held forms of investment, such as equities, bonds, units in mutual funds, and
- *Extreme risks*, which apply to new-style industries such as hedge funds, to highly leveraged entities, and to new instruments, such as alternative investments.[8]

An example of "extreme events" was the global hedge fund crisis in the autumn of 1998, when big funds speculated against the yen with huge financial bets, which they lost when it eventually became clear that the aftermath of the Japanese economic crisis was the opposite of what had been expected in terms of exchange rates. It is not investment but speculation and high gearing that brought down Long Term Capital Management (LTCM) in September 1998.[9]

Companies that overexpose themselves lose control over their future. In 2002 some, like Switzerland's Zürich Financial Services, dumped their CEO in the hope of reassuring the financial markets, but a change in management does not mean that a sick company will become healthy overnight. A torrent of red ink takes time to dry up. Zürich Financial posted a record $2 billion loss in the first half of 2002 and the heat was on its new CEO to:

- Replenish severely depleted reserves
- Cut costs all over operations, and
- Sharpen the insurance company's strategic focus.

Another Swiss insurance company, the Zürich-based Swiss Life, was on its third CEO in just one year (2002). The new boss, former Crédit Suisse Group executive Rolf Dörig, was hired in November 2002 to replace Roland Chlapowski, who had been sacked after only nine months in the face of a mounting crisis over accounting errors and management perks.

It takes not just one person but a whole team with skill and patience to turn a company around. Shinsei Bank is the reborn Long-Term Credit Bank of Japan (LTCB), which collapsed in 1998 under a mountain of bad loans and a run on its stock. LTCB was a huge bureaucracy which under political patronage provided low-margin corporate loans. When the Japanese government seized LTCB, it:

- Absorbed $37 billion in bad loans from its books, and
- Sold the remains to a consortium of financial firms.

This consortium, led by New York-based Ripplewood Holdings (which includes GE Capital and Mellon Bank), appointed Masamoto Yashiro, formerly of Citibank, as president of the reborn Shinsei Bank. Yashiro and his international team, mostly ex-Citibank executives, restructured the institution, overhauled its archaic IT system, rolled out a menu of financial products for retail customers, and started to transform the institution from a low-profile industrial lender to a top-flight commercial bank. The new management instituted rigorous internal controls and also cleaned up the balance sheet. But when it started calling in loans to deadbeat borrowers, relations with the government grew tense, and it was attacked by the Japanese press. However, the clean balance sheet policy paid dividends; Shinsei Bank had a $501 million profit for the year ended March 2002, while other Japanese money-center banks had lost billions.

* * *

What these examples, from the build-up to the bust of the bubble, have in common is *inadequate internal control* which should definitely include CEO virtue and performance. Paraphrasing Sun Tzu's *The Art of War*[10] it can be said that: If you know yourself, your company, its CEO, its board, its professionals, plus:

- Your company's exposure, and
- Your company's financial staying power

and, if you know your instruments, markets, counterparties, and their exposure, then you don't have to worry about the outcome of 1,000 risks. Chances are that the bursting of a bubble will leave you unscathed *if and only if,* you are ready for the event.

5   Cheer-leaders, equity traders, and true professionals

It needs no restating that "irrational exuberance" can lead to bubbles and bubbles are negative contributors to general prosperity. A major input to a bear market is the unearthing of accounting fraud, which acts as drag on business confidence. In their rush to build industrial empires, several CEOs failed to:

- Make their acquisitions stick together
- Convince investors that their strategic moves made sense, and
- Observe the time-honored business ethics of compliance with rules and regulations, as well as of transparency.

This gives business a bad name, in spite of the fact that one of the most basic reasons living standards have improved during the last 100 years is that companies have become much more innovative and productive. The majority of entrepreneurs and professional managers helped to drive that evolution by:

- Doing things efficiently, and
- Putting into practice ideas that transcended their company, their industry, and even their national borders.

By contrast, the minority damaged the economy through excesses which had many origins. One of them was the sort of leveraged promotions which, by feeding upon themselves, misled investors. Two books[11] convey to the reader the message that these engineered company upgrades work well because Wall Street is a promotion machine.

In the first, James J. Cramer, of The Street.com, says that he had been looking for stocks likely to move quickly on good news. Like Randolph Hearst in the early twentieth century, Cramer discovered the principle but also took care to provide the news. One of his staffers would call companies, looking to find anything good he could say about them. The synergy of being news provider and trader/investor seems to have worked well.

When Cramer discovered a stock that seemed ready to take off, or at least had something favorable about it that analysts didn't yet know, he would load up on options and stock. Then, after he had made his bet he would give the good news to his favorite analysts, so that they could go on with their promotion. In other words, in what can easily be seen as a conflict of interest, Cramer acted both as cheer-leader and trader through his hedge fund. The trader half of him would liquidate the position, for a handsome profit.

Nicholas W. Maier, the author of the second book, seems to have done some legwork for Cramer. In one of the cases he describes he was allegedly sent by his boss to an analysts' meeting to ask nasty questions about a firm which (also allegedly) drove down that company's stock. Maier has it that Cramer profited greatly because he was shorting the stock, but Cramer's lawyer denied most of the unflattering tales in the book.

Even if it is not the cheer-leader/trader himself who breaks news, this sort of story eventually becomes known and pricks the bubble; the end result is to dent the market's confidence. Running after a fast buck is precisely the opposite of the methods and processes developed by the successful leaders of industry such as Sam Walton and Henry Ford.

A characteristic of far-sighted business leaders is that they recognize the stimulus and threats of competition, and have the intellectual and emotional strength to deal with them through a longer-term strategic plan. They set the tone for industry, as their company:

- Becomes highly productive
- Adopts steady innovation
- Proves to be a genius in marketing, and
- Simplifies its organization and structure, leading to a dominant position in its line of activity.

This is the antithesis to the strategy of "smoke and mirrors" which characterized the big names from Enron to WorldCom, among many others. The promoters behind these brands were intelligent, but:

- They bent the standard of business ethics, and
- They cared mainly for the money to be made in the next three months – not for the longer run.

A lesson to be learned from the débâcle of 2000–3 is that cheer-leading and sound business practice do not mix. One of the most revered executives was General Motors' Alfred Sloan, the ultimate authority on managing large organizations. For nearly eight decades, no large company was uninfluenced by Sloan's concept of decentralized management. He came into a company that was cash-short, chaotic, and nearly bankrupt, and:

- Brought discipline
- Clearly defined the issues of planning, organization, and control, and
- Mastered the concept of market segmentation to target the company's sales.

Sloan understood what is today known as "consumer insight," by visiting dealers incognito to learn about buyer behavior and competitive offerings. This strategy had a famous historical precedent. In his time, Baghdad's Haroun Al Raschid was the most powerful ruler in the world:

- He wanted an accurate picture of what was happening in his kingdom
- But he also knew that his status prevented people from communicating truthfully.

He solved the problem by adopting a disguise and wandering through the streets of Baghdad, gathering intelligence. That is a strategy many modern CEOs would be well advised to follow. They may be able to learn much more about their employees, their clients, their products, and the risks their company is assuming. CEOs should not be mean operators or romantic dreamers who see a once-in-a-lifetime chance to reshape society. Wise CEOs should appreciate that while they appreciate the prestige of their position, results are what counts. The ability to deliver results on a sustained basis, as contrasted to the short-term flourish of Enron and WorldCom followed by bankruptcy, rests on four pillars:

- Insight
- Foresight
- Virtue, and
- Hard work.

All four are needed to increase the CEO's sensitivity to evolving market conditions and strengthen the management of change which keeps the organization's arteries from clogging up. This is more important than ever today because the post-Second World War globalization of business operations changed the perspectives under which business plans its activities and structures itself. An example of a professional manager with global duties is Roberto Goizueta, the long-time CEO of Coca-Cola:

- He proved that there was no such thing as a mature business, and
- He was able to define a long-term growth path for Coke.

Other CEOs also faced similar challenges, but they found out that the task exceeded their skills. Goizueta coined the term "global" for a company that was already seemingly everywhere. He also taught his executives that when they set goals for market share, they needed to focus on a broader perspective, not just the share of carbonated beverages. His broader market was water, not just soda. By this definition, Coke's 40-percent-plus market share became 3 percent, changing the company's view of growth. Goizueta gave real meaning to the word "diversity," developing a multinational talent pool. He also became an avid disciple of the idea of economic value creation. Creating more value became a strategic objective, but the market knew that it could depend on Goizueta's financial reports.

6   What differentiates us from our competitors?

Two key questions business leaders such as Sam Walton, Henry Ford, Alfred Sloan, and Roberto Goizueta asked themselves were:

- What makes our company different from other firms in our line of business?
- How can we distinguish ourselves from other players in a competitive market place?

Executives who can answer these questions are innovators, eagle-eyed cost-cutters, hard workers, and people to whom the employees look for inspiration – though they may also be controversial in their views. In essence, everything boils down to the question: What do we, as a company, believe in? Other questions are subsidiary, but also important. For instance:

- What is really supporting the business strategy of our organization in the longer term?
- How should we present our company to our customers and external audiences?
- How can we maintain market confidence?

These are by no means academic questions and the response should not be made lightly. Factual and well-documented answers help to:

- Set realistic and achievable targets
- Put in place proper human and financial resources, and
- Fine-tune the implementation of carefully designed business plans.

All business plans should consider the future evolution in the equities and debt markets, accounting ahead of time for the fact that reversal can be dramatic. Figure 1.3 presents an example, WorldCom June 2001–June 2002. As the company hit the skids its share price and bond spread over US Treasuries reversed course. The bill for the company's financial reporting malfeasance fell.

Enron and WorldCom will be remembered as mismanaged companies which fell on their sword. Others have faded away because, as a study by Kodak documented, six consecutive years of poor management brought a formerly great company to its knees. Nothing is more unstable than the hold a company has on the market. The case of Bloomberg and Reuters provides an example. Over the 1992–2002 timeframe, Reuters' share of the $6.5 billion financial terminals market, which it had helped create in the 1980s, fell from 55 percent to 39 percent. By contrast, the market share of its main competitor, Bloomberg Financial Markets, went from 5 percent to 38 percent.

Lots of differences characterized the two competitors. Bloomberg got about twice as much revenue per screen per year (some $16,000) as Reuters – and it also had a far better system of cost control. For these reasons, the market

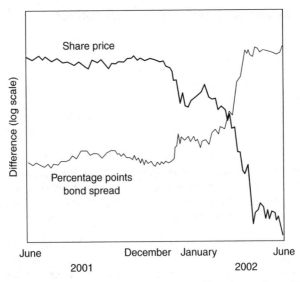

Figure 1.3   WorldCom: one-year trend in share price and bond spread over US Treasuries, June 2001–June 2002

pounded Reuters' stock. Over two decades investors saw Reuters go from innovator of financial services to a poorly managed company, with:

- No new products, and
- No long-term restorative.

Reversing a corporate downtrend is not easy. This was the challenge facing Tom Glocer, Reuter's CEO after July 2001. In his first year, he lurched from one crisis to another. "I'm not sure Tom ever expected he'd face a first year like this," Michael Nathanson, an analyst at Sanford C. Bernstein, suggested.[12]

One of the shocks was that customers defected in droves from Reuters' Instinet unit to cheaper trading venues after the Nasdaq began quoting prices in decimals. Instinet had accounted for 22 percent of Reuter's revenues in 2001, and 28 percent of its operating profits:

- Many companies find it difficult to crack how to get worthwhile innovations with a market impact
- The greatest challenge facing large established organizations is deliverable results, not vague statements of corporate goals.

Toshiba Corporation, for instance, expressed its business philosophy in terms of promoting corporate growth and improving its customers' quality of life. The five key company goals were: Promotion of globalization,

Business expansion, Strengthening of group management, Better intracompany developments, and elimination of environmental problems. None of these was a market mover.

Toshiba's globalization plan was to establish a business presence in the core world business regions. This was hardly innovative as Toshiba was already a global company, though (like Reuters) some of its core product lines were decaying with no killer products in sight. Under Toshiba's intracompany development goal, two specific subsidiary aims were spelled out:

- A total productivity campaign, where management developed a production and sales system that would minimize inventory
- A project to increase the proportion of high-value-added products manufactured by Toshiba.

The problem confronted by Toshiba, however, and by a score of other computers and communications manufacturers, was that the notion of value-added electronics products was totally protean while margins were shrinking and many companies made bloody cuts to their technology budget.

This is a challenge also faced by "Old Economy" companies. In its 2001 strategy to win small-car buyers General Motors lost an average of $2,000 on each of the half-million small cars it sold, losing $1 billion on small cars as it tried to prop up the sales volume of its slow-selling models with 0% interest on loans, rebates, and discount sales to car-rental fleets. None of these stratagems stopped the company's share of small-car sales from tumbling from 29 percent in 1998 to 21.8 percent in 2001.[13]

As these examples demonstrate, CEO malfeasance is only one of the major challenges facing business and industry. Unless a company is able to sustain leadership by making innovative products that people and other companies want to buy – and it is doing so at affordable cost – the market will turn away from it.

The years 2000–3 may be an epoch that many companies would be happy to see vanish in their rearview mirror, but overcoming adversity is not a short-term matter. It is a steady struggle requiring information, knowledge, and readiness to take action. Investors can choose wisely only by knowing the risk factors involved in both the inventory of assets held in their portfolio and in the new moves they are contemplating in the market. This cannot be done without market confidence, and this is basically what is targeted in the US Corporate Responsibility Bill of 2002.

7 Market confidence and the US Corporate Responsibility Bill

Conspiracy to commit an offense, fraud, wire fraud, perjury, tampering with witnesses, interference with commerce, and obstruction of justice are acts expected of the common criminals against whom Congress passed the Racketeer Influenced and Corrupt Organizations (RICO) Act. They should be no part of the arsenal of tools of daily business, because they pave the way for disastrous adventures which end by destroying market confidence.

Dr Sam Waksal was the founder and former CEO of the biotechnology company ImClone Systems. The government accused him of insider trading, perjury, bank fraud, and obstruction of justice. When he appeared in a New York court on August 12, 2002, Waksal pleaded not guilty to accusations of having allegedly tipped off family members and friends, such as Martha Stewart, to sell their shares in the company shortly before publicly announcing that the Food and Drug Administration had denied approval to its star cancer drug Erbitux. Waksal also allegedly fabricated a signature on bank documents and if found guilty faces at least twenty-five years in jail. He has also been sued by ImClone Systems over his severance pay. Martha Stewart is still under investigation for possible insider trading of ImClone Systems' shares, but on June 10, 2003, Sam Waksal was sentenced to seven years in jail for insider dealing. He will also pay $4.3 million in fines and back taxes. Judge William Pauley imposed the maximum prison term within federal guidelines, after prosecutors told how the once-celebrated scientist had refused to co-operate with investigators and "told numerous, separate and distinct sets of lies."[14]

Waksal pleaded guilty to six counts of fraud and conspiracy. He admitted trying to sell large chunks of ImClone stock in December 2001 after receiving a tip that the US Food and Drug Administration would reject an application to market its colon cancer treatment Erbitux. Moreover, he admitted evading sales tax on $15 million of art purchases.

Another business which hurts investors are the benefits derived by those favored with initial public offerings (IPOs). As an article in *BusinessWeek* pointed out, Disney CEO Michael D. Eisner, Ford CEO William Clay Ford, Jr., and several eBay executives, including CEO Margaret C. Whitman, received "hot stocks" from Goldman Sachs. Salomon Smith Barney also funneled IPOs to Qwest Communications' CEO Joseph P. Nacchio.[15] Other investment banks used profits to be obtained from IPOs as bait to get lucrative contracts for themselves.

Even labor bosses joined the bandwagon. ULLICO, Inc. CEO, Robert A. Georgine, is under criminal investigation by a Washington Grand Jury, as well as civil inquiries by the Labor Department and other agencies over profits allegedly made from a deal to buy stock in ULLICO, a union-owned company, just before shares were repriced to reflect the soaring value of an early investment in Global Crossing.[16]

In order to discourage such acts and prevent them from becoming normal tools of doing business the new US Corporate Responsibility Law foresees a maximum penalty of twenty years for such misdemeanors. Signed in July 2002, the law places personal accountability where it belongs: at CEO and CFO level. At the same time, it protects the business establishment, because the New Economy now depends so heavily on intangible assets. Critics say the new law puts a heavy burden on the shoulders of CEOs and CFOs, because it is not easy to value intangibles. But if the CEO or CFO cannot value their company's intangibles, nobody will be able to do so in any meaningful sense. Nobody else, including investors and regulators, can say what a company is worth in a factual and well-documented manner.

People wishing to escape personal responsibility rose against the Corporate Responsibility Bill over this issue. Others said that though what the new law demanded was necessary, there was no consensus on how to proceed. Still others added that the government was just trying to second-guess management intent. These are lightweight arguments. Expressing management intent entered the letter of the law not in July 2002 but in June 1998, with the Statement of Financial Accounting Standards (SFAS) 133, issued by the Financial Accounting Standards Board (FASB). It is nothing new. As for intangible assets, companies have been valuing and misvaluing them for a long time. An example is *goodwill*, such as the $50 billion 2001 and 2002 writedown by JDSU, a similar amount by AOL Time Warner, and, albeit at a lesser level by other companies (on the manipulation of goodwill, see Chapter 3).

It is simply not possible to leave the notion of intangibles out of the New Economy, because that economy is, to a large extent, built on intangibles. At the same time, this notion has been used by many companies to leverage their operations and grow their balance sheet. Nor is this phenomenon strictly American. Vivendi Universal, among many other French firms, has been doing it, and there are similar cases in Germany – Balsam, Flowtex, and Philipp Holzmann are examples.

A second argument has been raised against the Corporate Responsibility Law. Companies have been steadily feeding the market with inventive financial estimates which, incidentally, are heavy on intangibles. Proforma reporting, and Earnings Before Interest, Taxes, Depreciation, and Amortization (EBITDA), so beloved of financial analysts, are examples of unsound financial reporting practices (there is more on this in Chapter 3):

- If proforma and EBITDA were heavyweight statements, as their proponents said, then they would not have been so different from existing regulatory reporting
- If they were lightweight, then they should not have been used at all, rather than being employed to mislead investors and harm market confidence.

At Enron and WorldCom, as in so many other problem cases involving creative financial reporting, serious defects in corporate governance were uncovered post-mortem, after the company's bankruptcy. The fact that transparency was at a bare minimum hid the real figures for some time, but this could not last forever.

If there had not been misuse and misrepresentation of financial information, followed by top management abuse of corporate finances and some actual fraud there would have been no urgency for a new law. It is this abuse which underlined the need for re-establishing public confidence by putting a stop to the manipulation of the financial information provided to stakeholders. The new law therefore sees to it that personal accountability is increased across the board. The voluntary corporate governance code for companies has not worked well in an era of deregulation, globalization, technological processes, and innovation. The US Corporate Responsibility Act is a step in the right direction:

- Compliance with new, tougher financial reporting standards is now required by law
- The controversy surrounding this law shows, however, that there is still no consensus about the correct level of corporate transparency.

Enron, Adelphia Communications, Global Crossing, WorldCom, and other companies which failed in their management duties triggered a renewed debate on the role of top management accountability. Not only the markets but also supervisors need to rely on dependable financial reporting as well as on external ratings for enforcing the Basel II rules implemented since 2002. In the Enron case, rating agencies came under fire for having given the enterprise an investment-grade rating just before its collapse:

- The first golden rule of governance is that the markets should be able to obtain more up-to-date reliable ratings and that there should be penalties for misreporting
- The second golden rule is that accounting principles which produce reliable financial statements are by themselves insufficient if there is no credible institutional procedure for enforcing them.

Several European governments, and the Japanese, voiced concern over the international reach of the new US laws on corporate governance, transparency and accountancy standards – a negative response which is both irrational and badly timed. (Two companies have allegedly withdrawn listing applications with the New York Stock Exchange (NYSE).) Excuses can always be found for not doing something. One of the arguments advanced by Japanese and European firms working in the US and listed on the NYSE is that the accounting standard in America (US GAAP) and in their countries are different. This is a ridiculous argument – not because the accounting standards are not different (they are) but because these companies have had to adopt US GAAP in order to be listed on the NYSE. That was done years ago; there were initial problems, but they are over. Some countries, particularly France, have even permitted their international companies listed on the NYSE to report in US GAAP terms to their regulators at home.

The more profound reason for opposition to the Corporate Responsibility legislation is that top management is trying to avoid being pinned down over personal accountability. This has been a loophole for several decades, but the new law closes it. American companies have no option but to comply; as for the Europeans and Japanese, if they don't they will deny themselves access to the huge American capital market.

2
Mismanagement and the Firing of a Bad CEO

1 Introduction

It is always tough to get a bad CEO out of the company's system. The executive under fire will resist, and this will inevitably lead to in-fighting. When talking about how to get rid of a bad senior executive, Dr. Neil Jacoby, my Professor of Business Strategy at UCLA in the early 1950s, advised his students to give a bad CEO enough cord so he could hang himself. This, however, takes time.

In the early twentieth century John Patterson, then CEO of National Cash Register (NCR), fired an underperforming executive by removing his desk and chair, parking it in front of the company's factory, having it soaked in kerosene and set alight in front of the underperformer. Shortly after the Second World War, the then CEO of Montgomery Ward was carried out of the company's headquarters while still sitting in his chair. Armand Hammer, when boss of Occidental Petroleum, kept signed, undated letters of resignation from each of his board directors in his desk.

Edward I. Koch, the former mayor of New York, had a different policy for firing underperformers: "I just walked in and said: 'You have to go', and they said 'We are not going', and I said 'Yes you are, it's just a question of how you're going.'"[1] The boss did not bend when confronted by resistance. It's an advice of which cognizant readers should take note.

Whether in private business or in public administration, performance by the top executive and his immediate assistants makes the difference between success and failure in the short, medium and longer term. Jon S. Corzine is credited for getting the Wall Street institution founded by Marcus Goldman in 1869 back on track. He took the helm in September 1994 when Goldman had been derailed by:

- Huge trading losses, and
- Bad management decisions.

Corzine and then Goldman Sachs President Henry M. Paulson, Jr. quickly refocused the firm on client relationships, installed urgently needed risk controls, and tightened the management structure. A new risk management system and a revamped internal control assured that the company's CEO was again in charge, and Goldman Sachs quickly saw better days.

CEOs should be wise enough to follow President Lincoln's advice: "My mind is like a piece of steel, very hard to scratch anything on it, and almost impossible after you get it there to rub it out." Lincoln added: "Always bear in mind that your own resolution to succeed is more important than any other thing."[2] Success, however, should not come by cutting corners and biasing financial statements – an expedient but foolish act.

Thales, one of the eight sages of Antiquity, used to say that what one fool can do another can do, too. Dr. Carlo Pesenti once answered the complaints of the CEOs of his banks that I was taking them for fools with a short reply: "If you don't want to be taken for a fool, then don't do foolish things."

Nor is leniency towards a bad CEO a policy which bears fruit, whether the reason for getting the incumbent CEO out of the system is underperformance or malfeasance. The board and shareholders should heed the advice of an Athenian senator in Shakespeare's *Timon of Athens*: "Nothing emboldens sin so much as mercy."

2 Many of today's CEOs lack crisis experience

The CEOs of 2003 are younger than they historically used to be, which is a positive development. The downside is that they gained most of their experience during the 1990s, a period of record economic expansion, and therefore know precious little about when and how to appreciate that there are limits to growth, or what it takes to handle a crisis. According to a survey by Drake, Beam, and Morin of which I heard in the course of my research:

- Until 2000–2, the average CEO had never run a business during a recession
- Battle-hardened champions who had steered their business through ups and downs had been succeeded by "greener" people.

Table 2.1 shows the tenure of current CEOs. These statistics talk volumes about the risks of navigating in the treacherous waters of the recession which characterized the first four years of the twenty-first century. Experience is best translated in hindsight and foresight, which is very useful in the prevailing uncertainties with daily surprises characterizing the reaction of markets under stress.

Experience on how to deal with adversity becomes so much more important when the economy is down and everybody seems to be waiting for a lift which does not come. A study made by experts at Wall Street in early January 2003 projected that during that year, which was supposed to see a

Table 2.1   Cumulative statistics on tenure of CEOs, 2002[3]

Tenure (years)	Cumulative (%)
Less than 1	13.6
Less than 2	32.1
Less than 3	45.2
Less than 4	57.2
Less than 5	63.2
Less than 10	85.3
10 or more	14.7

turnaround, roughly 8 percent of companies with a BB or worse rating (non-investment grade) would default:

- One in 13 companies in the non-investment grade class declaring bankruptcy, and
- Among telecom and cable TV companies the ratio of junk-rated companies may rise to one in five.

This is not a time for inexperienced CEOs, or for people who cherish status consciousness more than action. Yet, surveys are demonstrating that today's CEOs are more status-conscious than their predecessors. Michael Milken said in the late 1980s, in response to a query regarding his title at Drexel Burnham Lambert: "I am some kind of a vice president. I am not sure exactly whether I am senior or executive or first. It keeps changing."[4] Milken was more interested in deal-making than in status.

"Greener" and status-conscious CEOs are *reactive* rather than *proactive*. One of the characteristics of "greener" people is that they cannot wait. Every day they search the Wall Street financials hoping that the economy will get better. But since April 2000, for more than three years, it seems that each day it refuses to improve or slides further downward. In the meantime highly indebted companies sink into more red ink.

Telecoms companies, particularly the sprawling huge former state monopolies or regulated industries excelled in sinking rather than swimming. France Télécom and Deutsche Telekom were at the top of the list of indebted entities, along with Verizon, British Telecom, and AT&T (on AT&T's mismanagement see p. 28). As a project I did in mid-2001 documented, in June 2001: France Télécom had a net debt of $51.2 billion, while Deutsche Telekom had a debt of $43.1 billion.

At that time other highly indebted telecoms with bleak prospects were: Verizon, with a $50.7 billion debt; British Telecom, $42.9 billion; AT&T, $39.3 billion; and WorldCom, $22.3 billion. The banks who gave them all these loans were also not blameless.

Judging from the level of their relatively short-term liabilities, these highly mismanaged companies were actively seeking more money. WorldCom attempted to raise another $11.9 billion through its largest ever bond offer, although its management were aware that bankruptcy could be only a few months away. When it came, WorldCom had debts in excess of $30.8 billion.

Denis Healey, the former British Chancellor of the Exchequer, is credited with what has become known as "The Law of Holes." It states: "When you are in one, stop digging." The CEOs of France Télécom and Deutsche Telekom had probably not heard of it. By December 2002 – that is, in a short eighteen months: the debt of France Télécom had grown to $70 billion, and that of Deutsche Telekom to $64 billion, an increase of 36.7 percent in the case of France Télécom and of 48.5 percent in the case of Deutsche Telekom.

In 2002, France Télécom and Deutsche Telekom fired their CEOs, but this did not change much, and would have gone under were it not for covert government support which continued as the debt kept mounting. The equity market took notice. Over his years of tenure as CEO of Deutsche Telekom (Europe's largest carrier), Ron Sommer presided over a 90 percent share price fall since the equity's March 2000 peak:

- The company was dragged down by its huge debt load and a management which had lost its sense of direction
- But the debt did not get any smaller just because Sommer cleared out his desk; it got slightly worse because he was given $15 million in severance pay.

This unsustainable debt of Germany's former state monopoly did not do much to improve the country's antiquated telephone system, except perhaps for East Germany whose phone network was renewed at Deutsche Telekom's expense – the government who had taken that decision heavy in capital costs did not compensate Deutsche Telekom for the expenses, as should have been the case. Investors must also take note that Deutsche Telekom's debt is currently rated three notches above junk only because the company is still a sort of state monopoly.

The new management of Deutsche Telekom has no margin for error. If something unexpected hits cash flow it will most likely be obliged to do a workout that will force bondholders (primarily international institutional investors) to accept less than face value. "Until you sort out the debt, you are just papering over the cracks," one analyst said. "Doing nothing is only risking more value destruction," Simon Surtees of Bear Stearns commented.[5]

The unloading of assets which were once considered to be Deutsche Telekom's core business is an option, but it's a buyers' market and they will not fetch much. Deutsche Telekom had negotiated to sell its six cable television networks as a single package, covering six regions and 10 million households, to US cable operator Liberty Media for Euro 5.5 billion ($5.5 billion), but the sale was blocked by the German Cartel Office. In August 2002, Liberty Media renewed its interest in buying the cable networks, through the interface of an intermediary, but said that this time it would not offer more than $1.5 billion.

Another possibility of unloading assets under fire-sale conditions was that of Deutsche Telekom's US mobile operator VoiceStream. Its timing in 2002 could not be more unfortunate as the market said that the parent company had lost control of its business plan, and there were no offers for more than 30 percent of the $26 billion Deutsche Telekom had paid to acquire upstart VoiceStream. At the time of writing, the sale has not gone through.

3   Mismanagement at AT&T

All the cases we saw in section 2 are examples of *lack of strategy* on how to avoid crises and how to handle them when they come. It is no accident that telecoms are highly indebted companies. In the late 1990s, along with technology and media, telecoms was the growth industry whose management misjudged the market's potential and greatly miscalculated the deadly effects of high debt which could be serviced through current cash flow.

What is surprising is not that mistakes were made; this is only human. The surprise is that highly paid CEOs, CFOs, and their immediate assistants, who should have known better, kept on repeating these mistakes – as if they were driven by an irresistible force to destroy their business.

In June 2001, Verizon (the former Nynex, a baby Bell) had a net debt of $50.7 billion. A year later, in June 2002, this had grown to $64.3 billion, an increase of nearly 27 percent. With an estimated 2002 revenue at Verizon of $67.5 billion, the debt load is more than 95 percent of the turnover:

- At WorldCom, just before its failure, the debt to turnover ratio was less than 88 percent
- At SBC, another of the baby Bells, the debt ratio stood at 47 percent of 2002 revenue – and even that was too high.

What the CEOs and CFOs of WorldCom, Verizon, and many other companies have failed to appreciate is that debt has to be *serviced*. This cannot be done effectively unless short-term liabilities are kept low relative to annual revenue, so that some of the profits can be diverted to paying interest and repaying capital. This is taught in the freshman year of business schools, but high leveraging is known to blur management's vision.

Deutsche Telekom, France Télécom, Verizon, Global Crossing, and WorldCom are not the only telecoms companies which mismanaged themselves at the height of the market. Another sad story is provided by the formerly proud and mighty "Ma Bell." Through the 1990s, a few years after the baby Bells gained their independence, AT&T went through a disinvestment strategy:

- Lucent Technologies (the former Western Electric) and NCR were the leading examples of disinvestment of assets

- Disinvestment was then followed by a mergers and acquisitions mania financed by means of a huge and unwarranted leverage.

With events in the telecoms industry volatile, and with debt running high, it was not the time to become more aggressive. Yet, as recently as 2000, AT&T was on a buying spree. C. Michael Amstrong, its CEO, spent $97 billion to acquire two big cable competitors, TCI and MediaOne, with the goal of making AT&T a leader in the broadband business. Investors were not happy:

- Wall Street analysts said that, by at least one indicator, cost per cable subscriber Amstrong paid double the cable companies' market worth
- Others suggested that this unprecedented expenditure, made in the name of synergy bundling of cable, Internet, wireless, and telephone services, was ill-judged in the first place.

In the opinion of some of the experts participating in the research meetings which led to this book, AT&T's strategic plan was wanting, if not outright flawed. What followed proved them right because synergy was never achieved by AT&T's top brass. Instead, the company faced declining margins in its core business and its stock headed south. With deliverables lagging behind, Amstrong then threw the concept into reverse. In 2001, AT&T's CEO announced that the company would be broken up into four pieces. The market did not applaud. A short time later Amstrong changed the game plan once more, leading to a deal with Comcast for a merger that would give the combined company some 40 percent of all US cable customers – with himself at the helm. The deal was confirmed on November 19, 2002:

- Comcast bought AT&T's cable system for $58.7 billion
- This gave it altogether 22 million customers in 41 states, but also loaded it with $30 billion in debt.

Aside from the debt, Comcast had also to take care of the fact that AT&T's cables' margin was just 25 percent, comparing poorly to its own 42 percent. The new owner was also faced with the challenge of upgrading 60,000 miles of AT&T cable. "Comcast will have to work hard to get back to where it is now," said Paul Wright, an analyst for Loomis Sayles which held 1.59 million Comcast and 883,000 AT&T shares. "That could take as long as three or four years."[6]

The only good news for AT&T shareholders was that the CEO who created the turmoil parachuted somewhere else. But at the same time the Comcast deal posed many questions. If indeed cable was AT&T's future, with Comcast taking AT&T's crown jewels it was likely that some other companies would get AT&T's low-margin leftovers and other damaged goods.

In December 2002 the talk at Wall Street was that both AT&T and WorldCom (if it came out of a bankruptcy protection) would need a white knight – probably SBC. That would be the end of the venerable telephone company whose Bell Telephone Labs were once the envy of the world.

Nor were investors happy with the fact that, while AT&T's equity was being managed in a questionable way, as documented by the beating the market gave to the company's stock, its top executives were being paid a high premium. In 2001, Amstrong took his full $1.8 million salary, though he got a reduction in his bonus, to $2.2 million. Good sense would have suggested that bonuses should be paid for first-class management, not for cases where the market votes with dollars against the people at the helm and their policies. Officially, AT&T said that Amstrong's bonus was for:

- Cutting debt by $22 million in 2001 (a debt largely created through his stewardship)
- Seeing through the sale of AT&T Broadband to Comcast
- Spinning off AT&T Wireless, and
- Unwinding its international joint venture with BT, into which he had led AT&T earlier on.

Bonuses should be given for merit and nothing in this list could justify a bonus. This has been a sad indictment of the demerits of a company's incumbent management, while the equity, the company's supposed crown jewel, also lost weight. When the Comcast merger was announced, the cable assets Amstrong acquired in 1999 and 2000 for more than $97 billion in AT&T stock and debt were sold for just $72 billion. Since then, the Comcast stock which AT&T shareholders receive has declined from $38 a share to below $30. These are numbers which underline the demerits:

- The assets AT&T shareholders got in exchange for their $97 million shrank to $62 million – a loss of about 35 percent – with more bad news in the offing
- The CEO, however, was paid handsomely for these losses. In 2001, Amstrong received millions in compensation, and further millions in stock options.

There was also the Citigroup, Weill, Amstrong, and Grubman affair. In an email, dated January 13, 2001, Grubman allegedly wrote to Carol Cutler, an analyst at a money-management firm: "I used Sandy to get my kids in the 92nd Street Y preschool [which is harder than Harvard] and Sandy needed Amstrong's vote on our board to nuke Reed in showdown. Once the coast was clear for both of us [i.e. Sandy clear victor and my kids confirmed] I went back to my normal self [on AT&T]."[7]

The subtext behind this was that Jack Grubman, a long-time bear on AT&T, upgraded the stock in late November 1999 to the equivalent of a "strong buy" from a "hold." Grubman's children were admitted into the school around the time that Citigroup pledged a $1 million donation, which came after Citigroup's chief executive Sanford I. Weill had urged Grubman to "take a fresh look" at upgrading the stock of a major corporate client, AT&T. Grubman did take a fresh look. He not only upgraded AT&T equity but also helped in selling shares of AT&T Wireless. Eventually Grubman downgraded AT&T again. By then, the shares had lost 50 percent of their value, going from $57.43 to $28.82.[8]

As if this damage to shareholder money was not enough, in 2002 AT&T's compensation committee voted the CEO an additional 1.4 million stock options, worth $32 million even at AT&T's highly reduced equity price.[9] It would be difficult to find a clearer misuse of incentive compensation.

Indeed, this is one of the reasons why compensation committees have recently received such negative publicity. Many investors say that committees are more interested in showering the CEO and company top brass with options and other benefits than in looking after shareholder interest:

- Shareholder value is protected only by tying compensation to true market performance, and
- It is destroyed by lowering the threshold of performance to negative values, so that options can be exercised at will.

In AT&T's case, as in so many others, management performance has dived and shareholder interests been ignored when the company spun off what itself considered to be its most promising operations, like cable and AT&T Wireless Services. Mismanagement left the formerly proud company as primarily a long-distance operator facing fierce competition, with revenues projected to drop 12.7 percent in 2002 compared to 2001, which was not brilliant either.

4   Beyond mismanagement: Enron, WorldCom, Qwest Communications, J.S. Sainsbury, and WPP

In 1953, one of my professors at UCLA taught that even human stupidity has limits, and that where stupidity ends conflict of interest starts. This is the story of events at Enron (examined in detail in Part II) as well as of several other companies whose performance left much to be desired.

At Enron, just prior to the company's bankruptcy, its CEO, Kenneth Lay, flooded the email circuits with assurances to his employees that all was well. Lay informed everybody who would listen that the company he was heading was in good financial health. Subsequently, it was revealed that:

- Enron's accounting had been manipulated
- Debts of about $23 billion had been hidden
- The auditors had collaborated, and
- The company's top management was aware of its real condition.

Within a few months after Enron filed for protection from creditors, 29 people from senior management have been indicted because they sold a huge amount of their Enron stock just prior to the crash.[10] By putting themselves and their own interests ahead of those of shareholders, and by misinforming their employees, the selected few collected hundreds of millions of dollars, while the company's rank and file and its small investors lost everything.

At WorldCom there was a similar story. It started with misinformation of stakeholders and was followed by indictments. On August 1, 2002, Scott Sullivan, the CFO, and David Myers, the chief controller, were the first of WorldCom's top brass to be arrested on criminal charges stemming from the $3.8 billion ongoing investigation into the accounting fraud that prompted the telecoms group's collapse into bankruptcy. Sullivan and Myers were charged with:

- Conspiracy to commit securities fraud, and
- Five additional counts of false filings with the Securities and Exchange Commission (SEC).

After the two senior executives appeared in court, bail was set for Sullivan at $10 million against the value of his property in Florida, and for Myers at $2 million against his two properties in Mississippi. In late August 2002 two WorldCom accountants, who had been promoted to "directors," also came under fire. However, the fortunes of Myers and Sullivan seem to have diverged. Experts interpreted a more reserved attitude in the prosecutors towards Myers and the two WorldCom accountants/directors, as an indication that the three were ready to collaborate, while the former CFO seems to have been singled out.

In 2000, Conseco spent $45 million to recruit CEO Gary Wendt from GE Capital. Despite the dismal results and the fact that in July 2002 the stock was hovering at $1, the board awarded Wendt an $8 million bonus. In August 2002, Conseco shares were delisted from the Big Board and by September that same year the stock was trading at 7¢.

Extravagant pay for underperformance was made not only at Conseco, WorldCom, Enron, and AT&T. AT&T alumni, Josef Nacchio, had become the CEO of battered Qwest well before the company slid down the slope. Nacchio had an annual salary of $1.5 million with a bonus of $3.75 million, in spite of disastrous financial results. He also made $300 million from executive options. Creative accounting at Qwest seems to have produced an unjustified increase in annual business by $1.4 billion; this is being investigated by the SEC. Emilio Gnutti, one of Italy's wealthiest financiers and a backer of the hostile takeover of Telecom Italia in 1999, was convicted of insider trading.[11] As we will see in Chapter 6, options and insider trading correlate, and they tend to increment the financial power a person commands.

The US was the first country to outlaw insider trading, with stiff penalties for this unlawful act. But in the 1990s, executive options (see Chapter 5) provided the ideal tool to circumvent the letter of the law, besides being misused to reward underperformance rather than top results.

Creative accounting helps in the misuse of executive options, because it has become a tool of leverage helping to beautify the balance sheet.

J.S. Sainsbury, the UK food chain, had to uplift its balance sheet; to do so, it underwent the pains of leveraging and outsourcing its real estate and its information technology (IT). When the tri-party deal was done with Sainsbury, Accenture (formerly Andersen Consulting), and Barclays Capital theoretically what took place was nothing more than outsourcing Sainsbury's IT to Accenture, following a decision by the board that IT was not its core business:

- Practically, this decision was wrong because IT was core business in merchandising, as in banking
- Because no merchandiser can allow themself to turn off the lights of their network, losing control of IT is like hostaging the future.

The hypothesis that outsourcing the IT was motivated by leveraging the balance sheet became a certainty when, on April 7, 2002, it was announced that Sainsbury intended to underline its recovery with a trading statement showing that it was gaining market share from rivals such as Tesco and Safeway and by an announcement that it had significantly improved its balance sheet and was investing £1 billion ($1.55 billion) in its recovery program, including store refurbishment and price cuts.

Unconvinced by Sainsbury's sales figures, some analysts were still questioning its recovery strategy. Philip Dorgan, a long-time critic of the stock, pointed out that while Sainsbury has been good at generating extra sales, it had still to prove it could grow profits as quickly. Ian Macdougall, food analyst with Williams de Broe, said that he was not wholly persuaded by Sainsbury's recovery: "I am not quite sure what the formula is. There has been a tremendous pre-rapport effort. But it is coming off a very low base and it will be hard to sustain it."

All sorts of industries fall into the creative accounting trap. In the UK, WPP (which owns J. Walter Thompson, Ogilvy & Mather and Young & Rubicam) showed a pre-tax profit of £411 million ($640 million) for 2001, with its accounts audited by Andersen. But a new analysis by accountancy firm Willott Kingston Smith (WKS), which specialized in marketing services, showed the profit would have been just £96.9 million ($150 million) if more conservative book-keeping practices, on takeover, had been adopted. Something similar had happened according to WKS, with WPP's year 2000 accounts. The gimmick used in beefing up the income statement was goodwill depreciation. Companies must account for the depreciation of goodwill in the businesses they buy over a fixed period, usually twenty years. Custom rather than an exact definition by law considers this to be the basis for a true and fair view of accounts. But WPP massaged its depreciation data with certain key acquired businesses.[12] Instead of the twenty-year basis, it put a value of £950 million on its balance sheet for its major advertising agency takeovers, because it considered them to have an "infinite economic life" given that they were big names (Enron and WorldCom were also big names till they crashed). By failing to recognize depreciation of goodwill in the generally accepted way, WPP boosted profits that would otherwise have reflected the declining value of those businesses and associated goodwill.

5   BCCI

In the annals of credit institutions, the Bank of Credit and Commerce International (BCCI) will remain the transnational company that was able to navigate between regulatory authorities in a variety of countries, expanding its network and avoiding scrutiny by supervisors into its money laundering and other activities. Life finally caught up with it and with this started the chain of indictments making the BCCI case one of the foremost banking scandals in recent financial history. In 1991 when the regulators shut down BCCI, its books showed $20 billion in assets, but some $5 billion was missing. The people running the bank had used their depositors' money, the New York grand jury said, "to expand the base of the criminal enterprise, to acquire and maintain political influence..." and to enrich themselves. According to the New York indictments:

- The key figures were BCCI's founder, Agha Hasan Abedi and its executive director, Swaleh Naqvi, both indicted in New York in 1991
- Lesser but still important players in the BCCI network were Gaith Pharaon, Faisal Saud al-Fulaij, Kamal Adham, and Sayed Jawhary.

The US indictment accused Abedi and Naqvi of running a criminal enterprise that had bribed central bankers and government officials. It also accused two senior U.S. executives, Clifford and Altman, of helping BCCI hide its illegal ownership of a US bank. Both denied the charges.

The Court papers said that one of the ways that BCCI had sought to win favorable treatment in foreign countries was to help nations – including Pakistan, Senegal, Zambia, and Nigeria – evade the fiscal restraints placed on them by the World Bank and the IMF. In 1979, when Pakistan's currency reserves were low, BCCI had made a $1 billion loan, but the proceeds were falsely reported to the World Bank and IMF as an increase in reserves.

This was the creative accounting predecessor of the "prepays" created for Enron by J.P. Morgan Chase and Citigroup (see Chapter 8). But BCCI went further. Again according to the New York indictments it defrauded organizations such as the World Bank and the IMF, and bribed central bank officials in more than one country.[13]

Curiously enough, as US political analysts pointed out, the Justice Department's contributions to the investigation were rather modest. The real initiative and energy came from Robert M. Morgenthau, the New York District Attorney. The New York indictments against BCCI therefore reached much farther than the federal ones. BCCI's operations in the US were a flagrant violation of US banking law. So how did BCCI successfully evade the federal bank regulators for a decade, and why was Congress rather lenient? How could a man like Clark M. Clifford, with an illustrious career that turned on his probity and sound judgment as an advisor to US presidents and Lyndon Johnson's Secretary of Defense, get into so much trouble? Clifford was even credited with having master-minded Truman's come-from-behind victory over Thomas E. Dewey in the 1954 election.

Clifford had been John F. Kennedy's personal lawyer, had gone on special diplomatic missions for Jimmy Carter, and was still prominent enough in 1989 for the speaker of the House, Jim Wright, to retain him as his lawyer when Wright was being investigated by the House Ethics Committee.

Clark Clifford's legal clients included corporations as Standard Oil, Du Pont, Phillips Petroleum, AT&T, RCA, TWA, and ABC. In the 1960s he was said to be the first Washington lawyer to earn $1 million in a year. By the 1980s he was a millionaire many times over. His explanation was that he had been duped by BCCI. The prevailing view in Washington's legal and political circles has been that, at rock bottom, Clifford's legal troubles were the result of hubris. After all the years of cutting deals, of wielding influence, he came to think that the normal rules did not apply to him. The message this story carries is that big egos are self-destructive.

6 Shareholders kick out poorly performing CEOs

"Re-engineering," "downsizing," "cutting costs," or "chopping dead wood" describe the practice followed by companies for slimming down by eliminating middle management and rank-and-file jobs. There are even computer programs which help in doing so. Software that fires employees with a simple press of a key is the latest way for employers to downsize.[14]

The $500,000 "fireware" developed by Business Layers, of Rochelle Park, NJ, dumps intended employees with a memo, closes their payroll accounts, cancels company credit cards, shuts down email, eliminates parking privileges, and locks down telephone extensions. Employees' names are wiped off any password or company account they have ever used, as well as their "need to know" privileges. The software also alerts security to collect any notebook computers, cars, cell phones, or any hardware or software equipment that's ever been allocated to the fired employee. About twenty-five major firms had downsized using this software in early 2002 (ACM Communications Report).

Firing a CEO is a much more involved enterprise, even if shareholders are increasingly vigilant and fight back. James D. Robinson III could not escape growing shareholder disgust with how he clung to power at troubled financial services company American Express. On January 30, 1993, just a week after he seemed to have secured his position, Robinson declared he would quit as chairman of the company. His decision followed resignations by IBM chief executive John F. Akers, and the CEO of Westinghouse Electric, Paul E. Lego.

This shareholder sweep of the early 1990s caused the lock-out of the post-Second World War generation of managers, a group some analysts called the most powerful ever. Swinging in behind them, and maybe pushing them out, was a new generation of younger managers, the generation which first performed, and then faltered, in the late 1990s.

Some experts say that even if the results with the new generation were not that brilliant, the sluggish corporate performance by former General Motors (GM) chairman Robert C. Stempel and Digital Equipment (DEC) chairman Kenneth Olsen opened up the road to CEO change. But did their successors, John F. Smith, Jr. and Robert B. Palmer, perform any better? Smith maybe, since GM is still around; but not Palmer who presided over the final demise of DEC. This is the law of *unintended consequences*. The real tragedy of corporate life is that:

- Changes occur only after it is too late, and
- Their aftermath can never be projected with precision.

Instead of capitalizing on opportunity, most companies are responding to crisis. When an entity is down, it is pretty hard to put it together again. The most visible result is embarrassment and deception, while the very reputation of the directors and of the new CEO is at stake. But staying with business leaders who are not in command is no solution either.

Take AmEx as an example. As problems mounted in the company's travel card operation and at its Shearson Lehman Brothers brokerage subsidiary, shareholders and a few dissident directors pressed for change at the top. James D. Robinson succeeded in salvaging the chairman's office for himself and the CEO's post for Harvey Golub, his choice as successor. Rather than keep battling, three board dissidents resigned. It was only the news of fresh losses at Shearson, amid record profits elsewhere on Wall Street, that provoked a new fury from investors which finally ousted Robinson.

BankAmerica's David Coulter had been chief executive of the newly formed BankAmerica–NationsBank merger only a few months when the enterprise announced a $1.4 billion loss; he fell on his sword as soon as the losses became public. Kenneth Burenga, Dow Jones' president and COO, resigned at 54 in the aftermath of the company's failed foray into the financial services business. Wall Street is always ripe with speculation that this or that CEO may be next, because he is accountable if something goes wrong.

The CEO of Salomon from 1983 to August 1991, John H. Gutfreund, enriched the company but also made some major mistakes, largely through substandard risk control. Perhaps the worst error was failing to inform the New York Federal Reserve Bank in 1991 when the firm found it had submitted a false bid in a Treasury note auction. While he was never charged with wrongdoing, Gutfreund resigned from Salomon and agreed to pay a $100,000 civil penalty. Another error was a pay deal with supertrader John W. Meriwether, which badly undermined the firm's compensation system. Gutfreund had made a name for himself because of being able to manage big egos, and because of his ability to gauge losses by the expression on a trader's face. Under his leadership much of the value of Salomon was created and then destroyed through a short series of flawed decisions.

Deeper personal accountability is the answer to these executive failures which can break and sink an enterprise. This deeper accountability existed in America, though it took some leave in the 1990s. Some say that personal accountability has never really characterized the less transparent environments of European firms, and European corporate leaders winced when a few heads rolled among them in the late 1990s. The most prominent were: Matthis Cabiallavetta, chairman of United Bank of Switzerland (UBS); Hans Wilhelm Gaeb, Adam Opel's supervisory board chief; and Gian Mario Rossignolo, Italia Telecom's chief executive. One of the major and persisting problems in Europe, in terms of CEO accountability, is that the CEO mantle almost comes with a sense of entitlement: this is a job to last for years, whether business is good or bad.

Exceptions do exist. In the early 1960s I was consultant to the executive board of AEG-Telefunken. The senior executive who introduced me to Dr. Gammer (the newly elected CEO) had warned me of the need to make a good impression: "This is the man who will lead our company for the next twenty years," he said. But business life took a different path, and the new CEO lasted only twenty months.

The more shareholders get proactive the less the CEOs can survive "whether business is good or bad." In Europe, as the cases of Vivendi, France Télécom and Deutsche Telekom in 2002 demonstrate, the travails of several companies now hit their CEO on the head. One reason is the result of globalization in investments: big international investors no longer tolerate losses or poor performance for long. To survive, CEOs need to be in the marketplace more than in the boardroom:

- Talking to customers
- Seeing people who are business partners
- Trying to sense what's going on, and
- Taking corrective action.

What is still missing is a culture making it mandatory that the CEO should be accountable for preserving sound business practices and directly responsible for results – in the short, medium and longer term. Personal accountability has been destroyed by lust, greed, overgearing, creative accounting, and the practice of unreliable financial reporting.

7   Charismatic and honest business leaders

Not every CEO is greedy – there exist notable exceptions. One that comes to mind is Raymond J. Noorda, who built Novell, one of technology's giants.

While his Novell stock alone made him nearly a billionaire, Noorda insisted on flying standby to get a senior citizen discount. Dining out, for cost control reasons, he liked the less expensive restaurants.

Noorda started at Novell in 1983 making $90,000, but three years later, when two of his sons began working at the company, he decided that for every dollar they were paid, he should earn one less. His salary dropped below $40,000. When his sons left in 1988, he didn't raise his wages; embarrassed board members raised his pay to $198,830 in 1992.

"I just don't like to spend a lot of money for things," Raymond Noorda used to say.[15] That was evident at Novell's offices, which were Spartan: employees referred to headquarters as the "space station." Even when company revenues were growing 30 percent – 40 percent per year, Noorda instituted spending cuts. This was his means of setting a standard at the company.

Another charismatic business leader, of the post-Second World War years has been Sam Walton, the founder of WalMart Stores. He was known for his masterful selling instincts and habit of turning up at stores to inspect the wares and inspire the troops. Walton became a legend inside and outside his company. Among his legacies was the cost-consciousness and the flexibility he built into the enterprise and the culture of an immediate response to problems which invariably come up. Flexibility and fast response were Walton's best known management principle. The first is exemplified by his ability to turn on a dime, which he conveyed to his immediate assistants. An example of the second was his ability to put his hands around the problem, so that the response was fast and factual. WalMart grew from a local store in Arkansas to the largest merchandising chain in the world.

Another great example of a very successful CEO who respected shareholders' money was Warren E. Buffett, the CEO of Berkshire Hathaway. Buffett, who is probably the most careful investor in life today, is known for his position that too many pay plans are "long on carrots and short on sticks."[16] He is against:

- The misuse of stock options by CEOs and their immediate assistants, and
- The lobbying against an accounting rule that would make companies charge options to corporate earnings.

Buffett pays himself a very reasonable annual salary of $100,000 with no bonuses or stock options, while shareholders have seen the value of their stake in the company rise steadily, with few exceptions (2001 was the only recent year with losses because of the impact of September 11 on the insurance and reinsurance industries).

The CEO of Berkshire practices what he says and has been castigated for it. Pay was a vital issue for Salomon Brothers when Buffett took the helm in the mid-1990s, following the disaster of mishandled treasury securities (see section 6). At Salomon, compensation in 1994 was $1.36 billion, two-thirds of total non-interest costs of $2.04 billion. In 1993, a record profit year, compensation had been $445 million higher, at $1.81 billion.

For Buffett, the pay question was not simply a matter of cost-cutting. High pay levels for certain individuals symbolized much of what was wrong in corporate America, particularly in the financial industry where bonuses had begun to reach for the stars. In the individualistic culture of the 1980s and 1990s which spread over the first lean years of the twenty-first century:

- Star performers received huge salaries which were not necessarily commensurate with their deliverables
- CEOs and other top brass who underperformed had the compensation committee award them even bigger handouts.

At Salomon Brothers, Buffett's pay scheme aimed to link pay to profits by setting a threshold return on equity. Below this, managing directors in the client-driven business were to receive a "relatively miserly" 35 percent of their 1994 compensation. If the return exceeded the threshold, the partners would take 40 percent of the profits. This was a very reasonable plan, but Salomon's fat cats rebelled.

What Buffett failed to realize was that even a powerful manager could not stand up to the proprietary traders who had made a dominant share of Salomon Brothers' profits in the late 1980s/early 1990s. This was just as true of John Gutfreund, who contributed to the huge bonus culture by caving in when the star traders asked for outrageous amounts of money. That set the tone for later disruptive battles over pay. Buffett's attempt to bring back discipline was a milestone, but his plan failed to tie bonuses to the firm's performance because things had already gone too far. Being an outsider, he lacked clout with the traders and his efforts led to a rash of departures by senior staff, helping to undermine his authority. He was therefore unable to redress a situation which had run out of control.

Buffett was much more successful as an investor where he applied the same wealth-preservation principles – as he says: "You can pay too much for even the best of businesses." "The over-payment risk surfaces periodically and, in our opinion, may now be quite high for the purchasers of virtually all stocks"[17] and he toned down his acquisitions policy. "We continue to make more money snoring than when active," he suggested in Berkshire's 1996 *Annual Report*: "Inactivity strikes us as intelligent behavior."

3
Creative Accounting, EBITDA, and Core Earnings

1 Introduction

Many companies are prone to use financial levers, such as gains from their pension funds, to boost reported profits. Until recently, this was a legal accounting practice, but many investors say it gave an overly rosy view of company results. After the 1999–2002 problems, increased scrutiny of accounting practices means that companies have to be very careful about how they beautify their bottom line. They now have to:

- Release more data to regulators and shareholders in their *Annual Reports*
- Avoid practices which the market considers distortions of accounting procedures
- Stop leveraging their profits by mixing pension fund gains and other one-off or non-core items, and
- Distinguish intellectual property income as a separate line item, instead of combining it with general management to make overhead expenses look lower.

Proforma financial reporting, in which each company draws up the accounting presentation as it pleases, and accounting manipulations like earnings before interest, taxes, depreciation and amortization (EBITDA) have made investors very careful about the financial numbers they are getting. Increasingly, stakeholders have come to understand that in the corporate world it is not exactly black and white when it comes to accounting procedures.

Creative accounting has many aspects, some of which are on the borderline between legality and illegality in financial reporting, while others are plain illegal but companies adopt them until they are caught. This sort of accounting is "creative" only in the sense that it uses reporting practices which masquerade as being compliant with rules and regulations but in reality are in conflict with them.

One of the commonest stratagems is to increase the level of complexity of the accounts, so that it becomes nearly impossible to untangle them. The

Byzantine book-keeping of the now-bankrupt Kirch Group, Germany's media conglomerate, proved an obstacle in reading its books after its bankruptcy. Some analysts say that a whole team of consultants, accountants, and Kirch employees labored to untangle the mess. In the longer term, creative accounting is counterproductive because it ends by misleading the company's own management. What happened at Kirch proved to be the Group's undoing. Fear of lack of transparency and hidden liabilities discouraged buyers such as Bertelsmann. For precisely the same reasons, Bertelsmann, who was initially interested in Vivendi, decided to opt out. According to published reports, it found the book-keeping too complicated.[1]

Like other overleveraged companies, the French conglomerate Vivendi-Universal was struggling to pay debt – some \$19 billion – after it sold its Scandinavian pay-TV unit to Norwegian telephone company Telenor, and its unprofitable Italian pay-TV business Telepiù to Murdoch. At the end of August 2002 it sold its Vis-à-Vis portal to Vodafone for a rumored \$148 million, one-seventh what it had cost the company to build it up. Together with weekly magazines, which were its crown jewels, Vivendi collected less than \$430 million, which did not even represent 2.3 percent of its huge debt.

Rather like getting drunk, creative accounting in the very short term lifts management's spirits – and sometimes the markets' belief – in the medium term its glow fades away; even worse, the beefed-up financial figures become a drag. In the longer run, manipulating the books ruins reputations and eventually sends companies to the abyss. Look at Enron, WorldCom, Kirch Group and Vivendi.

2 Rethinking the reliability of accounting

Events such as the collapse of Enron, Global Crossing, WorldCom, and even of not-for-profits foundations (see Chapter 6), have cast doubt on the reliability of accounting and auditing practices. Accountants, auditors, rating agencies, financial analysts, and the entities' own top management have all come under fire:

- Institutional investors have drawn criticism for accepting published corporate profit figures at face value, and
- Experts say that over-reliance on audited figures and on creditor protection acts has emptied several portfolios of their wealth.

It took the débâcle of 2000–3 to appreciate that overleveraging and overvaluing of company stocks is a negative. In the late 1990s, the so-called "Clinton years," both financial analysts and investors pushed growth companies to reach for higher and higher targets. The management of these firms was too eager to oblige, yet it should have known that no company could hope to double its business and profits forever. Senior management abdicated responsibility with creative accounting practices because it responded to the market's push with actions that generated long-term imbalances and led to a crash. This was by no means limited to startups. For mature companies which chose the same road look at Nortel, Lucent Technologies, Ericsson, Alcatel, and many other firms.

In retrospect, a sound longer-term policy would have suggested that managers must abandon the notion that higher stock prices are *always* better. All stakeholders should recognize that, beyond the fact that creative accounting is in the longer term harmful, an overvalued stock can be as dangerous to a firm as an undervalued one. Extreme events are full of risk:

- Meeting investor expectations in the longer run means willingness to take the necessary actions to eliminate equity overvaluation when it occurs
- Avoidance of overleveraging and the practice of factual reporting benefits all players in the market, because this is the best way to keep the company as a going concern and to maintain market confidence.

Even if analysts challenge senior management to reach for unprecedented earnings growth, it is the board's and the executive committee's unquestionable responsibility to explain why this is the wrong policy. Unfortunately, very often top management believes increasingly unrealistic projections and adopts them as a basis for setting goals for CEOs and their firm. At the same time, inflated stock prices encouraged many CEOs to make acquisitions and other large but doubtful investments in the unrealistic hope of sustaining high growth. The unwise trend of continuing to meet analysts' growing expectations becomes the rule. Some of the CEOs became media performers and quasi-celebrities, which helped to inflate their egos.

Technology companies were not the only ones to fall into this trap. On August 1, 2002, Warnaco, the maker of Calvin Klein jeans and underwear and Speedo swimsuits, said that the Securities and Exchange Commission (SEC) planned to charge the company and some former employees with breaking securities' laws, apparently stemming from accounting problems that had led the company to overstate profits and understate losses by $51 million between 1999 and early 2001.

This possibility of questionable financial reporting by a non-technology company was particularly significant because, among other things, Warnaco had been laboring under almost $3 billion of debt and it had also been out of compliance with several loan agreements. That is what can happen if good sense is forgotten and bad management practices come in.

The most common excuse for abuses in financial reporting is that management tried to capitalize on favorable market conditions which might enable their company to exceed historical performance levels. This is the wrong way of thinking and an unwise approach, because it leads executives and analysts alike to view unsustainable levels of growth as the norm – thereby leading to other mistaken decisions.

Leveraging, inflated gains, and hidden losses are not the only ways to manipulate financial results. Securitization of corporate assets with scant disclosure of embedded risk is one of the practices which contributed to them first masquerading as sound investments, then to spreading the impact of bankruptcy widely among investors. Many banks exposed on loans to Enron and WorldCom sold securitized products with a great deal of credit risk to institutional investors and to their retail clients (more about this in Parts II and III).

To recoup some of their losses, some credit institutions went short on the companies to whom they had loaned money, by using inside information obtained through their credit department. This reflects the recently developing notion that the culture of a corporation can produce malfeasance, destroying longer-term corporate survivability while gaining only a dubious sense of short-term "success."

People who are clear-eyed and have the right management culture condemn this practice. In December 2002, in an interview for CNBC, Dr. Peter Drucker said that some CEOs could see no further than the next three months. Drucker correctly condemned the practice; as an article in *The Economist* suggested, the consequences for a company accused of manipulating its accounts can be severe.[2]

Arthur Andersen is an example of the consequences of failure to act according to ethical standards. Many clients have deserted the global accounting firm, thousands of employees have lost their jobs, and the company's international network has crumbled:

- A criminal indictment can be the company's death warrant
- Banks and other financial companies who consider acting in a way that invites regulatory action, if not outright public condemnation, should think of the after-effects *before* taking that road.

There is plenty of evidence today that creative accounting practices are senseless. The government prosecutors know that they can choose a civil over a criminal charge because it carries a preponderance of evidence rather than proof beyond reasonable doubt. While the penalties imposed in a civil case may be less severe than those in a criminal one, the *reputational risk* is much the same.

As the events of the 1990s starkly demonstrate, creative accounting has reached the limits of how far it can go without invoking an inordinate amount of reputational risk. Stakeholders are becoming wiser and more inquisitive. Enron, Global Crossing, WorldCom, Kirch, Vivendi and many other meltdowns, have directed new attention to the ills of manipulated accounts and inadequate surveillance or transparency.

The consequence has been a loss of trust that needs to be won back, and this will not be easy as long as institutional investors and retail clients of banks and brokers are still being taken for a ride by risky new gimmicks like alternative investments.[3] Investment bankers have a conflict of interest in selling shaky assets; company CEOs have been manipulating accounts to suit their own finances, rather than their shareholders for too long; and certified public accountants (CPAs) have neglected their duties.

3   Understanding creative accounting

The Introduction should have drawn the reader's attention to the fact that creative accounting has many aspects. Some of them are qualitative, while others are quantitative; some have to do with book entries and with double books, others aim at manipulation of capital markets. Traders, for example, are using options to impact on stock indices, including the Dow Jones, Nasdaq, and London's FTSE 100. That is creative accounting "in the large."

Companies can set the stage for creative accounting by adding some sophisticated but highly risky ingredients to their recipe of financial deals. Exotic derivatives is a popular one, often done with the involvement of an investment bank. This can have dire consequences. Yamaichi Securities was Japan's third largest financial services company:

- In late 1996 it established a proprietary derivatives trading desk specializing in exotics
- One year later, it announced a $2 billion loss, and went bankrupt.

The cocktail of derivatives and creative accounting had led to an unprecedented amount of dysfunctional financial behavior. The *McKinsey Quarterly* (February 1997) includes some interesting references and also explains how certain ideas can lead to major short-term financial advantages.[4] One example concerns the aftermath of some off-balance sheet deals:

> The deployment of off-balance-sheet funds using institutional investment money fostered [Enron's] securitization skills and granted it access to capital at below the hurdle [minimum] rates of major oil companies.

A second example from the same source helps to explain how certain types of negotiations can lead to new business opportunities, altering the way financial work is traditionally done or a company's core business is served:

> Enron was not distinctive at building and operating power stations, but it didn't matter; the skills could be contracted out. Rather, it was good at negotiating contracts, financing, and government guarantees – precisely the skills that distinguished successful players.

As the 2002 *BusinessWeek* article suggests, credit for some of these moves goes to consultants like Doug Woodham. Woodham became vice-president at Enron Capital & Trade Resources, where he led a team that developed an electric power and natural gas hedge fund. Enron seems to have increasingly drawn on McKinsey partners with expertise in trading, risk management, and investment banking.

In the financial markets at large, derivative financial instruments, novel investment banking deals, and creative accounting have created a whole new generation of products that can be used to beautify the books. Older approaches like the liberty taken with write-off of goodwill now are falling under the rule of regulators (see section 6), while exotic derivatives can provide an unregulated field. Huge goodwill write-offs, for instance, were precipitated by the change of rules about how companies must account for *goodwill*, effected by the Financial Accounting Standards Board (FASB) in June 2001. Goodwill in the balance sheet is the intangible value assumed to exist when one company buys another and pays more than the acquirees' plants and equipment are really worth. That higher value can include brand names, patents, and presumed management expertise. According to the 2001 FASB reporting standards, companies no longer had to amortize goodwill by taking a charge every quarter. Instead, they could write off as much goodwill as they wished in the next reporting period (fiscal 2002). After that, they have to categorize goodwill, and account for it at least once a year.

Goodwill has been a huge loophole in financial reporting practices, but after Enron filed for Chapter 11 in December 2001 money managers started to scrutinize companies' books as never before, dumping stocks when they suspected manipulative practices in accounting. Because of Enron's bankruptcy market regulators are beginning to take a closer look at corporate accounting at large and goodwill practices in particular.

Following the 2001 FASB reporting standards, many companies felt that taking big write-offs during a recession could keep them from taking smaller ones later that could distract shareholders as the economy revived. They therefore intentionally depressed their results in 2002, in the hope that this would eventually allow them to inflate financial results in 2003 on a year-to-year basis. JDS Uniphase (JDSU) was the first to make a king-size write off of over $50 billion in late July 2001, the largest in US corporate history. Other companies were not too far behind. As of September 30, 2001, AOL Time Warner had $126.9 billion in goodwill and it took nearly 50 percent of that amount in write-off in 2002. As of September 2001, Viacom had $71.3 billion of goodwill, approaching its market value of $78.3 billion but Qwest Communications International did better than that. It had $30.8 billion of goodwill swamping its $23.5 billion market value at that date.

The equity of JDSU, AOL Time Warner, Viacom, Qwest and other TMT stocks were not the only ones that were hit as a result of huge goodwill write-offs. Shares in other companies fell as analysts issued conflicting research results on the quality of their accounting and debt levels. Rolls-Royce provides an example. In early 2002, Goldman Sachs issued a note giving a share price target of 100p for the jet engine maker, and said Rolls-Royce had:

- A combination of high debt both on- and off-balance sheet
- Significant absorption of future profits by non-equity partners, and
- Risk of a credit rating downgrade, expected to further depress the stock.

Goldman Sachs added that off-balance sheet debt was hidden but large, while Rolls-Royce also had significant off-balance sheet debt in its financial services division through aircraft and engine leasing companies and a power station developer. Dresdner Kleinwort Wasserstein, however, had a different opinion. Its aerospace analyst suggested that Rolls-Royce's balance sheet and accounting concerns were negatively weighing on the share price, but that they were well-known to the market and therefore could be discounted.

The irony is that there can be a downside in abandoning a creative accounting practice a company has used for some time. According to some expert opinions, one of the curious results of a change in current accounting procedures which have been so deeply embedded in corporate practice is that as companies come clean about their accounting method and stop massaging earnings as they have been doing for the last five or seven years, their stocks may suffer a prolonged drag. Financial analysts suggest that this is particularly a problem for companies that have been overstating earnings by as much as 15 percent annually over the past half dozen years. As a result of deflation in their leveraged financial figures, it is no longer possible for them to meet the numbers they have been reporting with the aid of creative accounting. This proved to be the case in a recession year like 2002.

4 Management ethics and financial disclosures

Management ethics and good business sense work in synergy. In the longer term, the market accords a *transparency premium* to the share price of companies who are willing and able to provide clear, consistent and informative disclosure about their operations. To be of value to investors, such disclosure must go beyond the general line of how the company works, to include the risks that are taken and provide an accurate understanding of economic drivers.

This information should be complemented by detailed financial results of the business. It is part of the ethics of top management to assure that financial disclosure is consistent and comparable within each reporting period, and between reporting periods, and that both quantitative and qualitative information is presented in as simple a manner as possible, reflecting the readers' ability to understand the company's performance.

Unbiased reporting standards are all-important in substantiating a strong commitment to corporate responsibility, in recognition of the demands made by different stakeholders: equity investors, employees, and the regulators.

A frequently encountered problem, however, is that corporate responsibility means different things to different people.

The principle which I follow is that core corporate responsibilities start and end with *ethical governance*. In terms of ethics, "what you see" is not what you get, because so many things are hidden. Ethics means *virtue* and as Socrates said virtue is knowledge and cannot be taught. This knowledge is constantly evolving, and often goes beyond formal legal and regulatory requirements, with the market reputation being the criterion:

- Management virtue and market discipline are twins
- Market discipline means growing demand for more responsible personal and corporate behavior.

Firms must meet this demand at an early stage, taking their responsibilities seriously and putting the stakeholders' interests first. A personal account-ability and corporate responsibility strategy has to be transparent and show factual and documented results for the efforts being undertaken. Measuring performance is therefore essential, and it should be done through compre-hensive and generally accepted criteria and standards. Standards should allow one to measure progress against objectives and make comparisons within and outside one's industry. The regulators have taken upon them-selves the promulgation of such standards, but a survey by the Basel Committee on Banking Supervision[5] pointed out that a rapidly changing business environment contributes to decreasing the lifecycle of prudential standards:

- Disclosure rates generally decreased as the sophistication and complexity of proprietary information increased
- Data about credit risk modeling, credit derivatives, and securitization was disclosed by fewer than half of the banks
- Only 11 percent of banks provided information about credit risk models that was comparable to data disclosed about market risk models
- Although almost all banks disclosed their risk-based capital ratio, fewer than half provided information on credit and market risk against which capital served as a buffer
- In 2000, the disclosure rate of *trigger events* that might affect the nature or cost of capital instruments shrank to 33 percent, down from 36 per-cent in 1999
- About 20 percent of the banks did not disclose how they determined when their credits were impaired or past their due date
- Only 7 percent of credit institutions disclosed the replacement cost of non-performing derivatives in 2000, down from 13 percent in 1999.

The Basel Committee report did not state it explicitly, but the reader will be excused from wondering if this 6 percent of credit institutions which failed to disclose the replacement cost of non-performing derivatives in 2000 dropped below the radar screen because their losses were so large. The old adage that "money buys power and power buys money" need to be adapted to reflect the fact that with leveraged instruments money can turn to ashes.

In terms of prudential supervision, the Basel Committee report made reference to the fact that in some countries, there was no definitive guidance in reporting on gains and losses associated with highly leveraged instruments. Some of these countries, it should be added, are members of the Group of Ten (G-10). Think about the absence of standards for reliable financial reporting in emerging markets.

Frank Partnoy gives plenty of examples of financial problems.[6] One of them concerned Japanese companies which had experienced significant losses. Worried about the upcoming fiscal year-end, they asked Morgan Stanley how they might be able to generate quick profits to hide their losses by using derivatives and creative book-keeping.

Numerous US banks, Partnoy says, were doing deals to generate false profits, accounting standards were lax and Japanese companies "would be able to hide the offsetting loss for years, perhaps for decades... Several firms... even admitted to dealings with organized crime."

Lack of transparency in financial reporting contributed a great deal to the market malaise which became evident in Japan from the late 1980s. Unable to see clarity in financial statements and unwilling to take inordinate risks, investors pulled more money out of US equity mutual funds in June and July 2002 than they did in the weeks after September 11, 2001. Unless:

- Opacity in financial reporting
- Senior management ineptness, and
- Lack of transparency in accounting

are checked, recovery can be aborted in a slumping market which brings more bad surprises. What investors today need above everything else is *confidence* and *reliability*. Weary of corporate bad judgment, many investors want to see CEOs and CFOs sign off their company's financial books, assuming personal accountability before they will buy stocks again. The US Bush administration has been right in its decision to:

- Double prison terms for CEOs guilty of financial fraud
- Freeze improper payments to corporate executives
- Force managers who benefit from false accounting to forfeit their gains, and
- Set the SEC to ban convicted chief executives from ever again serving on a board.

It is proper for all governments which have experienced such manipulation in financial reports to admit that the system itself has been corrupted and needs repair, rather than lobbying against the new US financial reporting standards. Many of Japan's most influential executives are concerned that the requirements laid down for CEOs and CFOs of companies quoted on the

NYSE are unsuitable for the Japanese corporate environment. A number of other companies have expressed similar worries.

Like some of its European counterparts, the Japanese Business Federation has been lobbying on behalf of the country's largest companies to exempt them from the Sarbanes–Oxley Act, passed in mid-2002 in response to the wave of corporate scandals. The Federation said that its members should be able to retain a more "Japanese-style" corporate governance regime, whatever that might mean.

As the careful reader will recall from the previous chapters, the SEC has passed a requirement that senior executives of all companies listed on the US capital markets swear to the accuracy of their financial statements. The SEC has indicated that it will not grant exemptions which might undermine the reliability of financial reporting practices.

Self-regulation might have been a preferable alternative to the heavy hand of government, but human nature being what it is, this does not seem feasible. Legal measures to reform business ethics seems the only way to restore market confidence, which in practice is what the 2002 Sarbanes–Oxley Act was all about.

5 Income statement, proforma, and EBITDA

Classically, a lack of significant amounts of informative detail have been included in income statements. The profit and loss account (PLA) merely recites the results of the past period and the amount available for appropriation. There is an absence of comparative information as to how revenues were realized, subdivided, or departmentalized. Yet, this would have been instrumental:

- In showing the *sources* and *results* of each major income-producing activity, and
- In furnishing data helpful in the determination of *trends in revenues and expenses*.

The question: "How much income detail?" suggests a fertile field of inquiry, while a preview of expected business results could offer a window into the future (see section 7, on forward-looking statements). At the same time, while the current structure of financial statements does not excel in informative detail, it does contain a standard form of data regarding:

- Interest on borrowed capital
- Amount retained in the business
- Taxes to government
- Compensation to employees
- Compensation to management, and
- Dividends to owners.

Such information enables investors to look at the balance sheet and income statement as instruments in the financial evaluation of a company's performance and in the equilibrium of the corporate equation. The classical way is to look at a company's financial rewards as being related to effort, initiative, and risk – with the capital they are investing having the promise and prospect of commensurate returns, as an inducement to taking risks. Such visibility, however, is destroyed with individualistic proforma reporting.

When in July 2002 the news about WorldCom's $3.8 billion fraud hit the market, few people remembered that this company and its top financial officials had been pioneers of a controversial method of financial presentation, hailed during the takeover boom of the 1990s as a sort of financial Messiah. *Proforma* accounting involved stripping all post-merger charges and other one-time expenses out of the company's results:

- The goal was to show what was claimed to be a "clearer picture" of a company's underlying performance
- Proforma reporting was then invariably manipulated to show a steady improvement in an entity's earnings.

WorldCom and many other companies profited handsomely from the lack of transparency which came with proforma reporting. But by depriving investors and analysts of financial detail, proforma left them dependent on the company's own interpretation of its financial results which might prove to be one-sided, biased, and misleading.

The practice became popular and, curiously enough, for several years nobody truly objected as long as WorldCom's and other companies' stocks continued to rise. These were firms enjoying a strong following among the analysts, and this shaped the financial markets' opinion. But holding the higher ground gradually meant bolder misrepresentation of financial data all the way to the $3.8 billion WorldCom crash.

The unreliability of a cooked-up EBITDA has been demonstrated on many occasions. A case in point is KPNQwest. In 2001, Jack McMaster, its CEO, proudly told *CommunicationsWeek International* that his company was EBITDA-positive[7] – one of the first of the pan-European new carriers to be able to say that it looked as though the firm was starting to generate enough cash to fund its operations. A year later, in May 2002, the crash of KPNQwest raised serious doubts over whether EBITDA was of any use at all in measuring either:

- The financial performance of businesses, or
- Their financial staying power.

The tech sector at large became, and remained, the home of proforma reporting. This persisted in spite of the principle that when it comes to how financial results are presented, it is in investors' best interests to value companies based on plain, old-fashioned reported earnings – as well as stress tests.[8] It is therefore surprising that earnings before interest depreciation and amortization:

- Has become the key indicator for new entrant companies, and
- It is seen by many as a proxy for operational cash flow, which is wrong.

A further irony is that by relying on EBITDA firms are effectively reducing their own chances of survival, because the sheer weight of costs supporting supposedly high earnings outruns the company's ability to turn up the corresponding volume of cash. Proforma reporting also masks the facts about financial solvency. All too often, investors have to wait until companies go into administration to find out the right information about the extent of liabilities and the liabilities' excess over assets.

One of the many reasons for investor misinformation was that proforma data were not audited. In fact, in the light of wide-ranging concerns about opaque accounting, it is surprising that investors continued to be happy with tech companies' tendency to release proforma results – or that regulators did not take steps to explore the balances in spite of the fact that proforma began drifting toward the area of financial reporting fraud.

The transition from lack of transparency and one-sided reporting to actual fraud did not happen overnight. It transited through earnings before interest, taxes, depreciation, and amortization (EBITDAO, the "O" standing for executive options). EBITDA is an inadequate guide to cash flow because it does not account for the company's capital spending:

- It does not show how much profit is actually turned into cash, or is tied up in receivables
- Nor does it show how much money banks and capital markets are willing to lend to the firm, and under what conditions.

Not only startups but also many established companies are enthusiastic users of EBITDA because it gives a starry picture of their performance, thereby allowing them to be "transparent" in their own terms, which often are quite remote from financial reality. Yet financial reality is most vital at a time when more resources are being devoted to the acquisition of financial assets than of non-financial assets. Figure 3.1 presents a decade of statistics from Germany.

I look at declarations that EBITDA reporting is "just fine," as nothing more than misleading words. "We are transparent enough that market and analysts can make their calculations the way they want to," said the CFO of Vivendi which even bases its bonus schemes for top management on EBITDA. This unrealistic (if not surrealistic) reporting explains why Jean-Marie Messier, Vivendi's ousted CEO, got an impressive pay of Euro 5.12 million ($5.12 million) in 2001 despite the fact that Vivendi announced France's biggest-ever corporate loss of Euro 13.6 billion ($13.6 billion).[9] There are also other stratagems which give manipulated financial reporting

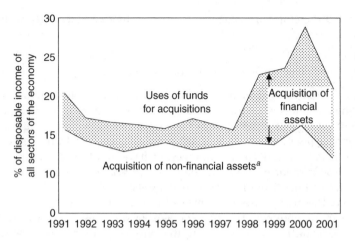

Figure 3.1 The growing importance of financial assets in a modern economy, 1991–2001

Note: [a] Based on statistics by the Deutsche Bundesbank, *Monthly Report*, June 2002.

a black eye. Vivendi includes in its profits all of the EBITDA of Cegetel, a telecoms firm that owns 80 percent of SFR, the second-biggest mobile operator in France. Vivendi owns 44 percent of Cegetel, and the liberty it takes is not justified by the fact that it has board and management control of Cegetel.

One way to demonstrate the weakness of EBITDA as a financial reporting tool is by appreciating that in 2001 Vivendi said it had produced a free cash flow of Euro 2 billion. This is EBITDA minus capital expenditures and holding-company costs, adjusted for earnings not turned into cash. Of these Euro 2 billion, Euro 1.5 billion came from the telecoms businesses. By contrast, free cash flow based on Vivendi's real stakes in its various companies was a far more modest Euro 800 million:

- Just enough to cover an estimated Euro 700 million interest charges on Vivendi's debts
- And it makes the Euro 1.2 billion dividend and related taxes it paid in 2001 a decreaming of assets.

As this example demonstrates, investors learn practically nothing about Vivendi's (and many other companies') financial health from EBITDA. If anything, they are misled. They don't even know where Vivendi finds the money for its dividend, except the classical method of raiding special capital reserves kept in the balance sheet of its holding company. After such reserves have been used up, the company will be high and dry no matter what its EBITDA might suggest. This is precisely what happened in July and August 2002.

6   Standard & Poor's core earnings

The reason for prudential financial reporting standards is to enable investors to realize what is happening to a company from the economic end. For this purpose, in May 2002, Standard & Poor's (S&P) proposed a new measure for corporate financial performance: *core earnings*. Its goal is to eliminate some of the popular financial reporting practices that companies use to bolster their figures. S&P says that core earnings will:

- Do away with stock options as regular compensation not deductible from income
- Exclude gains by pension fund(s) which belong to the reporting companies
- Include restructuring charges from ongoing operations, and
- Exclude gains and losses from one-tantum asset sales.

In that sense, core earnings can help to put some order into financial reporting practices where pension gains and other earnings flows, non-consequential to the company itself, increase the overall quantity of earnings and, as a result, make the company's stock worthy of a higher price/earnings multiple. At the same time, because options dilute the equity holding, it is only prudent to bring them into the financial reporting structure.

This is not the only weakness of current reporting practices. Recent corporate policies see to it that non-recurring charges start to recur too often, quarter after quarter, as an ongoing business. A one-off sale of property often biases the reported financial results. This is not income coming from a company's operating business, it is part of creative accounting which, as we have already seen, is destroying the dependability of financial statements.

Both investors and regulators are faced with a challenge. While a dynamic financial environment and the effects of innovation, deregulation and globalization impact on financial reporting, there is no denying that things have gone too far. For the benefit of all stakeholders, there should be some order in the way revenue and earnings figures are prepared, reported, and analyzed.

S&P's core earnings measure goes to the heart of a basic query: should analysts use operating earnings or reported earnings when valuing a company? It is becoming increasingly clear that reported earnings are not representative, as they provide anomalies like one-time charges that cannot be considered appropriate for evaluating an ongoing concern:

- In an economic downturn, the difference between operating and reported earnings expands as companies include more one-time charges than normal
- Alternatively, as the economic climate improves and translates into better corporate earnings, the use of one-time charges tends to decrease.

Standard & Poor's has proposed the use of core earnings in an effort to solve the problem of whether reported or operating earnings are the most correct method of valuation. Like operating earnings, core earnings would ignore one-time events resulting in income gains or losses, but would recognize expenses associated with the restructuring of ongoing businesses. They would also attribute a charge to stock options which the company may award to its CEO and other employees, as these are seen as a part of compensation expenses:

- No earnings would be attributed to over-funded pension plans
- But the cost of the amortization of unfunded pension liabilities would be recognized as an expense.

These are accounting changes proposed by S&P as a guideline to calculating the P/E multiple. Whether the accounting boards in the US and other G-10 countries will adopt these proposals is another question, and debate on this issue will probably keep the market busy for some time to come. To make a realistic comparison as to whether a company's equity is overvalued, correctly valued or undervalued, all creative accounting practices should end.

For the time being, this does not seem likely to happen. Instead, new instruments are being invented to bypass prudential reporting standards. An example is the *prepays*, complex financial transactions set up by Enron and two of its banks (as explained in Part II). Prepays appeared to be income-earning deals in energy commodities – hence assets – but were really loans and therefore liabilities (see also a similar setup by the Baptist Foundation, a not-for-profits, in Chapter 6).

"Enron loves these deals as they are able to hide funded debt from equity analysts because they, at the very least, book it as deferred revenue or … bury it in their trading liabilities," said an internal email at J.P. Morgan Chase, on November 25, 1998. The prepays hid from Enron's balance sheet an estimated $8.5 billion of debt (there is more on this on p. 115 below).

Examples like these underline the fact that the practice of creative accounting must stop, not only for ethical reasons but also because it is plainly counterproductive. As we saw in section 5, proforma reporting started as a way to bring financial reporting close to "real" operating earning, but ended by making a mockery of true financial figures and reports.

EBITDA beautifies the financial data of the most leveraged companies without reflecting on their (often downgraded) debt. Why not earnings before all operating expenses (EBAOE)? One of the problems with financial reporting is that once a bypass is found which permits companies to be less than frank in accounting, almost everybody jumps on the bandwagon and manipulated financial statements become a torrent.

An article in *BusinessWeek* suggested that research conducted by the University of Utah and Brigham Young University found the number of American companies abandoning the regulatory adherence to GAAP and outright adopting their own version of proforma creative accounting went from 181 in 1998 to 695 in 2000;[10] this is a 38,300 percent increase in two years. If such a ratio prevailed during the next two years, there would be 2,670 companies misleading their investors by the end of 2002, and many more than that in 2003. The same issue of *BusinessWeek* gave an example on how reporting on core earnings would affect the earnings figures which struck the public eye. General Electric's earnings per share for 2001, for example, would shrink from $1.42 to $1.11: 6 cents go because of charges from asset sales, 4 cents because of options, a big chunk of 19 cents because pension gains are no more part of GE's earning per share (EPS), and 2 cents for other adjustments.

The S&P core earnings measure is, in my book, a much more honest way to prepare, present, and analyze financial figures that reflect the company's bottom line. The ball is now in the regulators' court who must decide how financial statements can again become dependable.

7 Prerequisites for forward-looking statements

Practically all statements, other than those of historical fact, including statements regarding industry prospects and future results of operations or financial position, can be seen as forward-looking. Industry jargon uses words such as "anticipate," "believe," "expect," "project," "intend," and similar expressions. These characterize issues included in statements which typically:

- Reflect management's current expectations, and
- Are based on information which is inherently uncertain.

The challenge is to express this uncertainty in a formal, dependable way. Such need comes from the fact that accounting measurements must have form, which is essential to the recording and study of economic facts. Only then can forward-looking statements be the means of planning an economic product, or investment, in such a way as to provide incentives to all stakeholders.

This in a nutshell is the essence behind forward-looking statements. The goal is to go beyond accounting processes which yield transition summaries that reflect only past activities. The problem is that the challenge of giving a forward look to financial statements has not been attended with even moderate success, because the practice has led to abuses which do not permit us to:

- Understand the link between financial strategy and operating tactics
- Get valuable insight from the company's balance sheet and income statement, and
- Project future funding requirements, including factors giving rise to external financing.

In the complex business environment in which we live, a way to permit the translation of the present into the future appears to be rather urgently needed. Budgetary techniques in which many corporate managements have combined high levels of forecasting skills with the institution of devices necessary to control future activities suggest the need for possible supplements to regular financial statements without violating accounting practices or methods of reporting on completed transactions:

- This could be in the form of a projected virtual income statement, placed alongside the regular income statement of the completed year
- Such a virtual statement should be examined by the CPA for the reasonableness of its assumptions *and disclosures*, with their opinion of its fairness added to their certificate.

Management should have the ability to change its views as the market evolves, in a transparent manner. That is more or less what companies currently do when they revise their long-term sales forecast upward or downward. Nokia has stated, for example, that increasingly fierce competition increases the risk of commodization in the mobile phone business, which could depress operating margins.

Analysts may have other reasons for the revisions they make. In the case of mobile telephony, for instance, a reason may be the infrastructure business experiencing a flat period in the fixed network area; or the forecast that mobile communication network providers will have to live with falling 2G business with no income as yet from 3G contracts.

Users of forward-looking statements must appreciate that actual results may differ significantly from management's expectations regarding operating profitability, expected losses, net sales, cash flows from operations, and free cash flows, all of which are inherently difficult to predict. Indeed, actual results could differ materially for a variety of reasons:

- The rate of growth of the economy in general
- Prevailing market psychology
- Change in customer spending patterns
- The mix of products sold to customers, and margins derived from them
- Inventory management policies and practices
- Development of relationships with third-party sellers, and
- Foreign currency exchange and other risks.

Such risks may be specific to an industry and company, altering the forward-looking statement. There are also more general credit, market, and operational risks, each with its own impact. These, along with more general market uncertainties, may cause actual results to differ significantly from management's expectations. Such expectations may also have been too optimistic from the start – or simply misleading.

"(We are) still losing hundreds of millions [of dollars] a month," said Bill O'Shea, president of Lucent's Bell Laboratories R&D division, speaking to Total Telecom on-line news service in March 2002.[11] Other telecoms vendors had a similar reaction. Nokia said that its network equipment sales for the first quarter of 2002 were down and it expected a 25 percent year-on-year decline, compared to an earlier forecast of 16–20 percent for that part of the business. These are examples of deviations in real life from forward-looking statements, but as long as the hypotheses on which they are based are sound and are properly tested, forward-looking statements are worth their salt. They explain the need for project funding, alert to obstacles which might be encountered, and help investors in making a systematic review of performance. To achieve these results, however, forward-looking statements should provide a basis on which to determine the extent to which *objectives are being attained*. In every well-managed business:

- Objectives are established through the budget, and
- Performance is evaluated through periodic reports in which budgeted and actual accomplishment are compared.

The practice of forward-looking statements further underlines the need for solid accounting policies and procedures. To be adequately descriptive, an analysis of revenues and expenses – whether current or projected – must provide a classification of items which is stable and dependable, and should follow standard rules. This means that there must be top management direction and control of that activity, therefore personal accountability at the highest organizational level.

4

The Misleading of Investors

1 Introduction

"We are never deceived," Johann Wolfgang Goethe said. "We deceive ourselves." Goethe's dictum precisely encapsulates the plight of investors as they confront the volatility of their wealth, failing to appreciate that the markets are neither rational nor efficient, even if many experts think that they are that way.

There is plenty of evidence to back the statement made in the preceding paragraph, evidence showing that traders, analysts, and investors miscalculate in their decisions, as well as making systematic judgment errors. Individual risk preferences are profoundly influenced by how information, as well as misinformation, is presented to the individual decision-maker and to the market as a whole. For instance, investors act in a risk-averse way when making choices between outcomes which involve a higher amount of exposure. They also are subject to the "theory of noise," developed by Dr. Fischer Black, who describes many market moves as trading on noise *as if* it were information, even though from an objective point the different actors would be better off not trading or investing.

There is also enough evidence to document the fact that investors and traders generally make decisions using *inductive* not *deductive* processes. They base a good deal of their judgments not on what they know but on what they think *others believe* about likely market moves. They also use asset prices as proxy for aggregate expectations, a policy which can often lead to self-deception.

But investors are not only the victims of self-deception. Sometimes they are betrayed by the creative accounting of corporate management and their brokers. The analysts' opinion is often biased because of conflicts of interest in the top of the pyramid of the investment bank for which they work, the mixing up of equity analysis, and lucrative mergers and acquisitions business, as well as because of their own, personal reasons.

One of the case studies in this chapter is the action taken by New York's Attorney General against Merrill Lynch. Another is the betrayal of investors by bankers in whose hands they had put the management of their funds. Still another concerns the difficulty, if not outright impossibility, of recovering the money lost by investors by means that reflected a failure of ethical standards.

The Herculean task of cleaning up the mess created by conflicts of interest in the 1995–2003 period has largely fallen on two people: Robert M. Morgenthau, the Manhattan District Attorney; and Eliot Spitzer, New York State Attorney General, as well as their immediate assistants. In mid-September 2002, Dr. Morgenthau said in an interview with CNBC that his office had 550 assistant attorney generals working on cases involving conflict of interest.

The *District Attorney* is an elected official of a county, or designated district, with the responsibility for prosecuting crimes. These duties include filing criminal charges, or bringing evidence before the grand jury that may lead to an indictment for a crime. The *State Attorney General* is in charge of prosecutions and matters such as consumer protection, environmental law, supervision of trusts and not-for-profit entities, as well as other issues in which the state government may have a particular reason for protecting the citizen.

2 Efficient market theory and the facts of real markets

I have never been a believer of the so-called "efficient market theory," which I see as based on shaky, unproven grounds. This theory holds that the market is rational because information is instantaneously diffused and equity prices are determined by investors who care about just two things: the cash to be generated over the life of a business and the risk associated with cash receipts. The cases of analysts, traders, and investors who behave in this manner are, however, rare:

- The large majority fails to do its homework in carefully evaluating an asset's intrinsic value, and
- There is an active minority which is using equity analysis and stock picks to mislead investors (there is more on this below).

"Investors are waking up and realizing that Wall Street research is merely a marketing tool used for selling stocks," Kent Womack, Professor at Amos Tuck School of Business, Dartmouth College, says.[1] An example was provided by a memo to his bosses from Henry Blodget, then top-of-the line internet stock analyst at Merrill Lynch in 2000, stating that he had been involved in more than fifty-two investment banking transactions and that he had earned $115 million for the firm during that year.

In a March 1999 email, Blodget said: "We are now up to 11–12 internet banking transactions in the pipeline...The current schedule for this week...is 85 percent banking, 15 percent research." The prosecution stated that Merrill bankers used research as bait for investment banking business. In an April 2000 email, one banker wrote: "Do you think we should aggressively link coverage with banking – that is what we did with Go2Net (Henry [Blodget] was involved)."

The documents also indicate that Merrill's draft research and proposed rating changes were sometimes shown to the companies being covered, as well as to investment banking colleagues, ahead of time – despite internal rules banning this. In February 2001 a Merrill analyst sent an unpublished report to Tyco's chief financial officer with the note: "Please review asap. I will not send ID out until I hear from you first! Loyal Tyco employee!"

- Apart from hyping stocks through analysts' and brokers' promotions, there is also a "mass-syndrome effect" in the equities business
- When equity values move north the trend is to go for a fast buck and almost no one pays attention to the risks embedded in a dynamic market which can move either way.

Even lessons learned the hard way from major corporate failures which have happened in the past have a very short lifecycle. By 2010, after another market boom, few will remember what was taught by the bankruptcies of WorldCom, the National Century Financial Enterprises (NCFE), Global Crossing, Conseco, Enron, and others, as well as companies which wrecked themselves financially like Marconi, Vivendi, and ABB. Or about the dangers of responding to market pressures by setting unrealistic growth targets. Yet, much has been taught by the Lucent Technologies, Nortel, Ciena, Cisco, JDSU, Juniper, and other débâcles. All these companies were promoted as the new industrial wonders, run by management who simply could not do anything wrong. Complacency and conflict of interest all played their role. Complacency even hit the regulators who sat on their hands as:

- The volume of dubious equity research which hyped stocks soared, and
- Questionable practices in financial analysis and investment advice became commonplace.

"To the extent that regulators were aware that this was a speculative bubble, you could blame them just as much as everybody else," Roberta S. Karmel, a former commission at the Securities & Exchange Commission (SEC), now a Professor at Brooklyn Law School, says.[2]

A rational market should not encourage overpriced acquisitions and overinvestments because both are damaging to the long-run health of companies – and of the market itself. It matters little if the CEO claims some initiative or other conforms to company plans, expectations, and forecasts. Only in an irrational market do boards do their utmost so that the company's stock can trade at close to its peak value, while at the same time taking no steps to make their firm transparent to investors.

If the market were rational, CEOs would promise only those results that they had a legitimate prospect of delivering, and they would be willing to inform the market when they believed their stock to be overvalued. This is one of the fundamental prerequisites of well-informed financial markets, as well as of efficient resource allocation in a free economy.

If the market were rational, as theorists say, then the New York State Attorney General would not need to probe Merrill Lynch, Goldman Sachs, Crédit Suisse First Boston (CFSB), Lehman Brothers, UBS PaineWebber, and Salomon Smith Barney, among others. Neither would he need to subpoena their records. In a rational market, the *risk and reward link* would always be clear and the same is true of the evolution of both risk and reward. This brings up another issue:

- Finance theory assumes a linear relation between risk and reward
- But in a dynamic market risk and reward are rarely if ever linearly linked.

The fact that the tails of risk and return distributions are fatter than predicted by most economists, analysts, traders, and investors, is essential to understanding market behavior. Non-linearity should be factored into practically all investments, and when this is done the simplicity which classically characterizes the so-called "rational thinking" fades out of the picture. To limit wishful thinking, which has no place in a rational market, boards and CEOs must reconcile their own company's projections to those of the industry as well as of their rivals. Analysts should not develop unrealistic models of an industry's or company's growth. If their expectations lie outside what is widely viewed as a sustainable growth rate, they must be able to explain how and why their chosen company will be able to outperform their market. This is rarely if ever done.

CEOs should also contribute positively to the rational market process, which they don't usually do. Some executives are concerned that making the real situation clear to the analysts will reveal valuable information to their competitors. To this, there is a simple response: if one's strategy is based on one's competitors not knowing what one is doing, one cannot be successful in the longer term, no matter who knows what:

- Winning strategies have to be based on real foundations, and
- They must be backed up by real resources: human, material, and financial.

Not only is the market not rational, but the trend goes the opposite way. Starting around the mid-1990s, to keep the market at high gear and profit, some CEOs rapidly steered their companies towards creative accounting (see Chapter 3). They began to manipulate financial information and they tried to mislead the markets. Financial information turned out to be unreliable, investors became scared, and the bubble burst.

It is not only that Enron, WorldCom, and Tyco International had major accounting problems and members of their senior management were charged with malfeasance. Even some US mainstream companies were trying to evade taxes by setting up shell headquarters in Bermuda and other offshores, while other trusted, long-established entities were booking questionable revenues. The US and Western European markets reversed gear and entered into a spiral of recalibrating, and pressure mounted for measures which could ensure transparent, easy-to-understand financial statements.

What has been the role of regulators in all this? The job of regulators is to establish prudential standards, then ensure that the "rules of the game" are observed by everybody and that there is a level playing field. It is no business of regulators to see to it that the markets are efficient.

By law, the SEC is charged with reviewing the financial filings of over 16,000 US companies. It oversees a universe of brokerage firms and mutual funds, an industry whose assets grew more than fourfold in the 1990s. SEC has also the mission of:

- Ensuring the proper operation of the exchanges
- Seeing to it that there is no insider trading
- Watching over accounting transgressions, and
- Investigating whenever anything goes wrong.

Experts now say the SEC has not been given enough resources even to read annual reports. In a speech in 2001, one of the agency's chief accountants admitted that only one in fifteen annual reports was reviewed in that year.[3] This is an operational risk on SEC's part which, post-mortem, the Bush administration tried to correct by significantly increasing the SEC's budget.

The SEC and the Financial Accounting Standards Board (FASB), which is under its aegis, are also working to establish more credible financial statements. The SEC has ordered the CEOs and CFOs of the 1,000 largest US companies to attest personally to the accuracy of their financial statements, starting with their most recent annual report. The emphasis is on accuracy of financial figures which reflects on corporate governance; it is not on the efficiency of markets.

3   The contribution of financial analysts

What has been revealed by the market crash of 2000–2 is a huge deception of investors by people and entities which had contributed to the bubble of the last decade of the twentieth century. The positive development of that period has been the emergence of a new investor class which was subsequently let down by financial manipulation, managerial arrogance, and political complacency. During the second half of the 1990s, as practically all stock markets moved north, investors placed their trust and their future in the stock market. Subsequently they found out the hard way that a great deal of the boom was smoke and mirrors. In Germany, 5 million investors in Deutsche Telekom, for example, lost nearly all their savings.

This is one of the dramatic examples of what happens when investments are not subject to risk control and are not led by experience – even if, as George Bernard Shaw once said: "Experience is the name men give to their mistakes." From individual investors to pension funds, hype led them to embrace the high-risk side of the growth economy of deregulated markets, but they were deceived by insiders who hid the truth, manipulated company accounts, and rigged the odds against them.

Individual investors and institutional investors were stunned to learn of CEOs using their companies for personal enrichment and getting company loans to cover bad investments of their own. Top brass sold share at peak values, hiding the fact their company was weak. CEOs and CFOs benefited from a huge number of options without telling shareholders; but employees were locked into 401(K) plans while company stocks crashed.

During the stock market bubble of the late 1990s, no industry's stocks were as hyped as those of telecoms. In September 2002 the New York State Attorney General's lawsuit against telecom executives revealed that Citigroup's director of global equity research, John Hoffman, had warned Salomon Smith Barney's then-CEO, Michael A. Carpenter, in a memo in 2001 that he had a "legitimate concern" over "the objectivity of [Citigroup's] analysts." At a later meeting, Hoffman seems to have told senior executives that the firm's stock recommendations were "ridiculous on [their] face."[4]

The débâcle for the average investor and his personal savings or her pension plan was made worse by the fact many workers held company stock in their 401(K) retirement accounts. Some of these holdings were required by employers, partly out of loyalty and partly because they wanted to believe in their company's future, workers also placed their discretionary funds in company stock. In some countries:

- 90 percent of total pension plan assets, and
- Up to 75 percent of workers' discretionary contributions, were in the firm's own shares.

Few people really appreciated the risks embedded in this one-sided pension planning. Altogether, it amounted to a significant exposure because workers already had a big stake in their companies through their jobs. If the company goes under, employees and workers lose:

- Their job
- Their savings, and
- Their pension plan.

Alert investors appreciated that compared with the old economy, the New Economy called for more not less risk-taking. Continued technological and market innovation was essential, and this represented a greater amount of exposure. The problem was the manipulation of accounting and unsound financial advice, as well as the fact that there was no consensus about the dividing line between acceptable and unacceptable risk.

Here are some examples of misrepresentation of financial fundamentals and consequently of biased, even misleading, financial advice by the same broker (name withheld). On April 22, 2002, four months before Vivendi Universal crashed, the broker's financial analysts recommended the company's stock (American Depository Receipts, ADR) as "Strong Buy" and "Long Term Strong Buy":

> "Ahead of 1Q02 results we reiterate our Strong Buy recommendation on Vivendi Universal with a FY02 price objective of Euro 57."

> "We estimate Vivendi trades at just 9.4 × adjusted O3E EV/EBITDA, a substantial discount to its peer group of AOL Time Warner, Viacom and Disney at between 11× and 14× 2003E."

> "On revised forecasts, we expect 20 percent EBITDA growth in 2002, including USA Networks and acquisitions."

On April 22, 2002 Vivendi's stock stood at Euro 40.15 ($35.39), after a peak of Euro 142 in early 2000. By August 2002 the stock had crashed to Euro 9.70 – and with it the capital investors put in as a result of the "Strong Buy/Long Term Strong Buy" recommendation which they got from their broker.

Buy recommendations made by investment banks to their clients which turned sour can fill a book of dismal case studies. Take Broadcom as another example. The April 18, 2002, report by the same broker was neutral in the short term but it posted a long-term "Strong Buy." At the time, the stock stood at $38.76. The broker's report stated:

> "We remain impressed with the breadth and depth of BRCM's product portfolio, and its dominant market position."

> "We consider the stock a core holding for long term investors, and reiterate our long term Strong Buy rating."

Some four months down the line the "core holding" had collapsed to a little over $16 per share. The upbeat was not just poorly documented, it was misleading and incoherent. As the analyst wrote in his opinion: "Broadcom supplies Motorola with digital set-top box and cable modem chipsets. Revenues from its largest customer, Motorola, declined by 19 percent sequentially to $33 million to account for 14 percent of total revenues." Major clients of Broadcom were losing market share, but this seems to have made the securities analyst more upbeat.

Critics of the free market say that investments – particularly equity investments – are made in a world where falsity and truth are opposite sides of the same coin. This is not a realistic appreciation of the investment landscape.

In the general case, equities are not crooked deals, though there may be crooks dealing in equities.

And not only in equities, of course. During the last half dozen years, other brokers misinformed investors in order to hype risky derivatives instruments. Examples are Synthetic Bull Bonds and Podium Notes. They, according to the arguments written in their promotional literature, make it possible to combine the safety of bonds with the return potential of equity investments:

> "With Synthetic Bull Bonds, the investor assumes that the stock market will trend positively, while with Podium Notes, a sideways-trending market is enough to achieve a higher return."

Synthetic Bull Bonds are not bonds at all. In their background are market speculators paying an annual coupon to match the positive return on a share index. The average investor understands nothing about what it means to him, and to the pseudo-bonds, if the index fails to reach or exceed the knockout level during the year. Knockout derivatives are very risky instruments whose exposure is not well understood even by the experts:

- The "knockout" is set at the start of each year at a fixed percentage above the opening price for that year
- Should this level be exceeded, the investor no longer participates in the index, but receives a fixed payout, the rebate.

The risk taken by these investors is high and the return is low, but they don't know it. In the majority of cases, the rebate is below the yield on a comparable bond. Should the knockout level be exceeded in one year, there is still the opportunity to participate in the risks of another "annual performance" the following year, and so on.

The marketing of such fairly complex and unpredictable instruments to end-investors capitalizes on the fact that they don't have the know-how to appreciate the amount of exposure involved. As a result, they depend on the advice which they get from their banker, broker, or any other salesman – which is always positive till catastrophe hits and the investors' capital goes down the drain as will be the case with most "alternative investments."[5]

4   Investors must learn to manage their assets and liabilities

After having preached for twenty months, from May 2000 to December 2001, that the bottom has been reached and recovery was just around the corner, many analysts conceded that, at least in the technology sector, 2002 and possibly 2003 would be just as bad as 2001 when business customers had begun forgoing technology upgrades. Tight budgets put at risk the statements of many chipmakers, computer manufacturers, software firms, and telecoms.

Then, little by little, as the news of more sophisticated gimmicks in creative accounting came out, disclosures revealed that the much-celebrated corporate profits of the 1990s had actually been accounting manipulations. This was followed by huge write-downs with hundreds of restatements wiping out billions in earnings, while an unprecedented amount of debt was found to be hidden in off-balance-sheet partnerships and other cover-ups.

Suddenly, with accounting practices coming under close scrutiny, investors lost their appetite for overlooking heavy debt loads. Earnings and cash flows once again came center stage and they were much smaller than the mergers and acquisitions (M&A) addicts expected, leaving many companies struggling to pay their debt, or even to make interest payments.

Like the Lloyd's "Names" in England, some 100 million investors in America, about half of all adult population, can relate the loss of a big chunk of their wealth to these happenings. They took heart at the long bull market but they lost $5 trillion, or 30 percent of their money from the spring of 2000 to the end of 2002. Feeling misinformed and misguided, investors in 2001 alone undertook 341 class actions against brokers. Experts estimate that these lawsuits could cost the investment bankers as much as $14 billion to settle. The parties at fault are charged with:

- Issuing misleading prospectuses
- Taking kickbacks for IPO allocations, and
- Giving their clients bad investment advice.

Among deceived investors, "spinning" became a household word. It stands for awarding customers shares in popular public offerings in exchange for future investment banking business. This is one of the issues which New York Attorney General Eliot Spitzer has been looking at very carefully to assess possible criminal charges, including bribery.

On Wall Street, experts suggested that investment bankers should take spinning allegations very seriously, because the authorities seem determined to crack down hard on them. "The only way you're going to end this kind of practice, is to persuade people that they're doing it at the peril of criminal conviction," said William Galving, the Massachusetts Secretary of State.[6] Along with the State of New York, the Commonwealth of Massachusetts is after investment banks which acted illegally.

"Sunshine is the best disinfectant," Judge Louis Brandeis once said. By contrast, lack of transparency breeds conflicts of interest, promotes incompetence, and leads to excessive risk-taking. The case of "Names" associated with and financing the risks taken by Lloyd's insurance syndicates is telling. "Names" assumed unlimited liability to cover somebody else's insurance risks. What the centuries-old Lloyd's syndicates and today's alternative investments vehicles have in common is:

- The discretion with which the deals are put together, and
- The lack of rigorous risk control to protect the investor.

"Bad management" is the phrase most commonly used by Lloyd's "Names" – essentially its investors who unwisely accepted unlimited liability – as they faced bills for huge losses regarded as unprecedented in the insurance industry. The "Names'" homes, cars, and art collections were put up for sale to cover a torrent of red ink incurred through reckless insurance coverage by the syndicates.

Many "Names" who suffered great hardship believe that the Lloyd's syndicates' mismanagement worsened over the years. The lack of dependability in underwriting finally blew up like a volcano when Lloyd's reported record losses. Although disasters such as Piper Alpha, the Exxon Valdez oil spill, and natural catastrophes like Hurricane Hugo have contributed to these losses, those who have put their livelihoods at risk believe that:

- If the work of syndicates and agents had been more closely monitored
- Then the bills would not have been so huge because internal control would have seen to it there was discipline in underwriting.

When this "Names" disaster took place in the late 1980s to mid-1990s, many people whose assets went up in smoke complained that they had been insufficiently briefed on the risks. The same is true with other gambles like alternative investments, which is why the Lloyd's problems can be used as an earnest of things to come from the policy of selling alternative investments instruments to private individuals and pension funds.

In the background of both alternative investments and "Names" is the fact that investors are rarely up to speed with what is going on. In Lloyd's case, a large number of "Names" felt that their affairs were well managed until they discovered painfully that they had been mismanaged by reckless and ignorant underwriting.

Corporate governance left much to be desired; the syndicates were not vetted properly and the agents were not monitored sufficiently. Yet, they were gambling with the "Names'" entire wealth. Something similar happened with the boom and bust of the stock market in the 1995–2002 period, and the advice given to investors (see sections 2 and 3):

- In their dreams, investors expect very high standards, close inspection, scrutiny of account managers and investment vehicles
- In real life, however, it eventually becomes apparent that in many cases internal control channels are clogged, management is lax, or it has altogether abdicated its responsibilities.

Another similarity between Lloyd's "Names" and clients of leveraged financial instruments and equities that are not worth their salt is the fact that they were originally sold to high net worth individuals but then came down the marketing ladder and were being sold to everybody. Some banks advised their clients that 20 percent of their net worth should be in alternative investments; this is putting private individuals at very high risk.

A flat "20 percent of net worth" advice given to investors is worse than what has happened at the height of the 1990s bull market, when Jack Grubman, a Salomon Smith Barney telecom analyst, had "Buy" recommendations on practically all the companies he covered. Salomon was taking investment banking fees from telecom companies (almost $1 billion from 1997–2002), more than any other Wall Street investment bank. By February 2002, nine of the companies Grubman had promoted during the telecom craze were trading for less than $1 a share and at least four were in bankruptcy.[7]

In his book *Dot.Con*, John Vassidy makes the point that the analysts' opinions which they give investment banks are not one-way. For example, at Morgan Stanley Dean Witter, Mary Meeker hyped up nearly all internet stocks. But at the same time, in the late 1990s, Barton Biggs, chief global investment strategist, and Byron Wien, ex-chief investment strategist, were relentlessly bearish alongside Meeker's breathless "Buy" advice.[8]

Only post-Enron did investors start to be somewhat more careful with the sort of equities recommended to them by brokerages. A cleansing has been under way in the stock and bond markets, as private and institutional investors turned away from companies perceived to have flawed or opaque financial statements, and their paper was dumped because of their accounting misbehavior. Dozens of companies suddenly saw the need to restate their earnings, and make their balance sheets more transparent.

Even if this is not an industry-wide cleansing, the market has signaled that a reliable set of common accounting and financial reporting standards for all companies is absolutely necessary and must include:

- Uniform measures of true financial health
- Unencumbered cash flow, and
- Statements of true operating earnings.

This would help restore public confidence shattered by the decline of corporate codes of ethics, the buying off of professional watchdogs, the destruction of individual and pension savings, and the widespread corruption.

Legal action undertaken since 2002 will not altogether do away with malfeasance. That's why investors must learn how to *anticipate the risks*, and *mitigate* them. These are subjects that should be taught in every secondary school.

5   The New York Attorney General and the SEC

In early 2002, as investors' losses in the equities markets deepened, regulators from different US states moved ahead with a coordinated investigation of conflicts of interest involving stock analysts on Wall Street. Their action caused dismay in the securities industry. Officials from states such as New Jersey, Connecticut, California, Massachusetts, and others spent time with representatives of the New York State Attorney General, Eliot Spitzer, to study his work on Merrill Lynch. Spitzer had earlier disclosed some of the broker's internal emails showing that:

- Merrill Lynch internet analysts had privately derided stocks that they were rating as "Buys"
- While their investment bankers were earning fees from the companies issuing the stocks.

One broker's email said: "Excite@Home is such a piece of crap." As for GoTo.com: "Nothing interesting about this company except investment banking fees."[9] These are just two of the findings Merrill Lynch analysts exchanged with each other, while for the general public they maintained "Buy" ratings.

Both these emails were part of the evidence the State Attorney General's office gathered in its investigation. One of the charges against Merrill Lynch made by Eliot Spitzer was that the broker's internet research department was responsible for manipulating research coverage for the purpose of attracting and keeping investment banking clients by producing misleading ratings that were neither objective nor independent.

Merrill Lynch was also accused of having issued ratings that "in many cases did not reflect the analysts' true opinions of the companies" and, as the investigation files noted, analysts were advising the public to buy certain stocks, which among themselves they referred to by terms such as "dog" and "powderkeg." Eliot Spitzer charged that the brokers had converted its five-point rating scale (Buy, Accumulate, Neutral, Reduce, and Sell) into a *de facto* three-point system in which Reduce and Sell ratings were never given. This might have been the result of a serious breakdown of the "Chinese Wall" between Merrill's banking and research departments, leading to a situation where even the broker's highest investment rating could not be trusted.

Precedents added to lack of confidence on equity ratings. For instance, in 2001 Merrill Lynch paid a $750,000 fine to Massachusetts and another $7 million in mediated settlements to investors who had complained about the way a Merrill broker had handled their accounts. In the New York case, the bill of settlement hit $100 million, though Merrill Lynch admitted no wrongdoing, as such an admission would have left the firm open to shareholder lawsuits.

While brokers were hammered by heavy penalties, in early 2002 some experts started to discuss how equity ratings could be made more independent. Eliot Spitzer recommended significant structural changes, suggesting that Merrill should spin off its equity research as a separate unit. Merrill refused.

On Wall Street, many experts said that making equity research an independent business unit was not a practical proposition. The reason which they gave was that investment research was usually given away and its cost shared between the company's investment banking and brokerage divisions.

The experts' negative response was wrong, as Citigroup demonstrated later in 2002. Sanford Weill, the Citigroup CEO, decided that this was precisely what should be done. He divided Salomon Smith Barney into two independent business units: Salomon for investment banking, and Smith Barney for brokerage. Weill also put equity research at arm's length and chose a new CEO to head its operations.

While the State Attorney General's office was busy in prosecuting for malfeasance and advising on structural changes, the SEC, too, got in on the clean-up act. By late April 2002 Harvey Pitt, who was then its Chairman, announced that his agency was opening a formal inquiry into the issue of analysts' reports and recommendations. Pitt acknowledged Spitzer's role but said the states' effort would be part of the SEC inquiry. The state regulators were not in accord. They were ready to work with the commission but they also intend to pursue their investigations independently.

On Wall Street, the feeling was that investment bankers would rather work with Pitt than with Spitzer, hoping that the former would come up with softer terms. Prosecutors usually have hard questions to ask, and they are the parties who can bring the threat of criminal action.

To console themselves with the developing aspects of the investigation into investment advice and brokerage practices, some bankers said that state activism was not new, it had been evident since the famous cases against tobacco companies for smokers' nicotine addiction and similar events. Others added that the trend had accelerated, promoted by the sense that coordinated state action could go beyond initiatives in Washington. Some experts stated as a precedent the tobacco companies' astronomical $246 billion settlement of a state-inspired legal action in 1998.

In the meantime, different consumer groups and some lawmakers were accusing Harvey Pitt of being too close to the investment banking industry. Pitt met with the chairman of KPMG International, an ex-client of Merrill under SEC investigation for its audits of Xerox. Harvey Pitt denied discussing Xerox with KPMG, but this incident revived doubts about the independence of the SEC's chairman who later quit the job.

One of the experts in the securities business I talked to commented that as far as regulatory rules are concerned, the Attorney General's office can paint only broad brushstrokes – it cannot go into details. Having said that, however, he added that brushstrokes pointing at new rules in the making were not without common sense:

- Brokerages must reveal whether the companies they rate are, or are likely, to be banking clients
- Brokerages must also tell investors how their analysts' stock ratings correlate with changes in stock prices.

Among the forthcoming new rules is a stop to the practice of paying analysts bonuses for help on specific investment banking deals. But while these initiatives are necessary, are they enough? As the email exchanges between Merrill Lynch analysts and between them and their clients make clear, there is a need for tougher policing to assure the advice investors get is free from bias because of different business pressures. Among other things, the rating system needs a thorough overhaul. The current "Buy, Hold, Sell" system does not tell investors much, especially since analysts rate only 2.5 percent of stocks as "Sell." Adding a more detailed evaluation which includes *time horizon* and *risk* elements can provide better guidance. Furthermore, the history of the broker doing the rating should also be brought into perspective – including the efforts by the SEC to recover illegal gains.

The SEC collected roughly 14 percent of the $3.1 billion owed in so-called "disgorgement" cases from 1995 to 2001, as indicated in an analysis released by the General Accounting Office (GAO). The GAO concluded that many victims of financial fraud might never receive refunds. "Although the courts have ordered billions of dollars in disgorgement in the last decade, concerns exist about SEC's success in collecting these funds," GAO investigators wrote in a letter of July 12, 2002 that outlined the findings to the three House Democrats who had requested the analysis.

A tougher law is also needed to guard against CEO malfeasance resulting in investment losses. Richard Baker, of the US Congress, wants to let the SEC seize the personal assets of corporate wrongdoers, including mansions and retirement funds, and use them to help compensate stockholders who lose money from fraud.[10] This will go a long way in adapting to twenty-first-century business realities.

6 Learning from Mediobanca and Dr. Cuccia

In 1982 the late Dr. Enrico Cuccia was forced off the board of Mediobanca, Italy's foremost merchant bank, because he was past retirement age. Since Cuccia had been at the helm of Mediobanca for more than thirty years newspaper headlines hailed the end of an era. Subsequent events have shown how wide of the mark these projections were. In 1995, as Cuccia approached his 90th birthday, he made two giant deals that confirmed his unrivaled power of Mediobanca, taking the initiative in the two deals not as the CEO but as the honorary chairman of Mediobanca:

- Cuccia's admirers, who considered him one of the most astute financial minds of postwar Europe, were amazed at his audacity
- Critics, however, perceived the latest events as the actions of an over-powerful puppetmaster, who manipulated Italian finance.

Cuccia was able to use Mediobanca, formerly a state-owned bank, to consolidate his position at the center of an intricate web of holdings, including corporations such as Fiat, Pirelli, Orlando, Olivetti, Assicurazioni Generali, and RAS – the companies which dominated the Italian automotive, tire, office machinery, and other industrial sectors, as well as the two huge insurance businesses centered in Trieste. Commercial banks, which in Italy are limited to short-term lending, found in Mediobanca the way to expand their lending activities into the medium and longer term. With the 1990s wave of privatization, Cuccia enlarged his power in 1993 by gaining control of two of Italy's state-owned banks: Banca Commerciale Italiana (Comit) and Credito Italiano.

The government had ruled that no investor could hold more than 3 percent in a bank, but this obstacle was easily overcome: Mediobanca satellites simply took small stakes, giving Cuccia virtual power over Italian credit institutions other than his own.

On September 1, 1995, it was announced that the second largest Italian private industrial group had been born through the merger of the former Ferruzzi agro-industrial business with the chemical corporation belonging to the Agnelli family. The new entity, with a turnover of $30 billion and a monopoly over the Italian chemical industry sector, came under Gemina, a holding company controlled by an alliance formed by Fiat owner Gianni Agnelli, Giampiero Pesenti, and Mediobanca – with activities ranging from agro-industrial, to cement, chemicals and insurance (Fondiaria).

On September 7, 1995, Carlo DeBenedetti announced that, due to losses for four years in a row, he would push through a reorganization of his group (including computer-maker Olivetti and holding companies CIR and Cofide). The deal essentially amounted to a $1.4 billion rescue plan for Olivetti. The market was not impressed and after the announcement Olivetti, CIR, and Cofide shares lost more than 8 percent on the Milan stock exchange. The operation was a classic Cuccia rescue package. Dragged down by Olivetti's losses in personal computers and carrying an expensive commitment to the expanding telecommunications market, Benedetti turned to Cuccia, betting on his power to make friendly companies chip in, staving off banks and giving Olivetti another chance – this was Olivetti's fourth restructuring in a matter of a few years:

- The labor unions were furious about major job cuts, and
- Shareholders were getting impatient at broken promises of a turnaround.

Critics said that over nearly half a century Cuccia's deals had damaged the Italian economy because they held it back from modernizing as part of the European Single Market. After "SuperGemina," Italy's first- and second-biggest private groups could both be under the control of Agnelli and Cuccia, their combined sales being more than ten times that of their nearest corporate rivals, Fininvest or Pirelli. That deal also brought to a close the saga of Ferruzzi, the agrochemicals empire that had suffered from family feuds and the expansionism of the late Raul Gardini. In 1993, Ferruzzi had revealed huge, previously hidden debts, and admitted it had presented incomplete balance sheets. The news had caused panic; 80 percent of its loans came from Italy's top banks and there was concern some parts of the banking system might not survive the blow. Cuccia had stepped into the breach, and within two months had outlined a restructuring plan which got the banks on board. But the Ferruzzi case itself was a valuable lesson. Trouble had started in the 1980s, when Raul Gardini had tried to build a semi-public Italian chemical monopoly, first by buying the giant Montedison and then merging Montedison with the chemical division of ENI, the state hydrocarbons company created by the late Enrico Mattei. That private–public entity was to be called Enimont, but it never got off the ground owing to political opposition.

Ferruzzi never recovered from the loss of more than $100 million, because Gardini was forced out and the Ferruzzi family appointed a new, less competent management. In 1993, as part of the "Clean Hands" investigation into political corruption, Milan prosecutors started a trial for alleged bribes around the failed Enimont project. Gardini, no longer the head of Ferruzzi but still planning a comeback, was found dead having allegedly committed suicide.

In 1987, Gardini had tried to corner the Chicago soybean market with future contracts. When it became clear that the Italian financier might succeed, the Chicago Board of Trade, under pressure from the grain cartels, nullified his contracts.

The stamp of Cuccia's deals has been that, as a matter of policy, cash exchanges and asset swaps are favored over capital raising, and deals were announced without reference to minor shareholders: "Shares are counted by weight, not numbers," was an old Cuccia maxim. While brilliant in financial terms, Cuccia's deals lacked late-twentieth-century industrial logic. Analysts said that bringing publishing, insurance, cement, sugar, and electricity under one roof might have made sense in 1945, but no longer. A further unhealthy concentration of media power did not go unnoticed. "SuperGemina" brought four newspapers, Milan's *Corriere della Sera*, Turin's *La Stampa*, Rome's *Il Messagero*, and the *Gazzetta dello Sport* – under one roof.

One of the unwanted consequences of conglomerates with hugely diversified product lines is that management spreads itself too thin – and therefore management risk massively increases. Fiat provides an example. Its debt was downgraded, to junk status by Moody's, which gave warning of worse to come. In late 2002, the Agnelli family, which used its 34 percent stake to control Fiat, rallied around Umberto Agnelli's backing of an attempted coup to install new managers friendly to Mediobanca. Other Italian banks, however, objected to this move. They rallied around Paolo Fresco, Fiat's chairman, who was receptive of Roberto Colaninno's restructuring plan. Roberto Colaninno was an outsider who made a name for himself with Olivetti's takeover of Italia Telecom. Susanna Agnelli, Umberto's sister, became an influential voice. The family split, however, meant more problems for Colaninno's efforts over and above the fact that management risk during the late 1990s and early 2000s saw Fiat's car business decline to the verge of collapse:

- Its product range was weak
- Its market share was evaporating, and
- It had been hemorrhaging cash.[11]

In spite of these criticisms and of some unwanted consequences Cuccia and his policies benefited Italian industry and finance. When one analyzes the extraordinary success of Mediobanca over the years, one ends by recognizing that it has also had several positive aspects. Many of the negative aspects concerned the way of keeping the books. In the mid-1990s "Clean Hands" campaign, when asked by a magistrate whether he was aware that the Montedison balance sheet was misleading, Cuccia responded: "My dear chap, I have never seen a balance sheet that wasn't."

Double books are nothing new in Italy (and in most other countries as well), the difference being that in the mid-1990s Cuccia's political friends were no longer at the helm of the Italian government. It is therefore not surprising that shortly after the announcement of the big deals, Italian tax police entered the headquarters of Gemina on October 7, 1995 and took away thousands of documents and computer records. On the same day, Milanese judges announced they were placing ten senior Gemina officials under investigation for allegedly falsifying company balance sheets to hide $500 million in losses. The investigation, which also covered charges of insider trading and illegal slush funds, sent a clear warning that Italy's big business had some serious house-cleaning to do, something to which, until then, Italian finance had largely been immune.

"Italy cannot hope to have a modern stock exchange," Attilio Ventura said "when its most important elements continue to behave with very little transparency."[12] Nor can any other country hope to have a sustainable capital market when transparency is absent, investors are taken for a ride, and malfeasance is prevalent.

There is an irony in all this. In 2002, Vivendi's stock tumbled after the market understood the aftermath of its misjudged foray into Hollywood, through its expensive and irrational merger with Universal; a big chunk of Gemina's losses was similarly centered in Rizzoli's main publishing unit. Rizzoli had made a costly invasion of Hollywood by taking a stake in Carolco Entertainment; Rizzoli also controlled Fabbri and, according to some reports, it had "invested" unwisely in derivatives.

This is the second and most important lesson from this case study. The Italian market learned that with derivative financial instruments one can be at the top of the heap one moment and out of luck the next. In the mid-1990s Barings, the venerable British bank, went bankrupt for the same reason. But people never learn the lessons of the past.

7 Overexposure and reputational risk

As we have seen in sections 2–5 of this chapter, in the course of the 2000–2 market meltdown the reputation of some banks and brokers suffered because they had been cynically promoting bad investments to their customers. Others attracted the regulators' and legislators' attention for conspiring with corporate clients to cover up mediocre performance or corporate failure.

Risk-takers, however, loved the 2000–2 period. Overleveraging and taking on huge exposures proved attractive (though not necessarily profitable) to hedge funds and other investors, pension funds among them. Failing to account for possible damage to their reputation, many pension funds actively pursued supposedly higher returns with alternative investments. What pension fund managers failed to appreciate was that many of the alternative investments vehicles were based on repackaging of different risks with some sugar coating. Spreading risk through the financial system could reduce the impact on one single company of big defaults such as those of Enron and WorldCom:

- Banks got rid of a good deal of the risk they carried in their books
- But other institutions, including pension funds, ended up with too much toxic waste.

Every financial institution is open to this miscalculation of risk and return. American Express revealed in 2001 that it had made losses on derivatives, having failed to understand the risks while trying to boost its profits. Overexposure often comes from attempts to bolster investment returns. Life assurance companies locked into paying guaranteed returns bought bank credits to offset falling returns on other types of investments made in a low-interest rate environment. Then, suddenly, they learned the hard way that higher returns reflect much financial exposure, and with it comes a significant amount of *reputational risk*.

The alter ego of overexposure was the huge amount of *leverage* taken by companies, which can also turn into poison for investors. Leverage showed up most obviously in the US corporate sector, where companies geared up their balance sheets during the boom years of the mid-to-late 1990s. As the stock markets turned south, these highly leveraged companies were caught with falling revenues and the constant need to meet interest payments.

High leverage was created not only through borrowing but also by buying in a big way financial instruments based on somebody else's liabilities.[13] Life assurance companies, for instance, bought such dubious assets to keep their promises to pay out on death or on termination of policies. Aware that this is a house of cards which may collapse at any time, regulators need to insist on resilience and solvency tests to ensure that the insurers have sufficient assets to fulfill their promises. Some of these resilience tests, however,

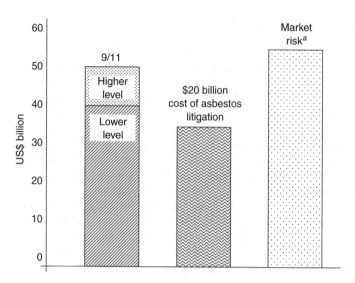

Figure 4.1 Capital depletion among insurers

Note: [a] Statistics from Geneva Association, *General Information*, 173, October 2002. Repletion was greater at market risk side, compared with 9/11 and 60 percent higher than the cost of asbestos litigation.

became elastic. As equity markets fell, the tests advanced by regulators hit insurers, particularly those with plenty of leveraged instruments and/or a significant amount of market risk. As some insurers risked going to the brink of bankruptcy, regulators relaxed their rules, as the UK Financial Services Authorities (FSA) did after September 11, 2001.

The new rule, hopefully temporary, is that insurance companies may report a guestimated value of their portfolio rather than one marked-to-market. Temporarily, but only temporarily, this can help to avoid a vicious cycle as falling prices oblige insurers to sell equities, this pushes share prices further down, and forces more sales of shares. In fact, as Figure 4.1 demonstrates, insurance companies lost more money from market risk in 2001–2 than from the tragic events of September 11. There is, however, a major risk attached to relaxed resilience tests:

- Market confidence can be undermined, and
- Reputational risk becomes more likely.

The post-Enron drying up of credit is not making things any better, and nor is the spike in energy prices. In the aftermath of the Enron bankruptcy, evidence emerged that the company had helped to create the California power crisis in 2000 and 2001. By manipulating the electricity market, Enron was able to boost prices and profits artificially while Kenneth Lay, its chairman, was blaming regulators for the crisis:[14]

- Enron's executives manipulated the energy market
- Misled the public and their own employees, and
- Created an environment of mistrust which fatally undermined credit.

Augmented by financial analyses by some brokers (see sections 3–5) this created an unwillingness to justify taking risks among investors when they felt they were being deprived of dependable financial information. The New Economy depends on innovation and vibrant markets, rather than the status quo, but it also needs an environment which is reliable. From August 2002, senior executives have been held criminally liable for their company's financial statements. This is compounded by the fact that the credit quality of companies has deteriorated. By the end of 2002, over $700 billion in securitized corporates were in limbo, as credit quality continued to fall.

Because bankers have significantly reduced tolerance for bad news from borrowers, small to midsize companies have become particularly vulnerable. Apart the scare about money lost at Enron, Global Crossing, and other high flyers in the late 1990s, many banks overrated the creditworthiness of small companies as borrowers, and lost money when the economy turned down. Reporting requirements after 2002 also amplified credit risk in the sense that they made it more visible.

Historically, credit-rating agencies tend to downgrade the bonds of several companies for every company they upgrade. But in 2002 the number of credit downgrades was equal to a 5:1 upgrade, the worst ratio since 1990. Even companies with good cash flow got a beating. AOL Time Warner usually generates plenty of cash to cover its debts. Yet, after its $54 billion write-off, its bonds, which normally yield around 200 basis points more than US Treasuries, have traded over 500 basis points. Investors have to learn to live with interest rate risk.

5
Top Management Pay and Options

1 Introduction

J.P. Morgan, probably the greatest banker of the twentieth century, thought that the ratio between the CEO's pay and that of the lowest-paid employee in the firm should be 20:1. Dr. Peter F. Drucker, one of the fathers of modern management, has repeatedly warned that the growing pay gap between CEOs and workers can threaten the very credibility of management. In the mid-1980s, Drucker said that no industrial leader should earn more than twenty times the company's lowest-paid employee because if the CEO took too large a share of the rewards, then this would make a mockery of the contributions of all the other employees.

A mockery of both employees and shareholders is precisely what has happened today. In 2001, CEOs of several large corporations – usually with the board's agreement – paid themselves 411 times as much as their average worker, more than 2,000 percent above what J.P. Morgan and Peter Drucker considered to be the limit. The money came through both base salary and options, in a year when the stock market was in deep depression.

An editorial in *BusinessWeek* in 2003 put this issue in perspective by stating that CEOs paid themselves and other top managers handsomely, while they often padded the bottom line with questionable accounting. The editorial states that senior management needs to pay a lot more attention to delivering value to shareholders:[1]

- The drive for higher share prices is not enough
- There have to be much improved profits and less self-gratification through options and fringe benefits.

As stock options became an increasing part of executive compensation, the enhancement of short-term stock prices turned into a personal priority for many CEOs and CFOs. This personal conflict of interest accentuated management's reluctance to undermine its own stature by surrendering another legend to the realities of business life: the quarter-over-quarter earnings growth.

Theoretically, a high stock price represents shareholder value. In practice, this is true only if the higher stock price is fully justified by industrial and financial realities. If it becomes a bubble, it will crash. Along with the explosion in stock values came an explosion in senior management compensation; by the late 1990s this had become a self-feeding cycle and engulfed other professionals, like leading financial analysts who shared in the bonus pools of their investment banking divisions, and were given incentives to issue reports favorable to deals involving their banks and the companies they covered.

Up to the moment the bubble burst, self-gratification was a vicious self-feeding cycle. Company overvaluations, executive options, and unrealistic analyst compensations influenced a flood of unwise investments irrespective of their intrinsic worth. Positive equity valuations and "Strong Buy" financial reports became part of a Ponzi game aimed at commanding multimillion dollar salaries, and investors were not up to speed with what was going on.

2 "Never have so many been paid so much for doing so little"

Paraphrasing Winston Churchill, "Never have so many people been paid so much for doing so little." With only a few exceptions, this is true throughout industry, and most particularly among those companies which misrepresented the facts and while performing badly sold themselves to investors as being the best. They become a symbol of the belief that the New Economy stock valuations could only go north, no matter how much of their performance was actually hot air.

There is nothing wrong about giving options to managers and employees of an enterprise. What is a problem is their abuse. At more than 130 major companies investors are aiming to curb such runaway compensation packages made by the company's board to the CEO:[2]

- Some 30 percent of all options issued by corporations are in the hands of the top five executives in each company
- Option abuses undermined rather than improved corporate performance in the 1990s.

While many old economy companies turned themselves into a parking lot for bright technologists, whose ability to generate ideas easily outstripped the capability of management to deal with them, a surprising number of New Economy companies were used by their CEOs as a vehicle for self-promotion. Liquidation bonuses paid to fired or departing staff at telecommunications, media and technology companies were a comparable abuse:

- *Der Spiegel* reports that Euro 15 million ($15 million) will be paid to Ron Sommer in settlement of his six-year contract at Deutsche Telekom, a company fatally affected by overexpansion

- Joseph P. Nacchio made more than $150 million worth of stock sales from Qwest Communications International, which is trying to survive under $25 billion of debt (see also Chapter 2), and
- The "golden parachute" for Lucas Mühlemann, chairman and CEO of Crédit Suisse Group, in spite of huge losses at Winterthur, a torrent of red ink at CSFB, and $11.8 billion paid for the unnecessary acquisition of DLJ in 2000.

To appreciate the true nature of Sommer's compensation, it is appropriate to recall that Deutsche Telekom has been buried under a mountain of debt and its shares dropped 58 percent in Sommer's last year in office. There is no excuse for poor executive judgment, and even less so for rewarding it. But it is no less true that most telecom companies' bosses got carried away in the 1990s boom. Sommer spent:

- More than Euro 11 billion ($11 billion) on 3G mobile-phone licenses in Germany alone, and
- Euro 80 billion ($80 billion) on a series of generously priced acquisitions which made little business sense.

As we have already seen, chief among the latter was the Euro 33 billion purchase at the height of the boom of VoiceStream, America's sixth-biggest mobile phone operator. Sommer also launched an ill-advised bid for Telecom Italia. Deutsche Telekom was beaten back after the Italian government sided with Olivetti, which saved Deutsche Telekom and the German taxpayers another mountain of bad debts.

Sommer and Nacchio are just two examples out of many whose tenure was accompanied by company disaster. The reasons for such disasters vary from one entity to the next; what is invariant is pay and options. Typically, corporate executive options plans include senior officers selected for participation by the board's Compensation Committee. Most often, these selections and accommodations tend to forget that even when business is good, high executive salaries are unwarranted. In 1990, Steven Ross, joint chief executive of Time Warner, got $78.1 million for doing his job. Stephen Wolf, boss of United Airlines, received $18.3 million, and John Sculley of Apple Computers $16.7 million.

Table 5.1 shows the wages paid at American firms in 1990. Over the years that followed, many of these executives and their successors have performed quite poorly. Michael D. Eisner, Chairman and CEO of Walt Disney, faces a board revolt over performance, a Securities and Exchange Commission (SEC) review, and big-budget movie failures.[3]

True enough, a dozen years down the line, the 1990 figures in Table 5.1 pale in comparison to what came afterwards. When in the mid-1990s Deutsche Bank bought Bankers Trust it had in mind to keep its CEO in an enlarged Deutsche Bank executive board. But then it found out that with

Table 5.1   Top dozen US highest-paid CEOs, 1990 ($ million)

	1990 salary + bonus	Long-term compensation	Total pay
Steven Ross (Time Warner)	3.2	74.9	78.1
Stephen Wolf (UAL)	1.1	17.2	18.3
John Sculley (Apple)	2.2	14.5	16.7
Paul Fireman (Reebok)	14.8	–	14.8
Dean Buntrock (Waste Management)	1.6	10.7	12.3
Leon Hirsch (US Surgical)	1.1	10.6	11.7
Michael Eisner (Walt Disney)	11.2	–	11.2
Joseph Williams (Warner-Lambert)	1.6	6.9	8.5
David Maxwell (Federal National Mortgage)	1.0	6.5	7.5
George Grune (Reader's Digest)	1.2	6.3	7.5
Roy Vagelos (Merck)	2.1	5.0	7.1
Rand Araskog (ITT)	3.8	3.2	7.0

about the $15.5 million Frank Neuman, BT's CEO, earned per year, he was costing nearly the same money as all other members of Deutsche Bank's board taken together: $16.4 million. So, they let him go, though the cost of his golden parachute was a cool $100 million.

Unreasonable salaries are very often also not commensurate with value to shareholders. In many companies with overpaid top executives what is expected in deliverables rarely materializes. Something has gone wrong with the way the pay-for-performance principle is implemented:

- CEOs' pay soared throughout the 1980s, and when recession hit in 1989 pay carried on rising; it did the same during the 2000–2 recession
- At most big firms the link between pay and performance was rarely watertight.

In 2001, Qwest Communications International paid Joseph Nacchio, who was then its chairman, over $27 million, more than six times his compensation of $4.22 million in 2000. The biggest share of that came from long-term incentive plans, with the rest from salary and bonus payments. Nacchio got a further $74.6 million in 2001 by exercising stock options. Over the same period the company's stock price declined by 64 percent.

Lucent Technologies, another company whose equity plunged, paid out some $16.2 million in retention bonuses to executives between January and May 2002, $4.5 million alone to chief operating officer Robert Holder. Yet, in order to reduce costs and survive Lucent had cut 50,000 jobs worldwide over 2001, and froze employee salaries from December 2000.

As of mid-2002, Global Crossing – a bankrupt company – was committed to pay a selected group of 417 employees a total of $8.25 million to remain with it, while it reorganized under Chapter 11. By contrast, in February 2001 the company had announced that it would be cutting off severance pay to thousands of laid-off workers. Management came under scrutiny for lump-sum pension payouts totaling $15 million, which it made to executives before the bankruptcy filing.

British–American NTL, another company which filed for Chapter 11 bankruptcy protection with debts of $10.6 billion, had earmarked some 10 percent of the equity of the restructured group for share option bonuses for its senior executives.[4] They got the equity and ran – and let other stakeholders, including the investors and the rank and file, suffer. Similarly, Flag Telecom, which filed for bankruptcy protection in April 2002, made bonus retention payments totaling $4.65 million to nine senior officers.

Another very questionable practice was the Euro 15 million *ex gratia* payment made to Klaus Esser, after he acceded to Vodafone's £113 billion ($170 billion) bid for Mannesmann, at a price 176 percent above its level twelve months earlier. In Germany, this fuelled an investigation that is expected to lead to charges of breach of trust against a number of supervisory board members, including trade union leader Klaus Zwickel, and Deutsche Bank's CEO Josef Ackermann.

I am against the heavy hand of government, but as far as executive pay and bonuses are concerned things have got out of control. All free market countries urgently need legislation enabling shareholders to have direct involvement in setting executive pay. In the UK, a move in this direction has come as a result of public outcry over executive payouts at failing companies such as telecoms equipment maker Marconi.

Whether the company is still a going concern or it has filed for bankruptcy protection, runaway compensation is a poison pill. Handouts are a fraud on shareholders, bondholders, and lenders, as it is money in effect taken out of their pockets. The trend accelerated in the 1990s:

- Rank-and-file wages increased 36 percent
- But CEO pay climbed 340 percent, ten times faster.

CEOs and their immediate assistants came to command such wealth in salaries, options, fringe benefits, and other compensation that the whole issue has got out of hand, and the money being paid counterproductive. Results became irrelevant, the only thing relevant was higher and higher pay: that is the growth philosophy of the cancer cell.

3   Unwarranted executive compensation

What is and is not an acceptable level of executive pay is not cast in stone. Still, as we saw in the Introduction, there are some unwritten rules about CEO pay which have to do with both ethics and good sense. Virtue and sound judgment go out of the window when, with the connivance of boards, compensation committees, and audit committees, the money made by CEOs and other company top brass escalates. Executives are not entitled to become rich at shareholders' expense.

There is no justification for increasing the compensation of CEOs from twenty times that of the lower-paid employees to 400 times or more at the expense of stockholder assets. Even in the years of stock market euphoria, companies that granted big salaries and lavish options to a small circle of top executives performed worse than those that distributed options evenly and fairly among all employees.

CEOs also benefited from the rich IPO grants that investment banks gave to their best clients in the 1990s. In September 2002 New York Attorney General Eliot Spitzer sued five telecom executives in order to recover some $28 million they banked from IPOs.[5] Spitzer's argument was that the money belonged to the company. The CEO, and others at senior management, got to buy the IPO shares – and profit from them – only because they held influential jobs: their companies were important clients to the investment banking section of the brokers.

The CEOs and other senior executives often responded that "they deserved them." To say the least, this is untrue; at worst, it is gross misuse of other people's money. Over the years CEO pay has become more variable:

- In the late 1980s, the highest-paid CEO in America was Chrysler's Lee Iacocca, who took home $20 million.
- Since 2001, the highest-paid CEO was Larry Ellison of Oracle, who made $706 million by exercising 22 million options, while he also sold another 29 million shares.

As 2002 came to a close, Oracle announced it would miss its earnings forecasts. This sent its stock plummeting; it also motivated investors into going to law. Though their main lawsuit against Oracle was dismissed twice, shareholders have persisted.

While in 2000–2 the economy dived and shareholders lost billions, CEOs of big companies, and some of the small ones, paid themselves even more than before. Compensation used to track performance and went north only when shareholder value in true deliverables was rising. Now big executive pay is disbursed independent of performance. As an article in *BusinessWeek* aptly noted: "When CEOs can clear $1 billion during their tenures, executive pay is clearly too high … the system is not providing an incentive for outstanding performance."[6] Options have become a huge loophole; they are no longer a compensation for results, but a means for self-enrichment at the expense of shareholders.

The fact that options have not, until recently, been expensed is partly responsible for this give-away of shareholder assets. If every option represented a direct hit on the company's bottom line, then boards would be much less inclined to spread them around by the millions, and lower performance standards so that rich options could be exercised even in lean years.

Commissions, too, were used as a way to defraud shareholders. In late February 2002, WorldCom suspended three sales executives and froze the commissions of at least twelve others as the telecoms operator probed its books to see if they had improperly taken credit for orders that had already been accounted for by other divisions of the company. In total, the company said that the employees could have accounted for as much as $4 million in illegitimate sales commissions.[7] The salesmen probably wanted to imitate the company's top brass, but there was also a failure of management control. This was hinted at by WorldCom's general counsel, who stated that because sales commissions and revenues were calculated on different systems, the investigation should not affect the company's earnings. This was a statement which left many Wall Street analysts puzzled.

Even pay cuts don't seem able to arrest the rising curve of executive pay. In 2001, Sanford Weill, the chief executive of Citigroup, took an 83 percent pay cut but this still left him with $36.1 million to take home. The stock of AOL Time Warner tanked because the company performed poorly; yet its four top executives collected stock options valued at around $40 million per head, even if they had to forgo their bonuses.

Some awards seemed especially irksome to shareholders. J.P. Morgan Chase, which had heavy commercial lending losses in 2001 "rewarded" William Harrison, its CEO, with a special $10 million bonus. Yet, because of losses in private equity, loans to Enron, and investments in Argentina, the bank's net income for 2001 fell to half its 2000 level.

Was the $10 million loan to Harrision a forerunner of a better tomorrow for the bank? Hardly. In 2002, J.P. Morgan Chase became subject to Congressional investigation and in October its stock traded as low as $15.26 a share – less than half its after-bonus January 2002 value. That same year the bank agreed to pay $80 million in fines, following investigations by the New York State Attorney General and securities regulators.

If investors in J.P. Morgan Chase were unhappy, so were those who put their assets in Qwest Communications International shares. They accused founder Philip F. Anschutz of unloading billions of dollars in equity before accounting problems came to light that sank the stock.[8] In other corporations, performance targets were lowered: in April 2001, Douglas Daft, the

CEO of Coca-Cola, was given a lower performance target to meet, and with it he got a generous helping of stock.[9]

Lavish executive options are not the only trick. Unwarranted loans to senior executives, and their later forgiveness, is another. Compaq agreed to forgive a $5 million loan it had extended to its CEO Michael Capellas, and provided him with a new loan to help with the tax bill. Bernie Ebbers, the CEO of WorldCom, borrowed $341 million from his employer, on which he was paying a little over 2 percent in interest.

Jacques Nasser, Ford's former CEO ousted by the company's controlling family in October 2001, was paid $17.8 million in wages and options. The package was awarded despite Ford making a $5.45 billion loss and Nasser taking "early retirement" at 53, after falling out with the company's chairman Bill Ford. He received a $1.7 million salary, $3.1 million other compensation, and share options that could net him $13 million profit. Nasser was also given 350,000 restricted shares worth an extra $5.3 million and was eligible to receive a further 750,000 shares if Ford met certain performance goals.[10]

Vodafone's stock fell like a rock in the depressed 2002 market, but on July 31 Sir Christopher Gent received a basic annual salary of £1.2 million ($1.9 million) as well as performance pay and bonuses worth up to a further £3.9 million ($5.4 million). Gent was also awarded 9.3 million share options at a strike price of 97p – the July 31 closing price.

"We seem to be giving rewards for failure [rather] than success," said Cyril Horsford, a retired lawyer, whose comments were typical of many shareholders at the Vodafone annual meeting.[11] Other disgusted stakeholders commented that businessmen in 2002 had gone a long way from the time when CEOs would never think of putting themselves before shareholders.

Compensation Committees of the boards do not seem to care a great lot about redressing the balance. The directors of a board are supposed to represent the shareholders and their interests – a notion which has been overlooked in recent years. Shareholders are not invited to board meetings, individual board members rarely speak out, and when they do so they just repeat the CEO's line. As a result, investors know nothing of what goes on behind closed doors in the boardroom.

Market confidence will not return as long as these things continue to happen, and many investors now are suggesting that the directors themselves must be disciplined. A ban on stock sales by board members for the duration of their terms would encourage them to be more vigilant, without fear of the short-term price declines that might follow the revelation of improprieties. Mandatory term limits such as a five-year term which can be renewed only once, and a cap on the number of directorships, to a maximum of three or four, would prevent board members from becoming entrenched in corporate bureaucracy. The fact that the board – the corporate authority supposed to supervise senior management and efficient performance of its duties – has itself got out of control is very much the aftermath of the lower morals of our time. It is a huge loophole in mismanagement, and therefore a catastrophe for shareholders who don't know whom to trust any more.

4   Executive mega-options

As a financial instrument, options are contractual agreements under which the buyer has the right, but not the obligation, either to buy (*call option*) or sell (*put option*) by or at a set date, a specified amount of a product at a predetermined price. Normally the seller (writer) receives a premium from the purchaser for this right; this is not the case with options granted by the board or CEO on company equity where the writer is essentially the shareholder – even if this is never stated in such explicit terms. Originally conceived to provide executives with a strong incentive to perform well over time, stock options have been often used to reward those executives who perform poorly. This is not just a 2000–2 phenomenon. Its roots date back much earlier. Advanced Micro Devices chairman Walter J. Sanders provides an example. His company's stock price declined 35 percent over the 1986–93 timeframe, but he got $29 million in option-based profits during that period. Another early example is that of the chairman of United States Surgical Corp., Leon Hirsch. He was awarded 2.8 million shares in just two years, 1991–3, while his company's stock underperformed the Standard & Poor's 500 index by 3 percentage points. Such awards are at the origin of so-called *mega-options* – grants consisting of at least 250,000 shares.

Because the regulators took no steps to stop this practice, and the market failed to exercise diligence and discipline, the number of mega-options issued by corporations kept on increasing at an unprecedented pace. Existing evidence points to the fact that the time for postponements of corrective action, and for half-measures, is gone:

- Analysts say that 2002 options would reduce S&P 500 earnings by 17 percent if they were expensed
- Misleading accounting for stock options conceals a significant transfer of wealth from shareholders and companies to their managers.

Because stock options have been so vastly misused, pressure has been building for treating them as *expenses* on corporate balance sheets. While it is true corporations will always need to provide compelling pay packages for top talent, it is no less true that they must also protect against shareholders' equity dilution. In spite of all the talk about shareholder value, concern for shareholders has taken the back seat for more than a decade. One statistic shows that in 2000 executive options amounted to an average of 19.7 percent of the profits of big American firms, and 72.8 percent among some information-technology entities.

When they were originally offered by startup companies in order to attract some of the best people at a base salary which could not compete with that paid by big firms, stock options were intended to give not just extra income but also a sense of ownership. Therefore, they were a good strategy. Eventually, however, all types of incentives and disincentives became over-exploited – as in the case of the rewards for poor performance discussed in section 3. Things were made worse by the fact that till mid-2002, when investors revolted, no company had expensed executive options, yet they had cost shareholders dear. Analysts at Wall Street have calculated that:

- Options generally take a haircut of 10 percent of annual company profits, though some banks like J.P. Morgan Chase give away a hefty 36 percent
- For technology companies the average rises to between 20 percent and 25 percent – and it went up to 80 percent in the case of Intel.

In other terms, the shareholder takes all the risks but gains 75 percent or less of the profits. This sort of heavy decreaming of return on equity (RoE) by management has become very similar to the policy followed by hedge funds. Based on available statistics, Tables 5.2 and 5.3 show how overexploited this business of options has become. In the small sample of these companies:

- Where there were profits, they were decreased by a ratio of 16 percent–80 percent
- Where red ink was the rule, losses were increased by 124 percent–1.057 percent.

Table 5.2   Decreasing the stockholder's profits, 2001 ($ million and percent)

Company	2001 net income	2001 net income minus option expense	Decrease in profits (%)
Microsoft	7,721	5,459	29
IBM	7,723	6,484	16
Intel	1,291	254	80
J.P. Morgan Chase	1,719	1,097	36

Table 5.3   Increasing the stockholder's losses to reward inefficiency, 2001 ($ million and percent)

Company	2001 net income	2001 net income plus option expense	Increase in losses (%)
Cisco Systems	1,014	2,705	266
AOL Time Warner	4,921	6,352	129
Yahoo!	93	983	1,057
Broadcom	2,742	3,408	124

When in the mid-to-late 1990s technology companies paid no dividend, the excuse was that they capitalized all profits to help themselves grow faster, while avoiding loans from banks. Now, in the market-wise first years of the twenty-first century, it emerges that the real reason was totally different– management took the money and ran.

Options can turn profits into losses, as happened in 2001 with Merrill Lynch, where $573 million in profits turned into red ink of $281 million; and with Siebel System, whose $254.6 million in profits would have become a loss of $467 million if it had expensed its executive options. In all these cases the shareholder was defrauded.

Even heavily indebted companies with a torrent of red ink give options to compensate their executives for incompetence. In 2001 this was the case with Lucent Technologies, whose unprecedented loss of $14.1 billion increased to $15.1 billion because of options; and with Nortel Networks, where an astronomical loss of $24.3 billion grew to $25.9 billion – with $1.6 billion in handovers in the form of executive options – in spite of the company's torrent of red ink.

Take Citigroup as another example. Between them, Citigroup's board of directors and senior managers own 85 million shares, worth $3.2 billion.[12] To make matters worse, shareholders are rarely if ever shown these figures in annual reports, yet it is their profits which fly out of the window. Options had not been expensed until mid-2002, and even then few companies decided to do so. Nor does the average shareholder know that, in the typical company, 80 percent of all options goes to the top brass.

This syndrome is not just a financial catastrophe for shareholders. It also impacts on employee morale, as Peter Drucker was quoted as saying in the Introduction. It is disturbing to see CEOs earning more than 411 times shop-floor workers; it is also immoral to see CEOs who have ruined their companies with stock options and other handouts.

Some 75 percent–80 percent of executive pay now comes in the form of options. For this and many other reasons expensing options by deducting the cost from P&L financial reporting makes sense. It will yield more accurate earnings numbers and restore investor confidence as well as help to reverse current trends. By being unaccounted for in P&L terms, companies feel free to award excessive and unjustified sums to top executives.

How should options be expensed? One way to measure the cost of stock options is to assign a value to options at the time when they are granted. Another, a simpler one used by government statisticians, is to count the net proceeds of exercised stock options as a payment by companies to labor. The latter has the advantage of measuring *actual cash* going to managers and other employees.

If an executive exercises ten stock options with a difference of $10 between the market price and the exercise price and then sells the shares, then he walks away with $100 in cash. In many cases, the company opts to buy back those shares and thereby effectively pays out the $100 to the employee. Applying this accounting model, one sees in retrospect that:

- The effective wealth transfer from options has been very significant, and
- Shareholders paid for all of it with profits which they lost and with dilution of their equity.

The option maturity is also a problem. Traditionally, most options have a life of ten years but few executives are patient enough to wait that long for their rewards and they typically exercise them after three–six years, or sometimes faster.

In former times company presidents who had to hold on to the shares for six months exercised options when the shares were likely to rise. But in 2001, at fifty big companies, the average CEO received options worth $6 million a piece. Under the "new ethics," it appears that chief executives of smaller companies developed a tendency to take option profits shortly before their stocks declined – leading to accusations of insider trading.

Worse still is the practice whereby many companies guarantee a price for these options which then turn into outright handouts. There are also other ways besides options of keeping the cost of remuneration off the balance sheet. These include esoteric schemes such as co-investment and carried interest, favored by investment banks and fund managers. Staff at Donaldson Lufkin & Jenrette, for example, shared $1.6 billion through their co-investment plans when it was taken over by Credit Suisse at an unreasonably high price.

In conclusion, expensing options will protect the shareholders' stakes and provide companies with funds by selling those shares in the open market. It will also bring more discipline to options allocation, discouraging grants to underperforming executives. The use of equity-based pay has created perverse incentives which should not be allowed to continue.

5   Why options can lead to trouble

No lesser authority than Senator Jon Corzine, member of the US Senate's Budget Committee and former CEO of Goldman Sachs, said in a television interview that: "Stock options led to misallocation of money and of power." I don't know if he had in his mind some of the executives who reaped the biggest rewards before their companies went bankrupt, Gary Winnick of Global Crossing, $512 million; Kenneth Lay of Enron, $247 million; and Scott Sullivan of WorldCom, $49 million, but this is not unlikely.

New York State's Attorney General, Eliot Spitzer, would not identify individuals or companies currently under scrutiny, but it became public news that several of the files on his desk were among the twenty-five top bankruptcies on the *Financial Times* list. The latter was the result of a survey covering salary and share sales between January 1999 and December 2001.

In his book, *Take On The Street*,[13] Arthur Levitt, Jr. says that when he became chairman of the SEC, in mid-1993, he found a controversy raging over whether companies should treat stock options as expense against earnings on their income statements – just as they treat salaries, bonuses, and other forms of compensation:

- Corporations insisted they should not, since no money actually flowed from the company's treasury
- The Financial Accounting Standards Board (FASB, the accounting standards-setter in the US) said they should.

In the opinion of the FASB, options involved real costs to shareholders. Therefore, in June 1993, it voted unanimously to seek comment on a rule that would make companies put a fair value on their stock option grants, and record that number as an expense. The pressure against expensing options, Levitt suggests, came from everywhere: big companies and small startups, particularly those in Silicon Valley. Politics played a role, both the big and the small were large campaign contributors. The core of the matter was this:

- By saying that non-expensed stock options were essential,
- They were arguing, in effect, that transparent financial statements should be secondary to personal, political, and short-term economic goals.

Dr. Alan Greenspan, the chairman of the Federal Reserve, suggested that a stock or options policy should require that rewards reflect the success or failure of managements' decisions. Better results could be achieved by tying option grants to some specific measure of company performance rather than to the overall stock market, which was meaningless when it cames to a specific company and its deliverables.

A factual and documented use of options, as a way of rewarding exceptional effort, is another reason for obliging companies to expense options. This could lead to the use of more restraint, as well as of better performance-based criteria. The fundamental principle is that incentive stock options cannot be turned into a gift, because this removes the value from the whole incentives scheme and, in many cases, it turns it on its head.

Part of the irony of runaway executive stock options is that the failures of Enron, Global Crossing, WorldCom, and many other companies, hurt both employees and shareholders but not the people at the top. As Alan Greenspan put it in May 2002: "There have been more than a few dismaying examples of CEOs who nearly drove their companies to the wall [but], nonetheless, reaped large rewards because the strong performance of the stock market as a whole dragged the prices of the forlorn companies' stocks along with it."

The fact that executive stock options are written off the balance sheet and not in the P&L statement has something to do with the miscalculations associated with their issuance. Some analysts say that Oracle's board would never have paid Larry Ellison $706 million in cash or any other form that would have to show up in the company's earnings statement. Indeed, that money came from exercising stock options which the company had given its CEO (see section 3).

One of the many aspects of the misattribution of money and power aided by lavish executive options is that the irrational and perverse practices which have entered accounting are kept away from the public eye. Oracle's income statement says nothing about Larry Ellison's stock options bonanza: It is as if it did not cost the company a cent no matter how large was the dilution of stockholders' equity, or the fact that options are by far the biggest component of CEO pay.

Critics say that executive options ushered themselves into the twenty-first century as a means to get rich quick. An example of options which may turn out to be a poisonous gift comes from a well-known financial institution. Under its equity plan, selected personnel:

- Receive a mandatory portion of their performance-related compensation in company shares, and
- Are also awarded a matching contribution in the form of additional shares or options on shares.

The exotic element comes in an added-value form of making participants eligible to receive a portion of their award in *alternative investments* based on a pool of hedge funds. This means that a major risk is assumed by the beneficiaries.[14] Another risk associated with executive options is that, in the meantime, the company's stock has tanked, or it disposes of the unit which granted the options.

Because Tyco's stock fell so sharply in 2002, many of the CIT employees' options became worthless, as they had an exercise price higher than Tyco's stock price. The only way out for them would be if Tyco's stock recovered within ninety days of the CIT spin-off; short of this CIT employees had no choice but to allow their options to expire unless a miracle happened.

The miracle which followed was Tyco's announcement that each of CIT's 5,700 employees would receive some new options in CIT when the company's offering was complete. CIT's top brass, however, was ahead of the curve as it received new options prior to the ordinary employees. In February 2002, Tyco gave 545 of CIT's senior people 1.2 million options to buy Tyco shares at $28.83 each, just above the low that Tyco reached early that month. Albert Gamper, CIT's CEO, received 200,000 of the options; four other senior CIT executives were given 50,000 each.[15]

With these different sorts of guaranteed equity handouts in the background, some researchers have shown that CEO pay has grown tenfold since 1990. Pay packages crammed with stock options allowed the boss's take-home pay to top $200 million in some cases. Only belatedly did Congress consider legislation to rein in stock options.

Up to a point, but only up to a point, this change in mood and in oncoming legislation has not gone unnoticed. According to Korn/Ferry International, a headhunting firm, nearly one-quarter of CEO candidates now hire outside consultants to pore over the books of prospective employers, looking for financial land mines.[16]

In conclusion, new rules are necessary to stop the dilution of corporate equity. Shares allocated to options at America's top 200 corporations grew to a remarkable 16.4 percent of shares outstanding by the end of 2000; it is estimated that they will be around 20 percent in 2003. As Warren Buffet says, in effect accounting principles offer management a choice:

- Pay employees in one form and count the cost, or
- Pay them in another form and ignore the cost.[17]

Because the same people who decide about distributing executive options are also those benefiting from them, the strategy is often used for self-enrichment. According to published statistics at the end of 2001, a few months before being fired, Jean-Marie Messier, CEO of Vivendi, had 592,810 stock options in his company as opposed to 152,090 in 2000, a nearly four-fold increase. Over the same timeframe, Vivendi's stock lost 75 percent of its value. Even when, in mid-2002, Messier was ousted by Vivendi's board, he kept the use of a $17.5 million Park Avenue, New York, apartment paid for by Vivendi shareholders.

6   Compensation Committees and executive bonuses

Federal and other taxes are not concerned with whether or not executive options are given for real performance or are simply handouts. The timing of handouts, however, helps in optimizing the tax bill – a fact often taken into account by Compensation Committees.

In the US, no taxable income is recognized by the optionee at the time of the option grant, or when the option is exercised. The optionee has to recognize taxable income in the year in which the shares are sold or otherwise made the subject of a taxable disposition. For federal tax purposes, dispositions are divided into two categories: *qualifying* and *disqualifying*.

A qualifying disposition occurs if the sale or other disposition is made more than two years after the date the option was exercised for those shares. Should this requirement not be satisfied, the result is a disqualifying disposition which, in a tax sense, is more onerous. Upon a qualifying disposition, the optionee will recognize long-term capital gain in an amount equal to the excess of the amount realized upon the sale or other disposition of the shares, then the excess of market value over the exercise price paid for the shares will be taxable as ordinary income to the optionee. Any additional gain or loss recognized upon the disposition will be recognized as a capital gain or loss.

At shareholders' expense, companies tend to compensate the fact that the optionee will, in general, recognize ordinary income in the year in which the option is exercised. This will be equal to the excess of the fair market value of the purchased shares on the exercise date over the exercise price paid for the shares. Compensation for taxes due is made in two ways:

- By increasing the amount of options granted, and
- By timing and pricing the handout so that the beneficiary can optimize his or her taxes.

Since death and taxes are unavoidable, it is a forgone conclusion that the optionee will be required to satisfy the tax-withholding requirements applicable to such income. In most cases, the Compensation Committee keeps this in perspective when in the first quarter of each year it sets targets in salaries, options, and other bonuses, based upon the recommendations of the CEO – who is at the same time the main beneficiary.

CEOs and Compensation Committees will usually submit for shareholders' approval a package of benefits to be disbursed over one or more years, without always accounting for the evolution in the company's financial position. In March 2002, Deutsche Bank asked its shareholders to authorize the award of Euro 1.80 billion ($1.76 billion) worth of stock options to top brass and senior employees:

- 25 million stock options to board members and executives up to May 20, 2005
- Behind it was a policy of introducing a more aggressive bonus-driven style of investment banking management.

Such a plan was a windfall for Deutsche Bank's management board members who would receive up to 10 percent of the 25 million options, while executives in associated companies and subsidiaries would get roughly an equal amount. At both Deutsche Bank and its associated companies, executives below board level were to be allocated up to 80 percent of the total, or 20 million stock options.[18] Critics said that the handouts could not have come at a worst moment not only for Deutsche Bank but for the whole German financial industry. In 2001 and 2002, Deutsche Bank's stock was down 64 percent; that of MLP, 96 percent; Commerzbank, 88 percent; Bayerische HypoVereinsbank, 83 percent; and Münchener Rück, 75 percent. The entire market capitalization of these six financial companies went from Euro 330 billion in 2000 to about Euro 70 billion at the end of 2002.

If banks were providing so much by way of executive bonuses, the stock exchange could not be left behind. EuroNext NV, the Dutch company who is the owner of the Paris, Amsterdam, and Brussels stock exchanges, established a two-tier price system for its share, loaded towards its own executives. The share price for the average investor was set at about Euro 25, but employees of EuroNext Paris can buy the shares at only 20 percent, i.e. for Euro 5, benefiting from stock options.

Some 200,000 stock was put into this scheme, representing something of the order of Euro 1 billion. A reason was also found for the handout. In early 2000, prior to the merger of the three stock exchanges, the Bourse de Paris set its value at Euro 2 billion. A year later, however, when the merger took place, other expertise determined that the real worth was Euro 10 billion – which explains why a French option of Euro 5 gives the right to a European option of Euro 25.[19]

The Bourse de Paris employees who benefited from that handout were not equal to one another when it came to dividing the windfall of profits; 600 lower management and employees had the right to buy an amount equal to one month of their salary. By contrast:

- The top brass was given the right to buy an amount equivalent to twenty-four months of their salary
- Since company salary levels also varied quite significantly from top to bottom, the benefit from these options differs by about a ratio of 500 : 1.

One can say: "That's life," but the problem of what should and what should not be done with executive options and other bonuses remains. The options' original goal of being a reward for performance and what the hand-outs represent in terms of shareholder equity are both up for review.

Any valid solution to the stock options and bonuses problem should account for the fact that they are both an extra, often unreasonable, compensation for executives and a major cost to stockholders, since their exercise dilutes equity ownership rights. For both reasons, it is important to provide all stakeholders with clear information on:

- The outstanding options
- The reasons why these options were given, and
- The value of the options given by any company in any year.

The latter should be deducted from revenue in that year, as a number of companies now assure us that they will do. On July 31, 2002, for instance, General Electric became the largest US company to announce that:

- It would treat stock option costs as expenses, and
- It would make senior officers hold stock for at least one year after exercising their options.

GE also said that its CEO and CFO had filed sworn statements with the SEC certifying that the group's accounts were true. Jeffrey Immelt, CEO, and Keith Sherin, CFO, affirmed the filings for 2001 and the first two quarters of 2002. "For me it was a no-brainer, we've signed similar statements for share-owners for many years," said Immelt, who also added that the group's decision to treat option costs as expenses was likely to have a only a small effect on earnings.[20] As we have seen in this chapter, however, the effect for other companies is quite major.

6

Responsibilities of Certified Public Accountants and of the Board

1 Introduction

Arthur Andersen, the former auditor of Enron and so many other companies in judicial trouble, said the fall-out from the company's demise had created opportunities, as well as difficulties.[1] This was a curious statement contradicting what the market thought about the auditors' responsibilities. The same day that Andersen made that statement, February 6, 2002, Deloitte Touche Tohmatsu became the next auditor to succumb to pressure for reform after the collapse of the US energy trading company.

The US–Japanese firm, which had long said it would keep its consulting and audit businesses together, reversed its position and stated that the two would separate. This is a decision which speaks volumes about the uncertainties confronting the big auditing firms, because of the conflict of interest between certified public accounting (CPA) and consulting that has developed over the years. In the aftermath of Enron's demise, experts now believe that regulatory scrutiny could result in restrictions on both:

- The *services* CPAs offer, and
- The kind of *relationships* they develop with clients.

A high-profile question facing the industry relates to the *conflicts of interest* inherent in accounting firms doing non-audit work for their clients – particularly as consulting work is so much more lucrative than auditing the books. Another issue is the lack of limits on the time for which firms are allowed to audit clients. Unlimited timespans in auditing missions help to create cozy relationships which can lead to conflicts of interest.

A third question is that of high auditing standards. Both internal and external audits should be done to well-established standards. The argument that the audit is no more than a contractual agreement between a company and its auditor, with standards subject to negotiation, is a sophistry.

The new mainstream thinking, one close to that of regulators, is that, for the public good, standards must be both high and uniform among all companies, and in all countries. These standards should also be made far stricter than they have been so far. In the UK, the Financial Services Authority (FSA), the House of Commons Treasury Committee, and the Review Board – the auditing profession's new regulator – are examining concerns raised about accounting and auditing norms since Enron collapsed in December 2001.

In the US, too, the spotlight has been placed on CPAs and the dependability of their audits, with the creation of a new supervisory board for CPAs. However, the emphasis on external auditors' responsibilities does not mean that there are no other parties accountable for the current situation of unreliable financial statements and the misleading of investors. Indeed, as we will see in section 4, a huge amount of responsibility falls on the board of directors and its Audit Committee.

The origin of the board of directors lies in the seventeenth century. It was one of the milestones in structuring the joint-stock company and, in all likelihood, it was first implemented by the English East India Company. After merging with a rival, the East India Company organized itself into a court of twenty-four directors, elected by and reporting to a court of proprietors – the shareholders. Since then, the role of the board and its responsibilities has evolved in a most significant manner, and so have the challenges facing the board.

As an article in the *Economist* aptly suggested: "What counts in the end is how directors behave and what questions they ask, not whether they have an ethics policy in place or can explain why they do not have a finance professional on the audit committee."[2] Ethics, however, shape the questions directors and auditors ask. Lack of ethics is a policy which many board and CPAs come to regret.

2   A history of audit miscarriages

The Arthur Andersen company, was founded in Chicago in 1913, and it came into national prominence in the 1930s, when J.P. Morgan picked the company to manage the restructuring of the electricity interest of Samuel Insull. As an entrepreneur, Insull, who had worked with Thomas Edison, had built a complex of electric utilities in direct competition with Morgan; but in the end, Morgan prevailed.

Subsequently, in 1938, Arthur Andersen (the person) was offered the chairmanship of the New York Stock Exchange, but declined the offer having chosen to concentrate on his company's business of accounting and consulting. In the 1990s, Arthur Andersen, a globalized company with significant accounting, auditing, and consulting business, played an important role in connection with energy firms – not only Enron, but also Calpine and Mirant among others. Andersen was also a driving force among the new telecom companies, where its clients included Global Crossing, Qwest

Communications, and WorldCom (see more on this below). Part of its own consulting business centered on how to structure telecom capacity swaps. Analysts at Wall Street say that Andersen literally wrote the book on telecom swaps, it also authored a White Paper on the subject which was widely used by other accounting firms and their clients.

This is, so to speak, the good news. The bad news is the audit miscarriages, often confirmed by grand juries (like Enron's), the courts, and costly out-of-court settlements. In June 2001 the auditing firm agreed to pay a $7 million fine, plus much of a $220 million class action settlement, to resolve charges that it had failed in its audits of Waste Management. While not admitting fault, Andersen accepted an injunction promising it would in future follow the law.

There were earlier problems, too. Andersen had failed to call Sunbeam to order for alleged creative accounting that inflated its financial results. In the aftermath, the auditor paid $110 million to settle shareholder litigation. As for the capacity swaps concerning Global Crossing, the accounting firm maintained that the Securities and Exchange Commission (SEC) had approved its client's accounting methods, and in any event it claimed that while it offered advice it did not structure or promote specific transactions.[3]

One of the scandals which hit Arthur Andersen's reputation hard was connected with its audits of the Baptist Foundation of Arizona (BFA), a not-for-profits entity which had allegedly broken the law. Without admitting guilt, in March 2002, the CPA agreed to pay $217 million to settle all pending litigation over its audits for the Baptist Foundation of Arizona, whose 1999 collapse:

- Was the largest Chapter 11 filing by a not-for-profits organization in US history, and
- Carried a cost to investors of nearly $600 million.

The Baptist Foundation was an Arizona religious not-for-profits organization, incorporated in 1948 for the purpose of providing support for Southern Baptist causes. Since 1984, BFA had engaged Andersen as its independent auditor. From that year until 1997, Andersen issued unqualified audit opinions on BFA's combined financial statements.

During these thirteen years, Andersen was also engaged by BFA and its attorneys to perform other accounting and auditing duties – as well as management consulting and tax advisory services. This led to significant conflicts of interest inasmuch as BFA's structure included a complex maze of for-profits subsidiaries whose accounting left much to be desired. Andersen:

- Operated a trust department
- Undertook a variety of investment activities
- Engaged in the sale of securities, and
- Served as a non-bank passive trustee for individual retirement accounts (IRAs).

The Baptist Foundation of Arizona was no ordinary not-for-profits. It raised funds through the sale of securities investment agreements (IAs) and mortgage-backed notes (MBNs). It then invested this money in real estate loans, real property, and different operating businesses. Auditing all this would have created a lot of work and, as the Attorney General's records show, the CPA did not discharge its responsibilities in a diligent way.

As stated in the Decision and Order (by Consent) No. 00A-98230-ACY, before the Arizona Board of Accountancy, even if it was a not-for-profits, because of its bank-like operations and products BFA faced problems quite similar to those that affect all banks and credit institutions. At the top of the list were issues of liquidity and asset quality.

But there was a major difference. As a not-for-profits, the Baptist Foundation claimed an exemption from Arizona banking regulations. Because of lack of regulatory oversight of its operations and sales of securities, BFA's offerings were not subject to the same scrutiny as a financial institution's products. This should have made Andersen, the CPA, much more – not less – careful in its auditing, specifically in terms of compliance.

Over the years, some deals and virtual companies seem to have been created around BFA. An example is New Church Ventures, a company which had no employees. BFA provided accounting, administrative, marketing and other support services for New Church Ventures which, for many years, included unaudited financial statements somehow integrated into the Baptist Foundation's own financial reporting.

Another curious entity was one known as Christian Asset Management; still another was ALO, a for-profits company engaged in real estate investments with numerous subsidiaries. One of ALO's purposes was to buy BFA's non-performing real estate investments, so that BFA could avoid recording write-downs and losses. (Note the similarity between this and Enron's partnerships in Part II.) By year-end 1997:

- ALO's total liabilities were $275.6 million
- This was way above its assets, leaving a negative net worth of $138.9 million.

The Baptist Foundation also served as a trustee for a number of trusts, including the IRA accounts which it marketed on behalf of its subsidiary New Church Ventures. BFA was thus subject to US Treasury regulations governing its fiduciary conduct as a non-bank passive trustee of IRAs. The trust's assets were not audited; they were disclosed in a footnote to BFA's financial statements audited by Andersen. But they were *not* marked "non-audited," as should have been the case.

In short, as the Decision and Order (by Consent) states, Andersen did not perform sufficient procedures, let alone due diligence, to determine if BFA was in compliance with relevant US Treasury regulations, in spite of the fact that, at all material times, BFA violated the Treasury regulations by actively managing the IRAs and collecting a fee to do so:

- Because BFA's net worth was actually negative, the Baptist Foundation was in violation of Treasury regulation on minimum net worth requirements
- Since related party transactions were not at arm's length, they inherently posed an increased risk of overstating results and defrauding investors.

As auditor, Andersen should have qualified its statements, highlighting such risks. It did not do so. In the trial connected to the Baptist Foundation case, the plaintiffs' lawyer maintained that Andersen had ignored warnings that the "charity" was a Ponzi scheme years before the Foundation fell apart.

While the Baptist Foundation promised that its profits would go to pay for Baptist charitable projects, this was not the case. Much time was involved in speculation and, as with Enron, the different fictitious vehicles provided the pyramiding tools. The shell companies bought real estate from the Foundation at inflated rates, with the BFA lending the money for the purchases. When in 1999 the Baptist Foundation collapsed, it owed $570 million, mostly to elderly churchgoers who has been attracted by: BFA's high interest rates and its (improperly) stated mission of using its earnings for good works.

Don Martin, Andersen's lead lawyer, told the jury that Andersen had been a victim of fraud by BFA. "It was a fraud. It misled investors. It defrauded its own auditor, Arthur Andersen."[4] This argument completely overlooked the fact that as CPA Andersen was paid a fee to discover and report the situation.

One reason the scheme lasted as long as it did, the lawsuits alleged, was that Andersen continued to certify the Baptist Foundation's financial statements and dismissed multiple warnings by individuals that BFA and the for-profits which it controlled was defrauding investors. A settlement was finally reached and Andersen said it had made a business decision to settle this matter, without admitting or denying any wrongdoing.

Under the agreement, Andersen's Phoenix office was placed under the supervision of a three-person oversight board established by the State of Arizona. The settlement also required retired Andersen partner Jay Ozer and Andersen principal Ann McGrath, who had led the Andersen team responsible for the Baptist Foundation's audit, to surrender their licenses to practice accountancy.

3 Did Arthur Andersen ring the alarm bells about Enron?

Following ten days of deliberation, on June 15, 2002 the jury decided that in the Enron affair Andersen had obstructed justice. While Andersen planned to appeal, the verdict essentially meant that the CPA would no longer be authorized to audit companies quoted on the stock exchange. Experts suggested that the reform of the profession, which was long overdue, should see to it that internal auditors and external auditors were not the same entity. This is what has happened with Enron, among many other cases. In a September 2000 letter, then Enron Chairman Kenneth L. Lay said that his company's use of Arthur Andersen as both internal and external auditor was "valuable to the investing public... given the risks and complexities of Enron's business." Lay's statement is, of course, nonsense. External auditors should *not* perform internal audits. The best approach would have been an outright ban, but the SEC was willing to accept as a yardstick that no company could rely on its independent auditor for more than 40 percent of internal audit services. This compromise did not please the big auditing firms, but stakeholders also saw it as a way to continue the conflicts of interest.

"[He] seems conflicted, like an Arthur Andersen auditor... " is a comment I heard on Wall Street, in a different case. Yet, in spite of the June 2002 jury verdict there was some evidence that at least in the case of Enron Andersen had timidly rung an alarm bell. As has been revealed post-mortem, Andersen had some doubts about the company's accounting practices, but the board had deaf ears. In February 1999, nearly three years before Enron's crash, the auditors described its accounting practices as "high-risk." David B. Duncan, who headed the Arthur Andersen team at Enron, informed the board's audit committee that:

- Enron's accounting was "pushing limits," and
- It was "at the edge" of acceptable practices.[5]

Headed by Richard Jaedicke, the Audit Committee of Enron's board seems to have taken no corrective action after being informed that the energy trader was a "maximum-risk" client of the auditor. Neither is there any evidence that the board's Audit Committee asked Andersen to adopt a more prudent approach in its auditing, given the revealed level of risk.

Enron, as a whole, seems to have had other priorities. In 2000, the Compensation Committee, chaired by Charles LeMaistre, approved $750 million in cash bonuses to the company's executives, in a year when Enron reportedly had net income of $975 million:

- The handout in bonuses stood at 77 percent of income
- The stated income proved in any case to be hugely inflated.

The real story was that of a torrent of red ink, but the Compensation Committee's decision stood – at the expense of the shareholders. The committee also approved a credit line for chief executive Kenneth L. Lay, that eventually reached $7.5 million; then, it allowed him to repay it with stock instead of cash.

How could this happen? The straight answer is conflict of interest at the level of the Enron board, which was sugar coated with a duty statement made of smoke and mirrors. A simple standard known as the *duty of care* should have guided the behavior of corporate board members, requiring that a director discharge his or her duties in good faith:

- With the care of an ordinarily prudent person, and
- In a manner which s/he reasonably believes to be in the best interests of the corporation.

Enron directors failed that standard miserably, and this seems to have taken place on repeated occasions. Board members never asked probing questions, nor did they follow up on critical issues that the board should monitor – for instance, the timid alarm bell rung by Andersen.

Post-mortem it also became known that directors got wind of Sherron Watkins' memo which spoke of many improprieties, but not a single one seems to have asked for a copy. "I am incredibly nervous that we will implode in a wave of accounting scandals," Watkins wrote in her (now famous) six-page memo to Kenneth L. Lay, the CEO.[6] Among other things, Watkins expressed concern over private partnerships subject to review by the finance committee, chaired by Herbert Winokur, but there is no evidence the board took corrective action here either.

Critics suggested that even if the CPA did inform the board of Enron about pushing limits and being at the edge, it failed to perform its duties in many other cases, though it did not fail in searching for excuses post-mortem. Arthur Andersen said that the CFOs of companies it audited, like Enron and WorldCom, had not told it of the manipulation of expenses, or sought its approval. But what is the purpose of an audit if not to ask focused questions about significant transfers in the accounts?

Interestingly enough, there is significant correlation between what has happened with Enron, the Baptist Foundation and WorldCom. Arthur Andersen was replaced as WorldCom's auditor in early 2002, by Scott Sullivan, the WorldCom CFO who was sacked after the problems were revealed. But this did not expunge WorldCom's previous accounting and auditing problems, nor did it relieve the CPA of its responsibilities:

- Andersen had a large auditing presence in energy and telecoms
- Both became areas under scrutiny in the wave of financial reporting cases.

Among Andersen's energy clients were Enron, Dynegy, and Halliburton. In telecoms, it looked after WorldCom, Qwest, and Global Crossing. All are names that appeared on the list of accounting investigations. The already battered auditing firm has been left with almost nothing further to lose, but individual partners – including former partners – may face prosecution, civil actions, or be named in shareholder lawsuits further down the line.

The senior partners who ran the relationships with Enron, WorldCom, and some other now defunct companies will probably be the first targets. In WorldCom's case, for instance, both regulators and prosecutors will focus on the fact that the accounting manipulation involved more than $3 billion of expenses in 2001 compared with a reported profit of $1.4 billion:

- Someone on the audit team should have spotted that, and
- Andersen's senior managers should have carefully checked the assets and their existence.

This is normal practice for an auditor; investors were certainly unimpressed by Andersen's statement about having been wrongly informed. After Enron, investors started to move away from any company that appeared to employ special-purpose entities, typically used by the energy company and by the Baptist Foundation to hide debt.

Institutions began to sell shares in companies audited by Andersen. All told, the auditing firm paid a high price for its unprofessional practices. Its dwindling group of audit clients has continued to shrink and the actual survival of divisions was by no means assured.

4   Audit Committees and the choice of auditors

Enron prompted a basic rethinking of how Audit Committees should be composed, paid, expected to perform, and made independent of the CEO's influence. A similar statement is valid about the duties and responsibilities of CPAs. Both will be examined in this section. The main tasks of Audit Committees are to:

- Oversee the external audit, and
- Monitor company finances.[7]

Over the years, however, Audit Committees have managed to reduce the importance of this mission by lowering standards in approving the hiring of external auditors, and signing off part of their accountability to the CPAs. However, apart from the fact that responsibility is never delegated, Audit Committees seem to forget that most CPAs come with big conflicts of interest, including multimillion-dollar consulting contracts with the company they are supposed to audit.

Audit Committees often also fail to ask the tough questions which are part and parcel of their job; their members are less than careful in exercising their duties. The case of Enron and Arthur Andersen are not one-offs. Outsider shareholders accused PricewaterhouseCoopers (PwC) of conducting dangerously lax audits of Gazprom, the Russian energy giant, depriving investors of vital information and sheltering its management from scrutiny over many questionable dealings.

This case is pertinent in the US, because investors have purchased Gazprom's American Depository Receipts (ADRs). Investment in Gazprom's ADRs were made on the basis of audit opinions provided by PricewaterhouseCoopers, but these proved to be flawed according to certain analysts.[8]

Experts say this is not the only case where PricewaterhouseCoopers seems to have had a conflict of interest. An SEC study, released in July 2002 showed that the CPA failed to make two companies, one of them Avon Products, correctly account for consulting fees they paid to it. Another alleged misbehavior was that PNC Financial Services used off-balance sheet magic to mislead investors into thinking it had got bad loans off its books when nothing of the kind had really happened. Yet the books were audited.

A major issue for investors was that, as external auditor, Pricewaterhouse-Coopers did not see the problems at Tyco International. Did the company's CPAs fail to probe Tyco's accounts, or were there other reasons? How did it happen that PwC did not catch wind of the massive loans and self-dealing that CEO Denis Kozlowksi, and other executives, allegedly engaged in? One would think that if the auditors could spot anything, it would be loans to corporate executives. But this did not happen.

Given the potential for abuse, the external auditors "should have reviewed all transactions between the company and its officers," Philip Livingston, CEO of Financial Executives International, a professional association of chief financial officers, says.[9] Such a review should have uncovered how Tyco loans had mushroomed far beyond anything the board authorized.

Still another case is that of the American subsidiary of Allied Irish Banks (AIB). The management of AIB said it was not blaming PwC for failing to detect the fraud it had suffered at Allfirst, its US subsidiary. In contrast to what happened with Barings' auditors, who were pursued in the courts by the bank's liquidators, AIB put this case on the backburner, yet its comments add fuel to the debate over the respective roles and responsibilities of auditors and company directors. Both auditors and company directors have come under serious scrutiny since the collapse of Enron in December 2001. On Wall Street, some experts say that the loss of $750 million by AIB may have involved collusion, which auditors have always argued is hard for them to spot. PricewaterhouseCoopers' last published audit, for the year to December 2000, nonetheless raised no concerns about the accounts.

Audited by PwC, the AIB annual report for 2000 said the CPA had earned Euro 2.5 million ($2.5 million) for its audit and received Euro 5.8 million ($5.8 million) for non-audit work, including a computer consultancy. These sorts of cases where consulting fees are more than double the auditing fees bring up the issue that to award big consultancy projects to auditors is looking for trouble:

- This is a relationship that might lead to conflicts of interest
- It is also controversial with investors, who argue that such contracts jeopardize the independence of the audit.

In the case of PwC, some experts suggested that the merger between Price Waterhouse and Coopers & Lybrand brought new challenges to compliance and also exacerbated the stock ownership problem: after the merger, Coopers' partners and staff had to divest shares they owned in companies audited by Price Waterhouse, and vice versa.

But analysts on Wall Street have been of the opinion that some of the required divestitures never took place. At the SEC's insistence, PwC hired a special counsel to conduct an internal investigation, which uncovered 8,000 violations, involving half the firm's partners. Some were major infractions – for instance, the heads of PwC divisions and top managers in charge of enforcing the conflict-of-interest rules owned stock in audit clients. Even PwC Chief Executive James Schiro owned forbidden stock.

The references made to PwC are not intended to imply that other CPAs have a clean bill of health. KPMG, for example, had similar problems. In April 2002, the SEC filed a lengthy complaint about KPMG's audits for its long-time client Xerox. It also notified the CPA that this complaint was part of a continuing investigation. This was not the only challenge KPMG had to meet. In April 2002, an audit of Comroad, a German technology company, by a new CPA firm also found 97 percent of Comroad's 2000 revenues to be fictional. Comroad's former CEO Bodo Schnabel is in jail awaiting trial, but it was KPMG which had originally audited the books and found no fault. This led to a massive re-audit. In the wake of Comroad, KPMG intended to go over the books of all thirty-five of its clients listed on the tech-oriented German Neuer Market.[10] There was a precedent for the German case. In Australia, in the early 1990s, KPMG settled for $100 million a $1.1 billion suit resulting from the audit of Tricontinental Corporation – a government-owned merchant bank.

Also in Australia, Ernst & Young was sued for a A$175 million by the liquidator of the investment bank Duke Group, and settled for A$35 million. In Canada, in 1990, Ernst & Young and a predecessor of Peat Marwick Thorne paid the major portion of a C$125 million dollar settlement in 1990 in connection to the failure of two Canadian banks.

Other penalties have been paid by auditors in England and in Luxembourg, where the liquidators of BCCI claimed $8 billion from Price Waterhouse and Ernst & Young. This was in connection to the 1985 audit of the collapsed Pakistani credit institution. Additional claims were filed in regard to the 1986 and 1987 audits, creating a trail of cases which is of interest to all shareholders, the CPAs, their clients, and the regulators.

5 External auditors' responsibilities and the cost of settlements

Apart from the ethical issues involved in the examples section 4 has presented, taking risks with substandard audits is bad business. Lack of compliance with rules and regulations is full of visible and hidden demerits. In October 1995, in the UK, a High Court judge found an accounting firm liable for negligence in permitting a loss-making Lloyd's of London syndicate to close its accounts. By implicating the syndicate's auditors, Ernst & Whinney (now part of Ernst & Young):

- The ruling gave out the message that the courts were sensitive to lack of compliance, and
- Made it easier to sue external auditors.

Settlements are very costly for accounting firms because as a rule they are partnerships and do not have a well-endowed treasury which could make the outlays out of current funds. Settlements have to be financed by the partners themselves, to satisfy the liquidators, or other parties who have suffered financial loss from an incomplete or improper financial audit. To protect themselves, up to a point, independent auditors may buy insurance (as we will see in the examples which follow in this section). With capital adequacy for operational risk brought under regulation with Basel II,[11] such insurance is clearly an option.

In the US, for instance, casualty insurers now offer cover for directors and officers (D&O). Today, such policies protect the personal assets of executives in securities litigation; tomorrow they may extend to other domains. But because of corporate malfeasance in 2000–2, premiums were expected to rise by up to 500 percent in 2003. Chubb, for example, raised its rates sharply after losing $1.16 on every $1 of D&O premiums it collected in the first three quarters of 2002. Rate hikes are also necessary to help insurers cover settlement costs from corporate fraud cases involving Enron, WorldCom, and Adelphia, as well as other firms.

Through payment of a premium, *operational risk* is exchanged for *credit risk* (see also section 6). Credit risk is not negligible, as many insurers have found themselves under stress because of September 11, 2001, asbestos litigation, natural catastrophe, and other events. D&O insurers are afraid that as stricter corporate governance measures take effect, shareholder class actions will proliferate. CEOs and CFOs are now required by law to attest to the validity of their companies' financial statements, and neither capital reserves nor insurance do away with the fact that senior executives of auditing companies must now watch like a hawk for compliance issues.

Two outstanding cases are Barings and BCCI. The administrators of the holding company of Barings, the British merchant bank that collapsed in February 1995, issued writs against the bank's auditors in the UK and in Singapore, claiming up to £1 billion in damages. In January 1996, the Barings liquidators started proceedings in the High Court in London against Coopers & Lybrand (now part of PricewaterhouseCoopers), and in Singapore against Deloitte & Touche.

The claim was "in respect of alleged negligence in the conduct of audits for certain years between 1991 and 1994." A spokesman of Coopers in London said the writ was a complete surprise, adding that: "We are not aware of any grounds for any claim against us." In January 1996, Deloitte & Touche in Singapore, also said: "The writ comes as a surprise. The audits of Barings Futures Singapore in 1992 and 1993 were conducted with all required professional skill." The counterparties felt otherwise.

In June 1998, Coopers & Lybrand and Deloitte & Touche offered to settle the £1 billion claims for £33 million ($51 million) – as reported in the London press. The damages claims in the action were estimated, before interest, as being at least £1 billion ($1.65 billion) including goodwill, or £560 million ($929 million) excluding goodwill. The liquidators reached their figure by considering in essence moneys which went out of Barings Futures Singapore on unauthorized trades after the date at which Nick Leeson's activities should have ceased and if the audit which was conducted had not been carried out in a negligent manner.

At no time was it sure the court would accept a claim of that kind and size, and while the difference between £33 million and £1 billion is 1:33, nothing is cut and dried in the world of auditor liability. Precedents were thin. As in the cases of Enron and WorldCom, CPAs tend to make the excuse that as far as the results of the audit, and the advice which has been offered, external auditors rely, in part at least, on the assurances provided by the company's management. In the Barings case, the external auditors asserted that at the time of the bank's collapse it had not signed its audit opinion and had not completed its audit work. Coopers & Lybrand maintained that it had not exhausted the audit work which could have led to the identification of Leeson's alleged frauds, which explains the auditors' efforts at arguing contributory negligence by various members of the senior management team at Barings.

Besides these arguments there was also a matter of insurance cover. Coopers' insurance cover was shown to be £47.06 million ($73.16 million) subject to an excess which had already been exhausted. Deloitte & Touche Singapore's cover did not exceed £55 million. The Barings' creditors included bondholders owed £100 million who were not repaid by ING, and perpetual noteholders owed another £100 million.

In its report into the collapse of Barings, the Bank of England's Board of Banking Supervision put much of the blame for the bankruptcy on Nick Leeson, the trader who ran up losses in Singapore. But it also mentioned a *lack of management controls* at Barings that allowed him to do so, as well as criticizing and questioning the actions of both firms of auditors.[12]

Just as interesting in terms of auditors' responsibilities is the liquidation of the Bank for Credit and Commerce International – but for a different reason. Accountants called in to wind up the books were accused in a confidential report of overcharging creditors by £1 million ($1.65 million) in the immediate aftermath of the bank's collapse. The report which brought these charges was commissioned by a court in Luxembourg, in January 1992, because BCCI was registered in Luxembourg. This report, by a panel of three independent experts, looking at the level of fees charged by the liquidators between the collapse of the bank and January 1992, apparently alleged that accountants Deloitte & Touche overcharged by 40 percent during the six months after BCCI closed:

- Deloitte & Touche contested the report at a series of court hearings, claiming that the experts who wrote it had no knowledge of the costs involved in a global liquidation of a bank with branches in sixty-nine countries
- But creditors' leaders hailed the findings of the panel as proof that the accounting firm had overcharged: "These people have been spending money like water," said one of them.[13]

Deloitte & Touche fiercely resisted any attempt to use the report of the experts in the BCCI case to drive down fees due elsewhere. It argued that the first six months of the liquidation required huge resources to be deployed to secure assets quickly. The accountants seem to have realized assets for creditors of $3.3 billion against global fees approaching $300 million – or 9 percent of the identified assets. Deloitte & Touche (which operated at the time as Touche Ross), also stated that the final ratio of costs to returns for the liquidation would show it had charged below the industry average of 10 percent. The firm said that it believed the experts' report tried to compare its fee levels with those charged for a routine auditing assignment. "This was more than a case of having to go in and change the locks," one of the insiders said at the time.

6   Audit reform, the auditors, and the board

After the scandals of Enron, Tyco, Global Crossing, WorldCom, and so many others, shareholders, bondholders, and regulators have been asking for radical audit reforms, as well as for greater internal checks on CEOs, their performance, their pay, and their ethics. A major part of this debate is focusing on how to strengthen:

- The boards of directors
- The audit committees, and
- The accountability of CPAs.

Companies now pay premiums to insure their directors against lawsuits.[14] These premiums have shot up by between 35 percent and 900 percent, depending on the business. If they can find an insurer willing to underwrite the risk at all, companies at greater management risk could pay $2 million a year for a $10 million policy.

The better solution is to arrest the growth curve of scandals. Some rigorous changes are urgently need, including more prudential supervision.

For this purpose, the SEC is pursuing changes to audit regulation and accounting standards. We have already spoken of the new responsibility of CEOs and CFOs to vouch personally for financial statements, which came into effect in August 2002.

Stock exchanges, too, are looking to make board members and senior executives more accountable for their actions. Acting at the SEC's request, the New York Stock Exchange (NYSE) has published new proposals to strengthen corporate governance for listed companies. An example is the demand that:

- A majority of the board consists of independent directors
- Audit and remuneration committees be composed only of outside directors, and
- Directors should meet each other and company managers without the CEO being present.

More rigorous measures for controlling management risk come none too soon, as conflict of interest has become routine and established rules of behavior are frequently broken. Enron's board, for instance, violated its own rules in order to allow Andrew Fastow, its CFO (currently under indictment), to benefit personally from the off-balance sheet partnerships that he set up.

Let nobody, however, think that CEO malfeasance never happened before, or that it could never happen again. The 2002 investors' revolt against abuse of company money by senior executive officers, and by the board, has several precedents. In the 1970s, many shareholders became particularly upset by public companies whose boards were beholden to powerful private interests, often the founding family or sources of finance and other business connections.

What is new now is the institution of a new independent board to supervise certified public accounts firms – and even that has had its problems in defining the board's precise authority and responsibility, and in finding a director who is acceptable to all parties. That says much about the likely pace and extent of audit reform.

Yet, after Enron and so many other misadventures within less than a year, practically everyone agrees that board members, CEOs, CFOs, and other senior managers, must be held accountable for the financial information, including losses and profits that they report. Practically everybody is also in accord that auditing firms should be on the front line of responsibility for their inspection of the books.

For senior company executives, directors and CPAs, there should be significant penalties, in addition to the punishment made by the markets, for those who falsify financial results or confirm the falsifications. Both "carrot" and "stick" are necessary to stamp out creative accounting practices and raise the threshold of ethics applied in financial reporting. A system of merits and demerits must be devised which creates for public CPAs, CEOs, board members, and senior managers an incentive to examine more closely:

- Financial performance
- Directors' independent opinion
- Auditing methods and results, and
- The general professionalism of public accounting firms.

The trouble is that the message conveyed by these four bullets runs counter to some of today's practices, whereby some companies foster an environment compromising the independence of external directors and of external auditors. It is therefore vital to reduce the potential for harmful conflicts of interest, including the amount of non-audit services a company can purchase from its accountants and auditors.

If an independent supervisory board is set up for CPAs, as is now happening, why should it not also be responsible for supervising Audit Committees? And why should it not include within its domain of responsibility independent credit rating agencies? With the internal risk-based (IRB) method,[15] and more generally Basel II, credit rating agencies play a critical role in the risk management and the responsibilities of boards and CEOs.

Not only CPAs, CEOs, CFOs, boards, and senior managers, but also investors should be held accountable as stakeholders in a company. As Scott G. McNealy aptly stated in an interview, investors don't have "to invest in a company that's going like crazy, [and] may be [its performance is] too good to be true … [They] ought to read the income statement, the balance sheet, and the footnotes."[16] A most interesting question is:

- How many investors actually read the footnotes?
- If they read them, are they able to understand them?
- If they don't, why are they investing in something that they cannot understand?

If a careful investor who exercises prudential judgment had investigated the extraordinary performance of Enron relative to other energy companies in the market, s/he would have been at least able to guess that Enron was an aberration rather than the norm. Indeed, it is hard to understand why everyone was not questioning what was behind Enron's spectacular rise, given the poor performance of the rest of the energy market.

If a company is too keen to avoid taxes, maybe this is only the given reason for moving to tax havens. The real reason may well be that its board and CEO have something to hide from prudential supervision, and they decide to move the company to an offshore with softer standards to avoid the watchful eye of regulators at home. The US Congress is now looking for means to prevent US companies from moving their headquarters to offshore locations, such as Bermuda, to avoid paying US taxes. Led by Richard Neal, proponents want to close a loophole that allows companies to avoid federal taxes through shell foreign incorporations:

- Well-known entities such as Tyco, Accenture, and PricewaterhouseCoopers have done this
- Even though practically all of them benefit from hundreds of millions of dollars in federal contracts.

There is a generally used semantic distinction made between tax *evasion* (the illegal avoidance of tax), and tax *optimization*. The sense of the latter term is that of using legal means to minimize the tax bill of an individual or an organization. Underlying this distinction, however, are ethical arguments as well as loopholes in legislation. Some of the cases currently under investigation suggest that "tax optimization" may not be the only reason for choosing an offshore location.

There is now considerable pressure on entities to differentiate in a factual and documented manner between ways of legally doing something, like avoiding taxes by exploiting loopholes, and a disregard for ethics, including moving offshore because there are other things to hide.

7   The evolution of regulatory legislation

It is always wise to study the evolution of legislation regarding financial crimes, as new ones like unreliable financial statements have joined older ones like money laundering. Every new piece of financial legislation, or regulation, can act as a harbinger of other legislation specifically designed for corporate manipulation of balance sheets, income statements, and other documents. Existing legislation may also be applied in novel, more rigorous ways. In the mid-1990s, the US government used the Racketeer Influenced and Corrupt Organization Act (RICO). This is the anti-corruption and crime legislation voted by Congress for punishment of gangsterism, but it was also used against Bankers Trust. The venerable bank was no mobster, but it had misused derivatives and (as the federal prosecutors said) taken some of its clients for a ride.

The study of precedents always serves to give perspective. The American government criminalized money laundering in 1986, with the goal of creating a weapon against drug trafficking. This law, however, is far-reaching. It prohibits financial transactions that involve gains from more than 160 illegal activities, including various types of fraud, foreign corrupt practices, arms smuggling, violations of US and foreign law such as extortion, fraud against banks, kidnapping, and terrorism. The interpretation and implementation of RICO has been strengthened over time, as evidenced by the criminal case brought against BCCI Holdings in 1991. More than any other, the BCCI case (see also Chapter 2) set the tone for the global reach of US law against financial crimes.

The international branches of BCCI's worldwide banking network tried to claim some of their frozen assets. They argued, without success, that under the laws of the various countries in which BCCI branches operated, each would be considered independent entities and therefore separate and distinct from BCCI.

The US government denied their claims because it considered a corporation and its branches a single entity. As the US government found, BCCI depositors, trade creditors, and other companies owed money under pre-existing contracts with BCCI worldwide were mere unsecured creditors lacking sufficient standing to make a claim against frozen funds:

- The claims of Credit Suisse, a trade creditor, and the claims of holders of letters of credit were denied
- The Organization of American States, a depositor, was also denied any special status.

The next major case in the progression of extra-territorial laws arose from Operation Casablanca. From October 1996 to April 1998, the US Customs Service operated a money laundering sting directed at Mexican banks. Three of them, as well as twenty-nine bankers from other countries, like Venezuela and Spain, were charged with laundering drug proceeds. Eleven other foreign banks also were named in various civil forfeiture cases and in administrative banking regulatory actions. Accounts in more than 100 banks worldwide were seized.

Bancomer and Banca Serfin pleaded guilty and were convicted of money laundering. Undercover US Customs agents, posing as drug money launders for Mexican and Colombian drug traffickers, made the case of a supposedly lucrative business to the bankers, and the latter fell into the trap by opening numerous bank accounts in the names of straw owners and using these accounts and their banks' US correspondent accounts to launder the money.

This is a harbinger of what will happen in the future in tracking down banks and other companies which persist in using unreliable financial statements. Among the significant criteria the government used to determine which banks to prosecute for laundering were the rank of the employee, the benefit accrued to the bank from the laundering activities, and whether the bank had any procedures that fostered the evasion of sound banking practices.

In the aftermath, a US Senate report recommended, among other things, that American banks be barred from profiling correspondent account services for foreign banks that are shell operations with no physical presence in any country. It also urged the creation of laws that would make it easier for law enforcement officials to seize laundered money from foreign banks' correspondent accounts in US banks and stepped up the scrutiny of correspondent accounts.

In response, the New York Clearinghouse Association proposed a code of best practice for correspondent banking. New legislation aimed to bar

American financial institutions from opening or maintaining correspondent accounts with countries or foreign institutions that posed a primary laundering concern, as determined by the government.

A new US regulation, which went into effect in early 2000, required the reporting of foreign holdings by US citizens, residents, and financial entities. Treasury Department regulations now require all entities with an interest in, or signature authority over, any financial account of $10,000 or more in a foreign country, to report the relationship by filing a Foreign Bank and Financial Accounts form (FBAR). The law applies to:

- US citizens
- Non-citizen residents
- Domestic partnerships
- Corporations, and
- Estates or trusts.

Failure to file an FBAR carries both civil charges and serious criminal penalties. This has been prompted by globalization. The shift towards internationalization of US financial regulations, to include foreign relationships, gained significant ground in January 2001 when the US government unveiled measures intended to discourage corrupt foreign officials from using US financial institutions to launder illicit funds.

These measures, issued jointly by the Federal Reserve, Treasury, Comptroller of the Currency, Federal Deposit Insurance Corporation (FDIC), Office of Thrift Supervision, and the State Department, are titled "Guidance on Enhanced Scrutiny for Transactions That May Involve The Proceeds of Foreign Official Corruption." While this is basically guidance which does not carry the force of law or regulation, the fact that it was issued by all major agencies with banking supervision authority made it much more than just "advice."

Among the practices recommended by such guidance are procedures for opening and maintaining accounts for senior political figures, their immediate family, and close associates. It also details a list of suspect account activities that should heighten a bank's scrutiny, like the routing of transactions into or through a secret jurisdiction, using of accounts at a nation's central bank, or employing government accounts as the source of account funding, frequent or excessive funds transfers, large currency transactions, and so on.

The serious reader should note these developments. The financial scandals which came to the fore in 2001 and 2002 had a precedent in money laundering activities in the 1980s. The legislation and regulation which followed them was punitive. In all likelihood, something similar will happen in the years ahead with fraudulent financial statements.

Part II

A Highly Leveraged Company, its Trades, its Accounts, and its Banks

7

Enron: The End of an Empire

1 Introduction

In mid-October 2001, the *Wall Street Journal* published a seminal article focusing on a handful of the 3,000 or so Enron partnerships, affiliates, and off-balance sheet operations. As the energy company's equity plunged, a Special Committee of its board was formed to investigate the allegations of illegal activities involving some of its people. This was a three-man committee which included two new directors. One of them was a former Lazard Frères partner; the other had close ties to Enron's Houston-based law firm, Vinson & Elkins.

The committee's report focused on the same small group of partnerships as did the *Journal,* and its findings provided the road map for the numerous Congressional investigations which followed Enron's collapse. A lesson to be learned from this experience is that, whether national or industrial, empires rarely have a slow painful death. Usually they crash and disappear, as Rome did in the classical era, and as did Portugal and the Soviet Union in the fourth quarter of the twentieth century.

The end of Enron's empire came in the first days of December 2001, when the formerly highly leveraged company filed for bankruptcy protection. It also laid off over 5,000 staff, some 25 percent of its workforce, and tried to sell assets to raise cash and reduce debts which stood at over $30 billion. Not surprisingly, as shown in Figure 7.1, Enron's equity value took a dive.

As an article in *The Economist* put it: "If there was a no-turning-back moment for the company it was the resignation in 1996 of the chief operating officer, Richard Kinder [who] had been the hands-on counterbalance to Kenneth Lay's networking with the rich and powerful."

The way dying empires often do, even on its deathbed Enron tried to strike back. It launched a $10 billion lawsuit against Dynegy, a smaller competitor energy company which had pulled out of a takeover bid probably made in the heat of the moment. Dynegy countersued, allegedly to get its hands on one of the dying company's valuable gas pipelines.

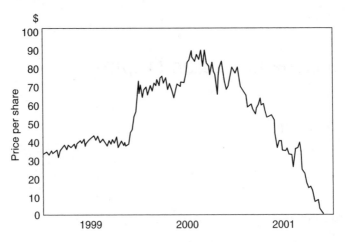

Figure 7.1　Enron pays the price for its high leverage and accumulated risks, 1999–2001

The collapse of Enron, which was until then the biggest bankruptcy in US history, is a metaphor for economic performance in the 2000–1 timeframe – post the 1990s bubble. It is also an example of how quickly and silently disaster can strike highly leveraged companies and deals. In the early 1990s, nobody would have suggested that what was no more than a medium-sized energy company whose main assets were gas pipelines and electricity transmission cables could be transformed so radically into an energy trader specializing in derivatives contracts; or that its failure might pose a systemic financial risk to the American economy and, by extension, to the global economy. Through high leverage, obscure deals, the support of some of the best-known banks (see Chapter 9), and the fact that it positioned itself as a global energy trader and derivatives dealer, Enron achieved the dubious distinction of doing a disservice to the American economy, to itself, and to its stakeholders.

2　Enron's deals

Though it started life as a sleepy gas pipeline company, under chairman Ken Lay Enron transformed itself into what was basically an investment bank specializing in the energy industry. In its filings with the Securities and Exchange Commission (SEC), Enron identified its business as a securities broker and dealer. This is the same classification used by Morgan Stanley, Goldman Sachs, and other Wall Street firms.

Was Enron a Texas gas company or a Wall Street investment bank? The best answer has been given by London's *The Economist*, which described it as "a hedge fund with a gas pipeline on the side." Enron created an over-the-counter derivatives market in energy contracts, becoming over the years a major dealer and player in derivative financial instruments (the section 4 and Chapter 8).

According to *Swaps Monitor*, at the end of 2000 – about a year prior to the crash – Enron had $201 billion in derivatives exposure. While this may seem peanuts in comparison to J.P. Morgan Chase's $24.5 trillion and Deutsche Bank's $9.1 trillion for the same period, it did make Enron one of the top derivatives holders. The toxic waste in its portfolio was also its downfall. The beginning of the end for Enron came on October 16, 2001, when the company stated that:

- It had lost $618 million in the third quarter, owing to write-offs of over $1 billion, and
- It was proceeding with early termination of certain structured finance arrangements, with a previously disclosed entity.

In a conference call on October 16, announcing the negative financial news, Ken Lay made a quick reference to a $1.2 billion write-down in the company's equity capital. This proved to be just the opening shot in a war of bad news. More announcements like that were to follow.

A day later, on October 17, 2001, the *Wall Street Journal* and other US papers began questioning Enron's book-keeping, charging that the company's actions raised vexing conflict of interest questions in its relationship to some of the partnerships it had created. The full extent of these partnerships and their deals would be revealed several months later, along with the role played by Andrew Fastow, Enron's CFO.

In a meeting we had in London in 2002, Moody's KMV, the risk management division of Moody's Investors Service, suggested that its credit risk model had foretold Enron's demise as early as August 2001. It did so by using the capitalization of the energy company as a proxy. If this is so, it is a very good example of the synergy which exists between *credit risk* and *market risk*.

In late August 2001, the SEC had begun an informal inquiry, soon upgraded into a formal investigation. The stock market also acted. Investors, sensing something was going wrong, acted to protect themselves rather than wait for official news. By October 15, 2001, the day before the fateful earnings announcement and conference call, Enron's stock had gone to $33.17 a share, a drop of 63 percent from its peak:

- As the bad news accumulated, Enron's stock went into a free fall, hitting $0.26 a share on November 30, down 99.7 percent from its peak
- This cut the company's once $66.5 billion market capitalization to just $193 million; a few days later, Enron filed for bankruptcy.

In retrospect, Enron's catastrophe had come not on account the $30 billion loans which banks had made to it but because this proved to be a company with a "black hole" of unknown proportions in its treasury. In the foggy bottom of its off-balance sheet and income statement were untold volumes of credit derivatives, including exotic contracts traded in the four corners of the globe. It is precisely these unorthodox financial deals that brought Enron down so fast once the market was able to scratch beneath the surface of unreliable financial statements.

Just as in the case of the collapse of Long-Term Capital Management (LTCM) in September 1998,[2] the only way the world's overstretched financial market supervisors could find out what exotic financial risks Enron had been running was by asking those banks doing business with it about their exposures. It was not the $30 billion debt that frightened regulators and investors, it was the unknowns. None of the banks that loaned Enron big money had:

- A complete overview of Enron's other exposures, or
- A thorough understanding of Enron's high leverage and its effect on its trading business.

The reason why it is so important to appreciate Enron's downfall is that what has happened is not so different to what happens today with hedge funds, funds of funds, and alternative investments offered to unsuspecting investors.[3] The other side of the coin is that investors ignorant of risks embedded in derivatives have been on another planet for twenty years.

Post-mortem, several analysts suggested Enron was a sort of hedge fund of the energy industry. Both over the counter and through its EnronOnline Internet energy-trading site, the company bought and sold electricity, natural gas, and other commodities worldwide. Being a major player, it was involved as a buyer or a seller in nearly a quarter of all US energy trades:

- Companies which sold to Enron through this online marketplace did so with the expectation that they would be paid
- If the confidence of payment is not there, companies cease doing business in that venue, and ask for immediate settlements of outstanding credit lines.

In the aftermath of Enron's downfall, both a Senate Committee and the SEC have been investigating the company's actions. What they have found is that the once-mighty Enron had been in decline not just at the end of 2001 but since autumn 2000. It was just that its health took a serious turn for the worse in mid-October 2001, the day it announced the $618 million third-quarter loss.

On Wall Street some analysts pointed out that superficially this hefty loss was not due to a drop in revenue, since reported revenue was up to a bubbly 59 percent in the third quarter of 2001 compared to the third quarter of 2000. Pragmatically, the origin of the loss was in the fact that Enron was running out of tricks which, until then, had enabled it to write off its losses in a way non-transparent to investors. That is why in, October 2001, it acknowledged a $1 billion loss due to its:

- Ill-judged water privatization business
- Sinking broadband communications' gambles

- Bad investment in the New Power Company, and
- Early termination of certain structured finance arrangements.

Mismanagement, high leverage, and derivatives were all present in its downfall. Indeed, with regard to the fourth bullet in the above list, Enron's equity capital had eroded in connection with the repurchase of 55 million of its own shares it had issued as part of a complex series of transactions with a "previously disclosed entity." This proved to be none other than a limited partnership created by Enron and run by the company's CFO, Andrew Fastow.[4]

The majority of analysts and investors on Wall Street were unaware of the magnitude of this hedging deal with a related private equity fund. As we shall see in Chapter 8, with the exception of Merrill Lynch almost nobody outside Enron seems to have had any information of the terms on which Enron had entered into different dubiously structured finance vehicles. The latter turned out to be just one of the company's many off-balance sheet devices, a telling example of the risks of murky investment funds and other secretive partnerships.

What was appreciated only post-mortem, when much more information on Enron's non-transparent business deals had become available, was that these different secretive partnerships were not just parts but were centerpieces of the company's Ponzi game. They helped to turn losses into profits through creative accounting deals, in precisely the same way that other illegal instruments like the *prepays* (see Chapter 9) helped to beautify the energy company's balance sheet until the final crash.

3 Enron's overexposure

Faced with a deteriorating liquidity position and having lost the market's confidence, Enron actively sought cash to fund its operations and pay down its debt. Reacting to a rash of downgrades by the major credit-rating agencies, the decaying empire tapped an existing $3 billion line of credit arranged through J.P. Morgan Chase and Citicorp, and used about $2 billion of that cash to redeem its outstanding commercial paper:

- Management characterized the action as a move to restore investor confidence
- But many analysts saw it as a sign of weakness, and a precursor of really bad news.

As Enron sought another $1 billion–$2 billion line of credit for future contingencies, the market reacted with another round of selling the company's equity short. Afraid that worse news was in store, investors dumped their Enron holdings, and traders found an opportunity to go short on the stock. When on November 28, 2001, Houston-based Dynegy pulled out of a deal to buy the company, Enron's attorneys at Weil, Gotshal & Manges, retained just a few weeks earlier, in October 2001, knew they had to act fast. Enron's stock was plunging below a dollar, its credit rating had collapsed, and creditors suddenly had the right to call in loans and seize buildings, pipelines, and other assets the company had put up as collateral.

The law firm threw everything it had into the case. Dozens of lawyers worked around the clock preparing a petition for Chapter 11 protection. As soon as they were ready they immediately filed electronically with the bankruptcy court – even though it was 5 a.m. on a Sunday morning. As an article in *BusinessWeek* suggested,[5] by the time the bankruptcy is over Weil, Gotshal & Manges could make as much as $30 million in fees. More than a dozen other law firms were also on the case, joined by investment bankers like the Blackstone Group, which is charging $350,000 a month plus a $35 million bonus if the company reemerges from Chapter 11.

Bankruptcies wipe out stockholders' equity, but they also generate a healthy cash flow for other firms. In 2001, 255 publicly traded US companies filed for bankruptcy, breaking the prior record of 176 in 2000. Some sectors have evidently been hit worse than others, particularly when faced with mounting litigation. Asbestos-related industries, not energy companies or airlines, provide the worst example with 600,000 plaintiffs, more than 6,000 defendants, and sixty-one companies in bankruptcy, as of January 2003.[6]

A peculiarity of the 2000–2 depression was that, unlike prior downturns where bankruptcies were concentrated in troubled industries like airlines, the market bubble's wave of failures was unusually broad, running across a wide range of businesses. These include Pacific Gas & Electric, United Airlines, LTV, Excise@Home, Fruit of the Loom, and Independent Insurance (UK). Mismanagement is what these very diverse companies have in common. Their board, CEO and CFO did not act in time to eliminate the risk that negatively impacted the company's stock price. When they did so by trying to strengthen the company's capital structure and enhance its liquidity, bankruptcy was a forgone conclusion. Mismanagement denied the company access to capital.

The August–November 2001 events which led to the downfall of Enron are a reminder to everybody that business is not just numbers in an inflated balance sheet. First and foremost, it is about the *confidence* a company inspires in the market. Usually, there are good reasons behind a meltdown. As we have seen, the biggest damage to Enron's brand name came with the release of third-quarter 2001 results that showed the huge write-off on broadband, water, and other bad investments.

Enron's rise and fall is an interesting case study for many reasons, not least among them the fact that many analysts and investors had not done their homework. My fifty years of business experience document that in every case where revenues suddenly spike to unprecedented levels, stakeholders are confronted by a financial iceberg where the 7/8ths of its mass of assets and liabilities, particularly the latter, cannot be seen:

- At Enron, revenues grew by $10 billion from 1998 to 1999, then jumped by another $60 billion, to $100 billion in 2000
- Profits before taxes rose by $1 billion in 1998, and by $500 million in both 1999 and 2000
- The gap between revenues and profits was widening and the company's return on capital was only 6.6 percent in 2000, less than rivals such as Dynegy and Williams.

Analysts with a sharp pencil should have noticed as early as 1998, as they did post-mortem in 2001, that Enron's trading margins were in no way commensurate with its big pronouncements about market leadership. It is therefore no surprise that these trading margins shrank further, until they collapsed: they went from 5.3 percent in early 1998 to less than 1.7 percent in the third quarter of 2001.

In fact, Enron's profit margins fell in spite of the company's practice of selling fixed assets and booking the gains as operating revenues – the sort of virtual company Enron wanted to be. In the last analysis it was not trading but financial engineering and creative accounting which ballooned the company's stock and bloated its balance sheet. Creative accounting practices included:

- Lumping assets such as pipelines into its trading business, and
- Using limited partnerships and other financial vehicles to inflate profits.

The ill-conceived forays into other industry sectors added to the company's troubles. Trying to stretch its brand name into new business areas, Enron grew the number and type of its contracts with some 8,000 counterparties. Its deals involved hundreds of business lines, ranging from credit insurance to metal trading, and it took ever bigger risks like trading telecoms bandwidth. Experts said that at the end the company's strategy had become Napoleonic:

- It tried to be a worldwide commodities broker and market maker to the whole world, and
- It operated twenty-four hours a day, trading with any party willing to accept just a BBB rating.

What is surprising is that the market tolerated this kind of wheeling and dealing. This speaks volumes for the mismanagement characterizing many firms. Eventually, the facts of life caught up with Enron, and the giant natural gas and electricity company filed for protection from creditors under Chapter 11 of the bankruptcy law, leaving its shareholders high and dry.

In licking their wounds, investors needed no reminder that Enron once had an outstanding market capitalization and ranked seventh on the

Fortune 500 list. At the end, its equity, which peaked at $90 a share, was trading as a penny stock. In the long run nobody, no matter how shrewd, can take the market to the cleaners – a feat which has happened in the short run more than once or twice.

4   Enron and LTCM

There are both similarities and differences characterizing the failure of LTCM formerly known as "the Rolls-Royce of hedge funds,"[7] and of Enron, the hedge fund with a gas pipeline. As Brian Toft said, LTCM did not fail because there was a problem with the data, the mathematics, or the computers that it employed. In the final analysis, it failed because of the assumptions and the decisions made by people about strategic issues and the way they handled these issues.

Based on this hypothesis, which is believable, Toft goes on to suggest that "*if* the kind of débâcle that was created by LTCM is to be prevented from recurring, *then* both regulators and the whole of the financial services industry need to understand how decision making processes and social behavior may affect people's judgment of financial risks."[8] The problem however is that:

- Investors are not so keen in learning from past failures, and
- As far as huge non-bank banks are concerned, there is no regulatory system in place to look after them.

The SEC does a very good job within the confines of its charter, but its charter is not like that of the Federal Reserve and of the Controller of the Currency (OCC) regarding the inspection of credit institutions. The Fed's and OCC's examiners have no mission for inspecting non-bank banks, like hedge funds. The Commodities Futures Trading Commission (CFTC) might have had such a mission if Congress had not clipped its wings (see Chapter 8).

Another regulatory domain where LTCM, Enron, and their like have much in common is the lack of a safety net to compensate the financially weak victims of hedge funds and industrial companies acting as hedge funds. The best example is the Federal Deposit Insurance Corporation (FDIC), which guarantees deposits of up to $100,000 per person, therefore providing a safety net. Some stakeholders with failed companies receive a triple hit as employees, investors, and pensioners.

Small investors and employees who got burned from CEO malfeasance were right when they said that they would like to see former Enron chairman Kenneth L. Lay, former CEO Jeffrey Skilling, former CFO Andrew Fastow, members of Enron's Audit Committee, top officials of Enron, and the partners at Arthur Andersen and Vinson & Elkins, personally repay the financial losses they had created.

The first of the top brass to face the consequences has been Michael Kopper, a former senior executive. He became a government witness helping the

Justice Department in the continuing investigation of his former boss Andrew Fastow. Kopper pleaded guilty to conspiracy and wire fraud. He agreed to pay back $12 million and could face fifteen years in prison but will not be sentenced until after the Enron investigation is completed.

"Disgorgement" has become a keyword in many investigations of senior executives' malfeasance. Whether one talks of employees, pensioners, investors, or individuals who were in all three classes, Enron's damage to individual lives was stupendous. The same is true of its damage to US confidence in the economy, and to the stock market.

LTCM, Enron, Global Crossing, Adelphia, Kmart, WorldCom, and so many other companies which failed because of their top management's fault, had no victims' fund. On the contrary, as we saw in section 3, tort lawyers did well while victims were further impoverished. This is a common characteristic of most failed companies. But there are also differences in terms of the aftermath between LTCM and Enron. Just before and after Enron, corporate bankruptcies and defaults soared; this did not happen with LTCM, in spite of the fact its event was preceded by the Russian meltdown and, a year earlier, by the downfall of the Asian economies – Thailand, Indonesia, and South Korea being the most pronounced.

As far as the 2001 events are concerned, the 255 public companies which filed for bankruptcy in that year alone left a hole of over $250 billion. This number of failures was up from 176 companies and way ahead of the $95 billion in assets in 2000. In the bond markets globally, a record 211 companies defaulted on $115.4 billion of debt in 2001, up from 132 companies and $42.3 billion in debt in 2000: the default rate for all bonds hit 4 percent in 2001, the worst year since 1991. Let us remember that the record for junk bond defaults was 10.9 percent in 1991, following the collapse of Drexel Burnham Lambert. The default rate on junk bonds in 2001 jumped to 8.6 percent from 5.7 percent in 2000.

Another major difference between the Enron/WorldCom class of events and LTCM is that the latter's losses were made good by its main shareholder, thanks to the able intervention of the New York Fed. In Enron's case, adding to investors' deception, huge liabilities had been shifted to a series of private partnerships, the confidence of investors was destroyed, and it was easy for corporations to hide the financial hecatomb until the day of reckoning.

Another lesson from the Enron/WorldCom events is that certified public accountants (CPAs) do not always do the external auditor's job with diligence. Enron's auditor, Arthur Andersen, was no stranger to this disease: the careful reader will recall the case study of the Baptist Foundation from Chapter 6.

In June 2001, the year Enron went bankrupt, Andersen paid $7 million to settle charges brought by the SEC over its audit of Waste Management, another company that had to restate its profits. Every fresh scandal of that type hits market confidence like a hammer. It also increases public demand for the independence of auditors. Indeed, the events of 2000–3 are the best evidence that the SEC should do what Arthur Levitt, its former chairman, has long requested:

- Ban accounting firms from doing consulting work for their audit clients, and
- Thoroughly update accounting and auditing rules including the definition of conflict of interest.

One of the reasons investors, even financial analysts who should have a sharper pencil than the average investor, did not understand Enron's books is because the company shifted many debts into off-balance sheet vehicles. The SEC should therefore tighten its disclosure requirements for all publicly quoted companies and discourage the practice of investing staff retirement funds in company shares, with the risk that the pension fund will go bust.

Still another lesson to be learned from the 2000–3 misbehavior is that companies must be thrifty with the money they spend on commissions. Top traders at Enron were paid average bonuses of $700,000 per head while the energy company was practically bankrupt and in takeover negotiations with Dynegy.[9] The discovery of the bonuses, which were paid to seventy-five employees and totaled $50 million, came just days after it emerged that Enron had also effected special payments to "profitable employees" after it had made the world's biggest Chapter 11 bankruptcy filing up to that date:

- These after-bankruptcy payments totaled $55 million, and
- They were distributed to about 500 employees selected by the company's senior executives.

There is finally a strong case for restating the rules of top management responsibility and accountability. Enron's senior executives were conspicuously absent from the first US Congressional hearing into the company's collapse; nor was Enron represented at a joint hearing by two subcommittees of the House Financial Services Committee.

By December 21, 2001, investigators with the influential House Energy Committee had requested interviews with senior company executives, directors, and members of the company's Audit and Compliance Committee. These included Wendy Gramm, an Enron director, former chairman of the Commodities Futures Trading Commission and wife of Phil Gramm, an influential Republican senator (there is more on this in Chapter 8). No subpoenas were issued for the mid-December hearing, although Congress had the power to require witnesses to appear.

Confirming that Lay would not be attending the Congressional hearing, Enron said: "This was an invitation, not a subpoena. We have just gone through a bankruptcy filing process that happened very quickly. We have numerous issues to deal with, with creditors, shareholders and employees, and we just believe we could not do an adequate job serving the committee's needs at this time."[10] But is this a valid excuse?

5   Lessons from Enron's bankruptcy

More than fifty years of professional experience have taught me that precious lessons can be learned through post-mortems. In the aftermath of the
fall of Barings, the venerable British bank, the Bank of England made a study
of the events behind its crash, and reached two conclusions. Both teach
something valuable:

- Barings' collapse was due to unauthorized activities that went undetected
  as a consequence of the failure of management controls of the most basic
  kind
- Management failed at various levels and in a variety of ways to institute
  a proper system of internal controls which would have informed it of
  malpractices and made it ahead of the curve.

As this section has demonstrated, the second conclusion by the Bank of
England fits Enron perfectly. But there is also an added-value element
brought to the fore through the Enron post-mortem: the company's top
brass seems to have made some particular contributions to the failure which
took place over the years and the final crash.

Just ten months before the bankruptcy of Enron, in February 2001, the
then company president, Jeffrey Skilling, suggested that the most logical
owners of the power plants and transmission grids were the big financial
institutions – not the energy company itself. Skilling, a former consultant,
based his opinion on the bank's access to cheap capital. Instead of owning
their core assets, energy companies like Enron should be the derivatives
traders and intermediaries, using a complex and dangerous mix of futures,
swaps, and instruments, and acting more like geared-up hedge funds than
classical energy companies.

This was, and it fully proved to be, a very dangerous strategy indeed.
Coupled with leveraged financial conditions and questionable accounting
practices that sort of strategy was supposed to give Enron, its energy derivatives trader, and the big financial institutions engaged in the geared instruments game, new income flows to keep them going (see Chapter 9).
Extended to other physical goods, the scheme was supposed to bring into
the bubble of the leveraged economy plenty of raw materials beyond financial instruments and energy supplies. The idea that energy companies
should disinvest themselves of physical goods and concentrate on trading
does not make much sense. Among other reasons, some of the big investment banks like Goldman Sachs, Morgan Stanley, and Merrill Lynch were
already active in the energy trading business, and with the fall of Enron they
have increased their hold over this sector of the market. The fact that
the United Bank of Switzerland (UBS) offered $1 billion to buy Enron's
energy trading business was proof of things moving in that direction, where
financial institutions become traders of everything.

Just prior to the fall of Enron, on November 29, 2001, the *New York Times* published an article stating that the market that Enron helped create would continue in a new form following either of the two alternatives:

- In a regulated manner, through a new clearing system
- Or, in an unregulated form with many different players, but few rules.

On December 3, 2001, the *Wall Street Journal* suggested that, although financial intermediaries are owed billions by Enron, there also are some winners that stand to pick up market share in the energy trading markets that Enron dominated. Right after Enron filed for bankruptcy it reached a deal with its two major creditors, J.P. Morgan Chase and Citigroup, for $1.5 billion in debtor possession loans. These are loans which sit at the top of the bankruptcy paybacks.

The interest of investment banks in taking over Enron's trading assets can be found not only in the fact that trading is their line of business, but also because its maze of partnerships made it very difficult for independent rating agencies such as Standard & Poor's and Moody's to verify many of its debts. Neither before nor after the bankruptcy did anybody really know *what* and *how many* off-balance sheet liabilities existed in Enron's books. What ratings should such a firm be given? What was the credit risk assumed by investors and counterparties?

Adding to leverage the accounting malpractices that overtook Enron, one gets an idea of the sort of shaky ground on which stakeholders and regulators found themselves. Documents from a May 1, 2000, meeting of Enron's Board Finance Committee revealed that the presentation of Raptor 1, one of the off-balance sheet vehicles, specified that it "does not transfer economic risk but transfers profit and loss volatility."[11] Another Enron invention was presented during an October 26, 2000, meeting for investors. It focused on the so-called "LJM partnerships," and underlined that accelerated earnings recognition for Enron was their major purpose.

As Chapter 9 demonstrates, these questionable instruments, and the shaky arguments behind them, did not discourage investors from pouring money in. Yet, Skilling's Raptor vehicles and Fastow's empty shells called LJM partnerships should have raised in investors' minds the question of *exposure without limits*. Risk and return are very difficult to quantify when it comes to off-balance sheet debt transacted through over the counter derivatives. And it becomes impossible with empty shells like the examples we have just examined.

Let us also recall that apart from the energy gambles, Enron was a major player in the credit derivatives market. It bought and sold these instruments as part of its own portfolio. The case of Mariner Energy, the little-known Houston oil and gas explorer, provides an example. In May 1996, Enron Corp. invested in the company. Mariner Energy was a private outfit with large but unproven fields in the Gulf of Mexico, specialized in risky though potentially rewarding deepwater drilling. These yet-to-be-explored oil fields could be worthless or they might turn out to be a potential goldmine. Such uncertainty made Mariner a perfect vehicle for financial manipulation:

- Every quarter, Enron's internal accountants recalculated Mariner's value, and for no factual reason the value went up
- By November 2001, just prior to the crash, Enron estimated that the value of its 75 percent take in Mariner had risen to about $350 million, nearly double the original investment.

Because of creative accounting, as those guesstimated "gains" accumulated they were applied straight to Enron's operating income, which significantly beefed up the company's financial performance. But like much else at Enron's accounting, the Mariner investment was overstated. Indeed, an informal internal study valued Enron's Mariner investment at about $150 million – less than half of what was written in the company's books.

Post-mortem, some of Enron's ex-employees said Mariner Energy was part of a larger story that still had not fully come to light: they alleged that the company had overstated the values of its investments in several private domestic companies in order to bolster its overall financial performance. Others suggested that Enron was a counterparty on $3.3 billion of credit derivatives rated by S&P, representing 12 percent of the $23 billion in this class.

6 The limits of creative accounting

In mid-to-late 2001, Enron was battling a cash crunch and a loss of investor confidence. This was partly due to questions about partnerships it had started and put under the control of its senior executives, partly because of having overreached its hand in leverage, and partly (if not largely) because of bad management. Investors feared that the company was using the partnerships to hide from the public eye losses and debt resulting from: huge liabilities,[12] highly speculative deals, and unorthodox financial transactions.

Nor were other decisions by Enron's senior management that clever. Five or six weeks prior to the crash at the end of October 2001, Enron announced that it would close its Singapore and London trading offices. This decision was taken only eight months after setting up operations in Europe, and it cost the company a great deal in write-offs.

It is surprising that former business consultants made that mistake, because they should have known that one of the worst policies a company can follow is that of start/stop:

- Starting something means putting up capital: financial and human resources
- Stopping it a few months down the line requires even more capital for zero results.

Start/stop policies and high gearing correlate, among themselves and with mismanagement. When they leverage their company to unbearable levels, its executives often forget that cash is king. While what has been classically considered legitimate transaction can generate cash, or so one would hope, leveraging and speculation absorb cash like a sponge. Speculation is usually done with other speculators who are themselves cash-hungry, and who are usually known to be short of liquidity.

Indeed, according to prudential management standards, the drying up of cash is the best indicator of progressive loss of the collective grasp of reality. Top management is no longer in charge of events, as demonstrated by a long list of companies like LTCM, Enron, Global Crossing, WorldCom, Deutsche Telekom, France Télécom, Vivendi, and many more.

It therefore comes as no surprise that hidden dealings and superleverage saw to it that Enron, the seventh-largest US company in its days of glory with $100 billion in sales in 2000, suddenly faced bankruptcy. Some analysts said that they would not have imagined such an outcome in their wildest dreams. Yet, as analysts they should have expected it: Enron had run out of cash. It is indeed a very bad sign that, by and large, financial analysts were taken by surprise. Their slow response was lamentable. Only in late November 2001, for example, rating changes by Crédit Suisse Private Banking (CSPB) downgraded Enron from *Buy* to *Hold* – while, at the same time, CSPB downgraded Heidelberger Zement, a premier cement company in Germany, from *Buy* to *Sell*. Heidelberger Zement, incidentally, is still a profitable firm.

Nor is it unusual that many among Enron's senior executives and board members, including its chairman and its president, pleaded ignorance as an excuse. After the crash Kenneth Lay, the former CEO, and Jeffrey Skilling, the former president, said that they did not know what was going on behind the books of the bankrupt energy trader because they were busy on other matters:

- Being busy is no excuse for being inattentive, and for failing to oversee the transactions which eventually ruined the company
- On Wall Street, protestations regarding ignorance about wrongdoing because of being busy in other matters earned Lay the epithet of "the most out-to-lunch CEO in America."

Investors, investigators, US Congressmen, and former Enron employees dismissed such top-management disclaimers. Could such disclaimers have any weight in court? In principle, they should not because a basic legal principle is that not knowing the law is not a defense. Similarly, in basic management terms, a person's accountability is a whole; it cannot be divided in parts.

In testimony to the US Senate Committee investigating the Enron scandal Jeffrey Skilling used the incompetence line of defense and pleaded ignorance to the financial misinterpretations that had eventually brought

Enron to its knees. What he failed to note is that this argument was incompatible with the findings of the internal Enron committee. The latter concluded that Skilling bore substantial responsibility, commenting that Enron's ex-president was accountable for assuring that those reporting to him performed their oversight duties, and that the internal controls the board put in place functioned properly.

"He has described the detail of his expressly-assigned oversight role as minimal. That answer, however, misses the point," the committee said. "Skilling certainly knew, or should have known, of the magnitude and the risks associated with these transactions."[13] He also knew, or should have known, that because of these dubious transactions and deals the company was running out of cash – and the day of reckoning was approaching.

Indeed, the investigators pointed to the pattern of deals Enron entered into with off-balance sheet partnerships, some of which involved Enron employees. It added that: "Skilling who prides himself on the controls he put in place in many areas at Enron, bears substantial responsibility for the failure of the system of internal controls to mitigate the risk inherent in the relationship between Enron and the LJM partnerships."

Part of the irony behind the drama is that as a former management consultant Jeffrey Skilling was very proud of these management controls he had supposedly put in place. Former employees say that under his influence, Enron became increasingly arrogant. There are other stories with the same egocentric message. Reports about meetings with financial analysts indicate that Skilling acted as if Enron was doing too well to answer to anybody, even to staffers who did not "get it." Yet, he must have known very well that the company:

- Was actually on its way to financial ruin
- Was getting increasingly short of cash, and
- Was tangled in a web of malfeasance issues.

As far as corporate law governance is concerned, executives such as Lay and Skilling who, because of their position, are required to make signed statements to the market about their company's finances, should not be allowed to plead ignorance as a defense. This sort of behavior has become a travesty of management. It is not improbable, however, that some of the people involved in alleged executive malfeasance will escape through legal loopholes. To establish civil liability, plaintiffs need to prove only recklessness on the part of executives, which is defined as an indifference to financial statements. With Enron, financial improprieties appear to have been central to the company's reporting and to its downfall, but only few top executives have so far faced prosecution. Yet:

- It is inconceivable that senior executives "did not know" and
- If they did not, their ignorance was so reckless that it became a liability to the stakeholders.

What the top brass of Enron did to all of the stakeholders: employees, pensioners, investors, regulators, and the American economy at large, is against the moral code of business – but it is not necessarily against the fine print of business law. Hence the difficulty in bringing them to justice. To re-establish a moral code of corporate conduct, not only top managers but also a company's outside directors should face *vicarious liability* for the corporation's faults, if plaintiffs can show culpability on their part – for example, if they can prove that a director deliberately avoided knowing what was going on. This demonstration is important because the courts say that one must show some breach of good faith.

The basic argument is that CEOs, their immediate assistants, and members of the board cannot just shut their eyes to corporate wrongdoing. They cannot profess ignorance of the company's deteriorating financial position – this is neither good faith nor diligence. It may not be a willful violation of the law – defined as a deliberate intent to break the law – but it is total lack of personal accountability.

7   Chapter 11 and prepackaged bankruptcies

Chapter 11 is America's approach to saving companies and individuals (more on the latter below) from short-term financial crises, if they have a potential long-term viability. Critics, however, say that the facilities Chapter 11 provides are widely abused and, as such, the after effect is to scare away new investors, even to destroy investments. Critics also add that Chapter 11 is failing to distinguish between:

- Operations worth saving, and
- Those that should cease to exist.

The people who are for Chapter 11 naturally have a totally different opinion. They say that it provides entities with a second chance, and the opportunity to redeem past mistakes. They also add that if Chapter 11 did not exist it should be invented, because by removing the stigma classically associated with bankruptcy it makes people more entrepreneurial and, in the longer run, more successful.

The critics of Chapter 11 do not accept this argument. They say that the removal of the stigma of bankruptcy leads to personal irresponsibility. They add that because of Chapter 11 competition in the market is being distorted and, at a time of globalization, such distortion is spreading beyond America to Europe and Asia, as US-registered operators drag their international assets into the US bankruptcy courts.

Proponents of Chapter 11 answer that many companies are emerging from bankruptcy in better shape, to the benefit of competition – including global competition. They further argue that Chapter 11 has been the mechanism that helped successfully to restructure industries as they have been moving from growth to maturity. It does so because it provides time for companies and their business partners to implement contingency plans.

Opponents of Chapter 11 respond that, as it now stands, it fails to reflect the concept of protection from court proceedings all the way up and down the food chain. For instance, it is not sufficiently protecting small and medium enterprises (SMEs) that service the big companies. Many SMEs are left with unpaid bills when Enron and its like seek protection from creditors. Indeed, many small US companies complain that:

- They suffer at the hands of huge corporations who can file for protection from bankruptcy and then emerge later with little or no debt
- What the SMEs are left with after the big guys' bankruptcy is that their former customers discharge their obligations and, hence, they collect little or nothing.

In spite of the protective walls built by Chapter 11, creditors are not giving up easily. In Enron's case, for example, they are determined to chase down assets the energy trader tried to keep off its balance sheet. Because Enron's bankers connived in this, by late September 2002 the creditors were mounting an aggressive new campaign:

- Targeting the bankrupt company's bankers and advisors, and
- Laying claim to assets from Enron's network of partnerships and special-purpose vehicles (SPVs).

Experts say that in all likelihood the money trail will eventually lead to the banks and other institutions that helped set up some of Enron's partnerships. Even if WorldCom's bankruptcy eclipsed Enron as the biggest corporate downfall in the US and worldwide, the energy trader's implosion remains one of the most complex ever handled by a bankruptcy court:

- More than 6,500 separate filings were made after Enron sought Chapter 11 protection on December 2, 2001
- But at the end of 2002, it was still unclear exactly how much the assets of the different Enron partnerships might be worth.

It is therefore not surprising in spite of Chapter 11 protection that creditors want to find out for themselves what kind of assets are left, and what they might be worth. These creditors know that they have to move fast because professional fees are eating into the pool of money that might be recoverable from Enron's carcass. As creditors prepare to sue the partnerships and the third parties that helped establish them (see also Chapter 9 on Enron's bankers), experts suggest that some of the biggest entities that were set up by Enron, or dealt with the energy trader, are at the top of the list of possible cash cows:

- Osprey, a vehicle structure prepared by Donaldson Lufkin & Jenrette (DLJ), now part of Crédit Suisse First Boston (CFSB).

- Deutsche Bank, and its Bankers Trust subsidiary (now called Taunus), which helped to sell the bonds of that vehicle, and
- Mahonia, an entity originally set up by Chase Manhattan, now part of J.P. Morgan Chase, accused of making disguised loans to Enron (the *prepays*, discussed in Chapter 9).

It worth recording that as a special investment vehicle (SIV) Osprey used Enron shares to bolster the partnerships' credit ratings. The goal was to draw in investors. Some estimates suggest that Osprey, and a couple of other partnerships (Marlin and Firefly, also devised by DLJ), contained about $4 billion of assets.

According to invoices filed into the bankruptcy court, Squire Sanders & Dempsey, a law firm acting for the creditors' committee, has research scenarios for recovery of assets from Mahonia and has elaborated some fraudulent transfer patterns for challenges to Osprey.[14] All this helps to demonstrate that SIVs and other creative accounting inventions don't only serve to overstate earnings and hide losses. They also:

- Open big holes to the protection from creditors' armory provided by Chapter 11, and
- Help in implicating third parties, like the Enron banks (see Chapter 9) which are not protected by Chapter 11 – and will not be protected till they file for bankruptcy.

Because Chapter 11 is often used by defendants, even some of its pros do admit that it has gaps. Where proponents and opponents of Chapter 11 are not so far apart is believing that it should not be used as a means to hide flawed management decisions, practice creative accounting, indulge in high-leverage financing, and keep malfeasance hidden from public view.

A point where practically all of the critics and some of the proponents of Chapter 11 concur in their judgment is the need for *time limits*. Conventional bankruptcy cases may last years, siphoning off large amounts of legal fees and absorbing considerable management energy as creditors war with company executives, and one another, to hammer out a reorganization plan.

The fast track is the so-called *prepackaged bankruptcy*. A firm using a prepack can emerge from bankruptcy within a few months, provided it can face certain challenges. To do a prepack a company must put together a plan and secure the approval of a minimum of 51 percent of its creditors who are holding at least two-thirds of the debt before filing for bankruptcy. The plan then needs a bankruptcy judge's approval. These prerequisites see to it that prepackaged bankruptcies are not a tool for everyone. While they have been around at least since the 1978 overhaul of the US federal bankruptcy code, it was only in 1986 that a major company, Crystal Oil, used this procedure. The idea began to take off as the high leverage of the mid- to late-1980s created more debt to squabble over and more creditors to do the squabbling.

This produced a need for a kind of fast-forward system, and companies turned to prepacks. Few deals can however be called successful. What is often overlooked by companies contemplating a prepackaged bankruptcy is that prepacks are not a penicillin for every troubled firm. They require a fortuitous mix of canny planning, enough amenable creditors, and the ability to face process risks.

Rushing a company out of court with a half-baked reorganization plan is like setting it up for another fall or outright failure. Prepacks are also not always kind to minority creditors. Because they telescope the process, they permit the majority to push plans down dissenting creditors' throats more easily than conventional Chapter 11 bankruptcies. Eventually, this can lead to more legal trouble.

While the case of restructuring Chapter 11 itself is gaining momentum a "better solution" is not that clear, let alone acceptable to everyone. That is precisely what also happened with regard to bankruptcies concerning private individuals. The new US legislation makes it harder for people to erase credit-card and other debt in the bankruptcy court. This has been the most sweeping change to US bankruptcy law in twenty-five years but opinions are divided. The best provision of the new law is that:

- Higher-income bankruptcy filers will not be able to walk away from debt they can afford to repay
- While at the same time the safety net will be preserved for others who truly need bankruptcy protection.

The US legislation applies a new standard for determining whether people filing for bankruptcy should be forced to repay debts rather than having them dissolved. If a debtor is found to have sufficient income to repay at least 25 percent of the debt over five years, or has at least the median income for his or her state of residence, a reorganization plan would generally be required. This makes the bankruptcy code more sophisticated. Only time will tell what sort of abuses will show up.

8
Assigning the Blame for the Enron Débâcle

1 Introduction

Victory, says an old proverb, has many fathers, but defeat has none. Enron ended in defeat. Who was responsible for its débâcle? "Its management," is an obvious answer, but it will be short-sighted if limited to its top brass. Even an answer which says: "all of the company's management," is partial.

The investors themselves played a part in Enron's débâcle because they were running after a chimera of higher and higher profits. The government, too, took a hand, since it failed to enact legislation which ensured that companies engaged in trading were meeting rigorous management criteria and capital standards before they were permitted to expand into banking-type activities. This is important in as much as non-banks can affect a broad range of investments, and influence the course of the economy as a whole – indeed, of the global economy.

Even post-Enron, it was not easy to pass legislation which established a sense of discipline. Dianne Feinstein, a Senator from California and former mayor of San Francisco, proposed a bill that would allow the Commodity Futures Trading Commission (CFTC), the US regulator of the futures industry, to set new rules for over the counter trading in energy and metals derivatives. Feinstein's initiative aimed to:

- Close an important gap in the current US regulatory framework, and
- Provide greater transparency in the pricing of electricity and natural gas.

The fact that this well-timed effort failed surprised many analysts. Apart from the psychological effect of Enron's bankruptcy, Feinstein had an important ally in the New York Mercantile Exchange (NYMEX), which also wants regulations imposed on its competitors in the over the counter markets. The proposed bill to regulate the over the counter market was the right deal at the right time – but lobbyists killed it. To appreciate NYMEX's position, the reader should recall that trading platforms like Intercontinental Exchange (ICE) and TradeSpark provide a facility for commercial entities to trade a wide range of contracts online.[1] Many of these contracts are based on energy, including forward, swaps, options, collars, and spreads. This is done outside the official exchanges, and beyond any sort of prudential supervision.

Yet, in spite of the urgent need for such legislation, particularly post-Enron, in April 2002 Feinstein's bill did not get the required majority in the US Senate. Experts said that if the Senate had voted on her proposal when she first brought it to the floor, at the peak of Enron's scandal, it might have passed overwhelmingly. A couple of months down the line (February–March 2002), a coalition of derivatives dealers and energy traders rallied against it. The Senate's sentiment changed, and this put Feinstein's bill in mothballs.

2   The Commodity Modernization Act

In the US, derivatives are regulated by the Commodity Futures Trading Commission (CFTC). This sort of activity has been a major extension of the agency's regulatory authority, if one takes as reference the Commodity Exchange Authority (CEA), CFTC's predecessor. CEA essentially regulated agricultural commodities, but with the Act of 1974 the existing supervisory authority for agricultural commodities:

- Was recast into CFTC, which became responsible for *all* futures contracts, and
- This new responsibility involved every type of financial contract, including the major trading innovations of the late twentieth century.

It is interesting to take note that the Act of 1974 did not define *futures*, but still required that they be traded on an organized futures exchange. A twist which came at the last minute changed that clause. Spotting CFTC's broad mandate, the US Treasury inserted an amendment (known as the Treasury Amendment) that excluded futures on currencies and government securities from CFTC jurisdiction. This exemption might have satisfied the Treasury, since it kept control of part of the futures' turf, but it left open the possibility of a subsequent battle over authority among regulatory agencies: the Securities and Exchange Commission (SEC), CFTC, Federal Reserve, the Treasury itself, and so on. The fact that banking regulators could not agree or did not agree left the over the counter derivatives market unsupervised. More precisely, it left it in legal limbo.

For instance, if the CFTC were to designate an over the counter swap contract as a futures contract – which it is – this would give the CFTC an exclusive jurisdiction over swap contracts. Furthermore, as a product, the swaps contract would be illegal unless it were traded on an approved exchange. Subsequently, the 1992 Futures Trading Practices Act exempted swaps and hybrids from CFTC jurisdiction. This, critics say:

- Led to several derivatives disasters in the mid-1990s and beyond, and
- Opened a gaping hole in the US regulatory armory through which Enron and other gamblers passed.

In November 1992, Enron, then a relatively unknown energy company, petitioned the CFTC explicitly to remove energy derivatives and interest-rate swaps from its regulatory oversight. Shortly thereafter, banks like J.P. Morgan and Chase Manhattan, as well as other energy companies including Exxon, Mobil, and BP, made similar requests.

The exemption was presented as "a minor technical change," but in reality it was a major legislative and supervisory issue. Effectively, it amounted to demolishing the existing prudential regulatory activities. By allowing over the counter trading of energy derivatives, which had previously been restricted to regulated exchanges, the government gave its blessing to a new era of speculation in the energy markets.

Huge losses and bankruptcies originating in over the counter energy trading were accidents waiting to happen. As far as its powers to grant an exception were concerned, a new management at CFTC capitalized on the authority the agency was granted by the Futures Trading Practices Act of 1992. This was signed in late October 1992 by President George Bush, Sr. and Enron was granted its exemption:

- In retrospect, the Gramm exemption (named after Wendy Lee Gramm, then CFTC chair) opened the door to a series of high-profile financial gambles in the energy domain
- Disasters followed, beginning with the $1.3 billion energy derivatives loss of Germany's Metallgesellschaft in December 1993.

This historical precedent is worth recording. In the US, Metallgesellschaft speculated with energy futures supposedly covered through other derivative contracts also signed in the US. But as happened in so many other cases with so-called "hedging" through derivative instruments, Metallgesellschaft's speculation turned into a time bomb:

- The "protection" which it provided proved to be asymmetric, and
- Metallgesellschaft capsized, though it later restructured itself as a much smaller company.[2]

Metallgesellschaft lost out and, to survive found itself obliged to leave the speculative side of the energy market. But other companies profited, at least for a time, and Enron was one of them.

In May 1998, under the chairmanship of Brooksley Born, the CFTC issued a concept release regarding the long-overdue US derivatives regulation. During her nomination hearings in 1996, Born had stated that some of the activities in the derivatives markets appeared to be illegal. In Congressional testimony, in April 1997, she warned that the so-called "Gramm exemption" could lead to widespread deregulation, which:

- Would greatly restrict Federal power to protect the market against manipulation, and
- Might promote fraud, financial instability, creative accounting, and other dangers.

In her Congressional testimony, Born added that such a state of affairs would pose grave dangers to the public interest. To appreciate how prophetic that was with regard to Enron, it is necessary to keep in mind happenings in the 1990s which led to a clash of wills (and of political power) between regulators and speculators.

One of the issues Brooksley Born had targeted in her Congressional testimony was the cancellation of the Gramm exception. This met with a wall of resistance. Enron used its lobbyists to push for more deregulation of the energy market, tried to influence events so that it was done globally, and (as so often) further leveraged itself. In fact, the more it leveraged itself, the more it speculated till disaster hit on December 2, 2001.

In 1998, however, Enron was all-mighty and Congress seems to have sided with the energy derivatives community, not with Brooksley Born. "In my view, there are no systemic problems in the OTC derivatives market," asserted Dr. Wendy Gramm, who testified to the House Banking Committee hearing. Gramm added that "instead of looking for regulatory gaps to fill with more regulation, markets, consumers, and the economy might fare better if efforts were spent looking for unnecessary regulatory burdens to eliminate."[3]

Senator Phil Gramm, then chairman of the Senate Banking Committee, supported his wife. He promoted the 1999 legislation known as the Gramm–Leach–Bliley Act, killing the Glass–Steagall Act of the 1930s Depression era, which had built a wall to separate commercial from investment banking. The attack against CFTC's regulatory position produced the Commodity Futures Modernization Act of 2000. This act:

- Opened the door for greater speculation by Enron and others, and
- Legalized the exemption on energy derivatives granted by Wendy Gramm.

It might have been reasonably expected that in the aftermath of Enron's collapse the political climate would have changed and Diane Feinstein's regulatory proposal would have gained a significant degree of support. The economic and financial climate of 2002 was totally different from that of 2000 when Congress had approved legislation that largely exempted over the counter energy and metal regulation as part of the Commodity Futures Modernization Act. But, as we saw in the Introduction, this was not the case. Deregulation was given no chance to protect companies from crashing because they speculated too much, and spread themselves too thin.

3 Deregulation

The end of the 1970s, under the Carter Administration, were stagflation years. After a decade of a financial depression because of two oil shocks, spikes in the gold price, and inflation, people and companies were looking for change. In that climate, the idea of banking deregulation became a ripe fruit. Personally I have always been for deregulation, but in retrospect one has to admit that along with the benefits came a number of unwanted consequences. One of them was the shift to favor a certain type of speculation. This was further accelerated by the Kemp–Roth Economic Recovery Tax Act of 1981. The Kemp–Roth Act handed out huge tax breaks to real estate investors, triggering a boom in metropolitan real estate markets which eventually wrecked both the real estate and the banking industries.

Experts suggest that the transformation of the economy into a deregulated enterprise took another step in 1982, with passage of the Garn–St. Germain Depository Institutions Act. This targeted greater freedom for commercial banks and the Savings and Loans Institutions (S&Ls). The Garn–St. Germain Act:

- Lifted existing restrictions on the S&Ls, allowing them to make commercial real estate loans, and
- Partly contributed to the real estate bubble of the 1980s, bankrupting the S&Ls.

Another unwanted consequence of a deregulation which simply lifted restrictions rather than modernizing them and adapting them to new business realities, has been the rush into derivatives. A direct consequence of speculation was the bank-bailout law, the Financial Institutions Reform, Recovery and Enforcement Act (FIRREA) of 1989, which set up the Resolution Trust Corporation:

- To manage and dispose of the assets of failed S&Ls held by the US government, and
- Clean up the mess created by speculation without limits, including the tsunami of junk bonds.

The S&Ls were not the only institutions to suffer from the bubble of the 1980s. According to Wall Street experts, in November 1990, the New York Fed quietly seized control of Citicorp. The Boston Fed took control of the Bank of New England (BNE) which had collapsed because of derivatives and the real estate bubble to give time for its $36 billion derivatives portfolio to be unwound (an operation which took a year to complete).

While BNE went bankrupt and Citibank faced serious problems, a number of commercial banks – Chase Manhattan, Chemical Banking, Manufacturers Hanover, and Security Pacific – were said to be on the sick list. The latter two did not survive for long as independent agencies, while Chemical Banking eventually took over Chase Manhattan.

Federal regulators closed the Bank of New England in January 1991, and in July and August came a wave of mergers involving six of the twelve bigger US banks, with Chemical taking over Manufacturers Hanover, BankAmerica, swallowing Security Pacific, and North Carolina National Bank (NCNB), which had already acquired the Republic Bank of Texas, taking over X&S/Sovran to form NationsBank (which a decade later acquired BankAmerica, and adopted its name).

Some of the experts said that this consolidation was inevitable. Others, however, pointed out that the banks which fell to suitors or searched for a white knight had wounded themselves – which was one of deregulation's unwanted consequences. Another consequence was a growing saga of hedge funds now at somewhere between 4,000 and 6,000:

- The 400 biggest hedge funds have between them a capital estimated at $500–600 billion, and
- Because they are in the habit of leveraging themselves to the tune of 20, 30, 50 times or more their capital (LTCM was leveraged at 35,000 percent), they have become a sword of Damocles over the market's head.

By leveraging themselves by a factor not far from 50 on average, hedge funds control some $25 trillion – more than all the G-10 stockmarkets together – at bargain basement prices.[4] A comparison between the unregulated hedge funds and other non-bank banks with the regulated banking industry, helps better to appreciate the layers of prudential supervision which are missing from the world's financial system.

Let us take as an example the case of a European money center bank operating in the US. In addition to the direct regulation of its banking business in its home country (be it England, Germany, Switzerland, or anywhere else), this credit institution is subject to US regulation by the Board of Governors of the Federal Reserve System under various laws, including:

- The International Banking Act of 1978, as amended
- The Bank Holding Company Act of 1956, as amended, and
- The Gramm–Leach–Bliley Financial Modernization Act of 1999.

The Bank Holding Company Act imposes significant restrictions on US non-banking operations and on the credit institution's worldwide holdings of equity in companies operating in the US. It also features several restrictions on transactions between its US banking offices and its non-banking subsidiaries.

As for the Gramm–Leach–Bliley Act, it has modified existing financial laws, including laws related to the conduct of securities activities. Various restrictions that previously applied to bank holding company ownership of securities firms and mutual fund advisory companies have been removed. The overall regulatory structure applicable to bank holding companies, including those that also engage in insurance and securities operations, has been revised, but there is still prudential supervision by the Fed, the OCC and the FDIC for all credit institutions.

One is well advised to contrast these regulatory relationships with the legal limbo of over the counter derivatives trades which, in violation of good sense, continues to persist (see section 2). In the Bankers Trust–Gibson case, for example, the CFTC promulgated the notion that Bankers Trust was a *de facto* commodity advisor and had violated its fiduciary obligations to Gibson, despite the fact that the security in that case was a swap and thus exempt from CFTC regulation.

In the Metallgesellschaft case (see section 2), the CFTC ruled that the German company had entered into illegal futures and options contracts with its customers because these were established outside an exchange. At that time, however, the CFTC was being eased out of regulatory activities, its supervisory authority was trimmed, and we saw what happened to Enron and energy futures.

One of the major twists regarding CFTC came in May 1998 with a concept release asking whether the agency's jurisdiction over over the counter derivatives markets was sufficient. The release caused anxiety among securities firms and banks. It also brought into action Fed Chairman Alan Greenspan and Treasury Secretary Robert Rubin, both fearing that their turfs would be invaded by the CFTC.

There is no denying that a focused approach to futures regulation is urgently needed to clarify what is still an uncertain regulatory domain. This, however, first and foremost requires clear definition of the risks involved with over the counter derivatives and identification of the nature of prudential controls – followed by concrete legislative action. This issue is both *technical* and *political*. At the political end, Congress should specify which derivatives markets really need to be regulated and how. It is totally rational for the CFTC:

- To regulate futures trading on organized futures exchanges
- But leave unregulated other futures trading in the over the counter market, which accounts for about 78 percent of all derivatives deals.

Such contradictions in regulatory legislation are unfortunate because the use of effective regulation as a language helps translate complex and frequently nebulous patterns into more precise policies and practices. The latter serve to align and mobilize all traders into actions supporting a properly functioning market. As we saw in section 2, the Commodity Futures Modernization Act moves somewhat in this direction, but it has also created major exemptions from CFTC regulation for certain types of futures markets:

- What is designated as "contract markets" are subject to complete regulation
- By contrast, transactions involving leveraged derivative financial instruments are subject to little or no regulation.

Particular attention needs to be paid to markets exempt from the CFTC's supervisory authority, even if the CFTC is responsible for monitoring these markets for fraud. The Modernization Act also gives up the exclusivity doctrine, at least for the newly approved futures on individual stocks, by providing that the CFTC's regulatory authority be shared with the SEC – which leads to another legal limbo. All this is pertinent to this chapter's theme because it documents that the débâcle of the huge "hedge fund with a gas pipeline" is not just a one-tantum affair. The conditions which predict that it will repeat itself are still present, and "Enron risk" has many incarnations. Its control is an integral part of a process of restructuring the US and the global financial markets. This is a basic reason why Enron's gambles, mistakes, and misjudgments should be seen as lessons of what should not be repeated in years to come. This is the theme of the following sections.

4 Consultancies, the media, and class actions

Whether an outfit is an investment bank or a consultancy, the advice it provides to its clients is increasingly found to be the origin of strategic moves by top management, some of which turn sour. McKinsey, for instance, helped Enron formulate its now-discredited broadband strategy (see section 5), in which it built a high-speed fiber network which remained largely unused. It represented a huge financial burden to Enron, and contributed to its downfall:

- Over several months, the consultancy assisted Enron in gauging the size of growth of the communications market
- But, like Enron and most of the telecoms, the consultants didn't see the coming communications industry meltdown.

BusinessWeek mentions a former Enron senior executive who suggested that McKinsey consultants wielded influence throughout the company: "They were all over the place. They were sitting with us every step of the way. They thought, 'This thing could be big, and we want credit for it.'"[5] In the end, the consultancy was part of Enron's problem rather than of its solution.

Whether the consultancy is right or wrong in the strategic direction which it recommends for its clients, its advisory services don't come cheap. As the article in *BusinessWeek* had it, an unidentified company which was McKinsey's largest client paid some $60 million for the advice it got in 2001. Enron paid "only" $10 million in annual fees in that fatal year. McKinsey is a consulting company which services 147 of the world's 200 largest corporations, including eighty of the top 120 financial services firms. Its operations are global, including a network of eighty-four worldwide locations with a consulting staff of 7,700 and revenues of $3.4 billion. This huge network is managed by 890 partners who: keep close watch on client accounts, and ensure that the cash flow generated from fees is steady and growing.

BusinessWeek mentions among McKinsey's clients some big-name firms who failed in 2001–2: Enron, Swissair, and Global Crossing were all McKinsey clients that filed for bankruptcy. Other companies which were McKinsey clients and failed in the late 1990s included Kmart, Exide Technologies, and NorthPoint Communications.

The Enron affair also focused attention on the role played by the media and by financial analysts who propped up the stock almost to its last day. The media never questioned Enron's model of "supergearing." Yet, journalists pride themselves as being investigative analysts *par excellence* – a function they perform more effectively in politics, the Watergate scandal being a prime example. One of the major contributions of the media is to create a personality cult of the leaders of large corporations – Alfred P. Sloan (of General Motors, GM), and Jack Welsh of GE (General Electric) were examples. The difference is that both Sloan and Welsh were first-class organizers and hard drivers of people; they were at no time the sort of gamblers who brought their companies to bankruptcy:

- At both GM and GE, better organization and greater efficiency paid lasting dividends
- By contrast, the turning of gas and electricity into geared financial products was done with disregard for assumed risk, and led to a crash.

In the case of Enron, the media promoted the company as an "innovator of capitalism," and "a great place to work." It is difficult to explain this collective press myopia which is one of the unwanted consequences of the personality cult. This "herd syndrome" of Enron worship can only partly be explained by the fact that big modern companies are expert in managing their communications strategy and public relations affairs. While most of what is reported by the media is based on official company announcements, including their stated proforma earnings, cash flows, and breakthroughs, there is absolutely no excuse for not questioning the "obvious."

Investigative journalists owe it to their public and to themselves to be skeptical. There is also the behavior of certified public accountants (CPAs), eager to rubber stamp the accounts. They, too, should be expected to challenge the "obvious" in a company's accounting statements and financial reports. As we saw in Part I, this was far from always being the case.

Lack of dependability by professional watchdogs, and the subsequent big financial failures, led to public outcry. In 2002, Enron, Arthur Andersen, a couple of law firms, and some global banks were named in two class actions, as current and former Enron employees and holders of Enron equity and debt sought compensation for losses suffered in connection with the company's collapse. Enron itself may be bankrupt, but other entities are still around and they can be sued for compensation.

The lawsuits touched upon a fundamental issue in the Enron affair: the fact that the energy trader did not act alone, but was part of an organized network of abuse of power at the expense of its bankers, shareholders, bondholders, and employees. The class actions are expanded versions of suits filed earlier in US District Court in Houston against a narrower range of defendants, one by Seattle-based lawyer Steve Berman and the other by San Diego-based William Lerach.

The Berman suit made the bolder charge that Enron, five investment banks, Arthur Andersen, and the Houston-based law firm of Vinson & Elkins were all part of a conspiracy to defraud Enron employees. The suit states that they were guilty of violations of the Federal Racketeer Influenced and Corrupt Organization Act (RICO). As we have seen, while it was originally designed to fight organized crime, RICO has both criminal and civil provisions.

The Lerach lawsuit does not contain the RICO charge but it has a larger list of defendants than the Berman suit, including another law firm (Kirkland and Ellis), and nine commercial and investment banks: J.P. Morgan Chase, Citigroup, Bank of Amercia, Merrill Lynch, Crédit Suisse First Boston, Lehman Brothers, Barclays Bank, the Canadian Imperial Bank of Commerce, and Deutsche Bank. The Lerach suit states that: "Enron was a hall of mirrors inside a house of cards – reporting hundreds of millions of dollars of phony profits each year, while concealing billions of dollars of debt that should have been on its balance sheet…Enron has turned into an enormous Ponzi scheme – the largest in history."

5   Lessons from Enron's failed broadband venture

The theme of this book is *management risk*. Enron's failed broadband experience is one of the best case studies from the late 1990s on the after effects of mismanagement. Only fools will run into a new industrial market because other people have done so, attracted by the glamour of communications-for-everybody, no matter the cost, pitfalls, or actual market potential. One should expect to make a profit commensurate only with the skills and effort necessary and the risks which are assumed in that operation.

In January 2000, when Enron's star was at its summit, Andrew S. Fastow, its CFO, wanted to raise $400 million for a partnership he controlled. This was known as LJM2 Co-Investment LP. Different funds, like the Houston Firefighters Relief and Retirement Fund, were invited to contribute.[6] Other contributions came from investment bankers working for Merrill Lynch (see Chapter 9). As revealed after the bankruptcy, Enron needed LJM2 to bail out some of its other failed efforts at creating new markets for commodities trading. In fact, with the money it raised LJM2 bought part of the 18,000-mile fiber-optic cable network, in a transaction that generated a $67 million creative accounting profit for Enron – but not for the shareholders, for whom the real accounting picture was bleak. Because of major losses in mid-November 2001:

- Enron decided to pull out of the telecoms business and put its network up for sale
- This gave financial analysts another sign of the coming tough times facing bandwidth traders.

The foray into telecommunications was initially heralded by Enron's top management as another breakthrough. Suddenly, however, Enron Broadband Services was identified by the parent company as a non-core business, and put a $600 million price tag on the unit, which included the 18,000 kilometer-long fiber network. The "For sale" sign sharply contrasted with the previous strategy where Enron had planned to become an internet protocol (IP) and bandwidth traffic maker, claiming that it would leverage this business unit, capitalizing on its expertise in trading energy swaps and other derivative instruments. Another claim by Enron senior management was that it would invest more than $600 million in the broadband business within twenty-four months. In the real world, all this was no more than high-profile empty words.

To appreciate the chemistry of Enron's broadband deal, and how it came down in flames, it is appropriate to recall that the company's much-leveraged broadband venture capped a decade of transformation for the whole firm. After having morphed itself into the dominant trader of natural-gas futures, controlling as much as 30 percent of the gas futures contracts traded on the New York Mercantile Exchange, Enron was searching for a new growth market and it stumbled on a perceived potential in the telecoms domain.

For some time the deal-making in broadband seemed to have worked, carried along by the telecoms wave. Enron thought it had repeated its previous success in trading electricity and weather derivatives. Jeffrey Skilling, who was then Enron's president, promised investors that the company would deliver 20–30 percent profit growth annually by applying the same strategy to new markets, emerging as the biggest player in each field. Broadband was a case in point, but not the only one.

In this game plan, Enron began trading in metals, lumber, and broadband, setting up companies such as NewPower Holdings to tap deregulated electricity markets, and the Azurix Corporation to buy and sell water. However, none of these ventures generated the profits promised by Skilling, and some started to lose big money.

By the third quarter of 2001, as Enron's end approached, gas, power, and weather trading had brought $717 million in pretax profit, but losses from other operations had reached double that, to the tune of $1.4 billion. Liabilities topped profits by a ratio of 2:1, and among these huge liabilities was Enron's broadband business, which had managed a loss of $80 million on revenues of a mere $4 million. Management risk had reached a new peak. Although this $80 million was an "improvement" of sorts over Enron's second-quarter loss of $102 million from broadband, the drop was worse in terms of revenues, which stood at $16 million in the second quarter of 2001.

Dynegy, which at the time planned to buy Enron, had also been losing money on its global telecoms business, but at a slower pace: $15 million in the third quarter of 2001 versus $21 million in the second quarter.

These hefty losses in broadband communications by the two energy companies, in a field outside their core business, were part of an overall trend. The bandwidth glut meant that exchanges saw prices tumble on many routes in 2001. Most operators and exchanges had only themselves to blame: by dumping capacity on exchanges they were solving a short-term problem, but they were creating a huge long-term liability.

Placing previously unavailable communications capacity on exchanges, meant that prices fell even more quickly. The business plan of Enron, Dynegy, and the other broadband competitors was rotten because, in the aftermath of the internet's major setbacks, market conditions for a favorable trading environment simply could not materialize. Financial analysts said that while IP traffic and bandwidth might be the future, in 2001 the switched voice market was still significant:

- Bandwidth was liquid only on certain point-to-point routes, such as that between London and New York
- While speed of execution is key in trading, it is generally difficult to buy and sell capacity quickly because local loop access is still a bottleneck.

This belated discovery that the bandwidth market was not elastic was in itself an example of management risk. The mismanagers panicked and searched for means to get out of the red-ink hole. Buying and selling fiber-optic bandwidth became a business that embodied many of the corporate practices that led to Enron's bankruptcy, including the use of Ponzi schemes. According to regulatory filings:

- Assets were sold to partnerships controlled by Fastow, and
- Proceeds from the transactions were used to mask mounting losses at other divisions.

Market deception became the game plan. By hiding the losses from the public eye through the different partnerships, all income suddenly became the good earnings that investors were shown. This is a highly improved version of EBITDA (see Chapter 3). With bandwidth, as elsewhere:

- Enron officials overstated the value of the business
- Misled investors about the volumes being traded, and
- Acknowledged losses only when the company was on the verge of insolvency.

Even after the bankruptcy Enron's top brass was not forthcoming with information. Andrew Fastow, like Kenneth Lay, invoked his Fifth Amendment rights before a US House Committee investigating the company's failure. Management risk hid behind the ruined walls of a former empire.

While Enron was a going concern, the secrecy enveloping the losses helped up to a point, but not beyond. Lack of transparency made it possible that less than a year before its bankruptcy, in January 2001 Enron executives could tell investors the company was on its way to dominating the broadband market worldwide. According to their (wrong) estimates, that market was poised to top $500 billion by 2005 "because of the explosion of the internet."

At an investor conference in Houston, Kenneth Lay said that the company's broadband division had reached the critical mass it needed, and then CEO Jeffrey Skilling promised enormous growth prospects for the business. The broadband division, Skilling stated in an interview in March 2001, was worth $36 billion, or $40 a share. This was stated at a time when Enron's stock traded at $70. Nine months down the line, the whole company crashed.

In retrospect, one can see that Enron survived for a while because it absorbed the losses from its broadband business and other product lines by shifting debt off its books via the dozens of private partnerships set up by Fastow. Only the company's assets were visible. With one exception (in August 2001), financial analysts did not challenge these numbers and Enron shares rose 87 percent in just one year (2000).

The exception was Chung Wu, a UBS PaineWebber stock advisor. On August 21, 2001, he told clients they should "sell" their Enron shares – and he was fired by the broker that same day.[7] Informing clients is an analyst's duty, but some companies interpret it as being a deadly sin. Suppressing an independent opinion is another aspect of management risk.

The high fliers of the casino economy of the late 1990s did not hesitate to violate of business ethics. Samuel D. Waksal, for example, pleaded guilty to serious charges of securities fraud, perjury, and obstruction of justice,[8] and others are still awaiting trial. In Enron's case, Fastow pleaded not guilty to seventy-eight criminal counts of fraud, conspiracy, money laundering, and obstruction of justice, yet the facts of using special purpose vehicles (SPVs) to hide debt and inflate profits allegedly exist:

- Even though the partnerships were supposed to be separate entities, Enron guaranteed the debt they issued
- When Enron's shares began falling in 2001, the company became liable for off-balance sheet debt.

Since misfortune never comes singly, these events set off a chain reaction that caused Moody's Investors Service and Standard & Poor's (S&P), respectively, to cut Enron's credit rating to junk from Baa1 and BBB$^+$. These downgrades scared off customers and ultimately brought Enron to its knees. "The broadband deal was the beginning of the end," says Ogan Kose, a crude oil trader who was one of 4,500 employees Enron fired in early December 2001. "Instead of writing it off, they continued to carry it."[9] And they did everything possible to hide it from investors.

6   Enron, EES, and outsourcing

Unlike other energy companies which back their trading operations with hard assets such as power plants, allowing them to guarantee a supply chain to a buyer, Enron worked furiously to shed power plants and oil- and gas-generating fields. Its management believed it could earn higher returns using its trading and technology expertise to tap assets owned by other entities in markets including not just oil and gas but also steel, pulp, paper, and broadband communications. This strategy of disinvestment of real assets was a major contributor to the fact that Enron suffered from a crisis of confidence.

Confidence crises were fed by the drying up of cash and credit, while nervous markets led to more confidence crises. This created a vicious cycle, which is the no. 1 reason for Enron's meltdown.

The lack of confidence *is* a management risk, and a major one. It was magnified by unreliable sales figures, inflated profit projections, and creative accounting used in the company's financial reports. The sales force at Enron Energy Services (EES) seems to have been routinely inflating profit estimates for long-term contracts they were negotiating, which boosted the reported short-term profits.

But life caught up with both the salespeople and the company, with many deals turning out to be loss makers. As a report in the *Financial Times* suggested, according to allegations by former employees, EEC racked up losses of more than $500 million despite reporting a $103 million pretax profit in 2000.[10] Reminiscent of derivatives trading, salesmen were paid huge commissions on these deals without much responsibility for how the contracts they signed performed later on.

This is one of the reasons why management quality at Enron was so poor. It also makes EES an interesting case study in outsourcing. This subsidiary was founded in 1997, and it sought to convince businesses to outsource all of their energy needs to its parent firm. The range of products and services was wide – from electricity and natural gas to workers who would maintain boilers.

Superficially, the operation was successful. After three years of operations, EES had signed long-term contracts worth more than $30 billion. But according to some reports, the insourcer's compensation system had incentivized the salesmen to sign a number of flawed deals. They were paid commissions based on upfront earnings the company could book on these long-term deals, even if pricing was not transparent let alone optimized, and future payments were neither predictable nor certain. This created a situation open to abuse. Before the policy was changed in 2001, the EES sales team could routinely guarantee customers generous discounts on large deals without making sure that those savings were feasible. Several contracts also made no provisions for price increases over their lifecycle, leaving Enron and its profitability exposed.

Analysts on Wall Street also suggest that Enron's senior management endorsed the salespeople's business behavior because it contributed to the company's short-term profits. Cash was running short at a time when other ventures, such as broadband trading, were not bringing in money. But EES was the antithesis of what serious insourcing/outsourcing agreements should look like.[11] Companies that hope to succeed in their outsourcing and insourcing agreements need to appreciate what the issues are from an *integrated perspective*, including that of their business partners. They should plot a strategy to overcome present and foreseeable roadblocks by becoming aware of lessons learned by other companies that have "been there." One of the basic requirements in testing information technology (IT) outsourcing deals is to understand what is meant by "due diligence;" how a back-up strategy will work; what to do if the insourcer defaults; how an exit strategy can be implemented; and what happens with operational risks all along the contract's lifecycle:

- Does the insourcer observe IT standards, including those of an open architecture?
- Does the outsourcer takes the risk of finding himself locked into parochial and high-cost solutions?

Years of experience have taught me the importance of *a priori* norms and of thorough testing. Both seem to have been totally absent from Enron's outsourcing practices. Testing is necessary on both the outsourcer's and the insourcer's side; and it should be targeting precise goals. A *testing plan* must be the *alter ego* of every outsourced service. No words are strong enough to underline the importance of a written testing plan for everything being outsourced (or insourced). In connection with IT, for instance, this must set out:

- Objectives
- Testing environment
- Testing tools
- Methodology
- Schedules
- Financial resources
- Human resources, and
- Fall-back position.

As a basic management principle, there are always prerequisites to be identified and met. From what has become known about EES nothing of the sort took place. The goal was allegedly simply the fast buck which could inflate short-term profit figures:

- Failure to plan for longer-term conduct of a profitable business can create serious problems further down the line
- Failure properly to identify and correct outsourcing/insourcing problems as they appear will threaten the safety and soundness of both business partners.

Senior management, and not only middle management directly connected with outsourced/insourced services, must also be prepared to face the problems connected with outstanding contracts. In outsourcing/insourcing terms, many of these problems are *cultural*, leading to agency costs and subutilization of resources. Other problems are *technical*: technology moves fast, and so does obsolescence in skills, software, hardware, and systems solutions.

A third major issue is the lack of first-class *methodology*, which seems to have characterized Enron, except for the methodology of Ponzi games with its dubious partnerships. Closely associated to the absence of an insourcing methodology which could provide a sustained profitability base was the alleged lack of quality control criteria at EES. These should be both quantitative and qualitative – and they should be contractually defined between outsourcer and insourcer. Their absence is still another aspect of management risk.

7   Enron and emerging markets

An act in the ongoing drama of emerging markets which shocked America in the mid-1990s was the scrapping of Enron's big deal in India's Maharashtra state. According to Indian sources the company benefited from favorable bidding procedures and contract terms – kickbacks – made by corrupt politicians. An article in *BusinessWeek* said that Michael J. Kooper, Fastow's former lieutenant who pleaded guilty and collaborated with prosecutors, "disclosed that he had paid kickbacks to Fastow and his family in some of their … deals."[12]

Kickbacks and other types of payoffs are nothing new in developing countries. A senior executive of Enron conceded that in the Indian energy deal as much as $21 million was spent on "educational expenses."[13] The World Bank refused to finance this project, and the Planning Commission of the Indian Government had serious objections to the prohibitive costs of the contract.

Ingenuity in creating schemes which end up by defrauding investors are sometimes promoted by brokers who work in the investor's home country. A few years ago, the US House Committee on Commerce, Consumer and Monetary Affairs held hearings on telemarketing fraud at which witnesses testified that investors lost billions of dollars. The outcome of these hearings was that such overseas investments became a fast-growing segment of fraud. All sorts of promoters offered overseas investments involving energy resources, strategic and other precious metals, currency speculation, junkbonds, foreign banking instruments, through what they advertised as "no risk" high-yield certificates of deposit. Among the examples presented to the House Committee was that of a Missouri man convicted of masterminding a fraudulent gold contract scheme. That Missouri case cost US investors as much as $100 million, including $15 million for the residents of Bozeman, Montana. The self-styled commodities expert who set it up had previously run only a small mirror and tile installation firm. He based his contracts on what were supposed to be 5-ounce gold bars produced by South Africa's Impala Mines which, investigators learned, had never dealt with the man and did not produce 5-ounce bullion bars in the first place.

Investors are simply too careless to do, and a good number of them are outright incapable of doing, their homework. But also the deals presented to them are camouflaged. Very often, the overseas investment schemes have also involved shell offshore banks in the Pacific or the Caribbean, as well as high-pressure "boiler room" telephone-sales operations, usually based abroad.

The House Committee's report raised concern over offshores that, through liberal banking laws and tight secrecy restrictions, allowed or encouraged dubious banking practices. An official of the US Office of the Controller of the Currency described these deals as "prostitute banking." One of the witnesses to the House Committee who was arrested and pleaded guilty to racketeering, theft, conspiracy, and securities charges in Pennsylvania, testified that he worked as a salesman in "boiler-room" operations in Manhattan and California for ten years.

In the 1990s, the Department of Justice made a sweep which arrested hundreds of fraudulent telemarketers, and many were sent to prison. In 2000–2, however, big-company Ponzi games defrauded investors at a rate the telemarketers would never have dreamed off. One example is the case of the securitization and marketing of loans to companies with high probability of default, which we shall study in Chapter 9.

9

The Bankers of Enron

1 Introduction

Among the bankers of Enron, J.P. Morgan Chase and Citigroup came in for much criticism. Both analysts and investors believe that they were the big credit institution losers in the Enron débâcle. J.P. Morgan Chase, for instance, provided a wide array of financial services to the bankrupt entity, which ranged from commodities trading to commercial loans, investment banking advice, and deals such as the *prepays*. In the wake of Enron's bankruptcy J.P. Morgan Chase was forced to write down $451 million in the fourth quarter of 2001, while leaving more than $2.5 billion of potential losses on its books.

William Harrison, chairman and chief executive of J.P. Morgan Chase, acknowledged that the second-biggest US bank had lent too much to Enron. His remarks, reported by Bloomberg, came as banks on Wall Street were getting to grips with what, in December 2001, had been the largest corporate bankruptcy in US history. "Harrison's troubles are hardly over," a 2003 article in *BusinessWeek* said. "The odds are rising that Morgan will lose its $1 billion suit against eleven insurance companies over surety bonds on trades made by Enron. Insurers allege the trades were actually loans"[1] – more precisely, loans masquerading as trades, something one does not expect from a responsible bank.

Second among big Enron lenders was Citigroup, the largest US bank, which recorded a $228 million pretax write-off in the fourth quarter of 2001 owing to Enron. Bank of America (BoA) took a $231 million loss and the official who headed BoA's energy resources investment banking practice resigned. BoA and the Bank of Wachovia seem to have taken a more conservative write-down on their unsecured exposures, as contrasted to companies such as Citigroup, J.P. Morgan, and Fleet Boston.

Credit institutions do not generally disclose detailed information regarding individual client exposures, citing confidentiality as a reason. Table 9.1 presents a collection of statistics from different sources regarding domestic and

Table 9.1   The biggest creditors who lost from Enron's bankruptcy

Institution	Country	Estimated exposure ($ billion)
$1 billion or more		
J.P. Morgan Chase	USA	3.3
Citigroup	USA	3.0
Bank of New York	USA	2.4
Bank of America	USA	1
Below $1 billion but above $200 million		
Fleetboston	USA	
John Hancock	USA	
Suntrust	USA	
Wachovia	USA	
Aegon	Netherlands	
Canadian Imperial Bank	Canada	
Crédit Lyonnais	France	
Ing	Netherlands	
Sumitomo-Mitsui	Japan	
Tokyo-Mitsubishi	Japan	

foreign banks with significant exposures to Enron loans. Other domestic credit institutions which lost money include Bank One, KeyCorp, National City, PNC, US Bancorp, and Wells Fargo. Among foreign banks are Abbey National, ABN Amro, Crédit Suisse, and the United Bank of Switzerland.

Some of these banks, like J.P. Morgan Chase, were also prominent lenders to other high-profile companies that filed for bankruptcy in the early twenty-first century, including Kmart, Global Crossing, and most particularly WorldCom. In J.P. Morgan's case, the bank's CEO predicted that Enron's shadow would continue to affect people's views of the market and the political world for some time to come. He also touched on problems at the bank's private equity business, J.P. Morgan Partners, whose portfolio is one of the industry's largest. In line with an old principle in finance that bad news never comes singly, J.P. Morgan Chase was forced to write down $1.3 billion on its holdings in 2001, largely due to souring telecoms and technology investments. In hindsight, the bank had too much capital committed to the fast-track business sectors of the mid-to-late 1990s, and when the market soured loans, investments, and the trading book bled. This is one of the foremost lessons from the case studies on Enron's bankers in this chapter.

2   Enron, its bankers, and its investors

In its December 2, 2001 filing, Enron listed $49.8 billion in assets. It identified its debts at $31.2 billion, but Wall Street analysts suggested that the energy company has at least another $27 billion–$30 billion in off-balance sheet debts not yet mentioned. This would have pushed its total debt figure past $60 billion; in fact, some analysts claimed that the company's debt liabilities were actually $80 billion or more.

The list of Enron's unsecured creditors was a *Who's Who* of the banking world. It was fifty-four pages long, and included twenty-two major institutions: J.P. Morgan Chase (formerly two different entities: J.P. Morgan and Chase Manhattan), Citigroup, Bank of America, Bank of New York, Merrill Lynch, Goldman Sachs, Morgan Stanley, Lehman Brothers, UBS, Crédit Suisse First Boston (CSFB), Barclays Bank, NatWest, Société Générale, the Canadian Imperial Bank of Commerce, the Royal Bank of Canada, the Bank of Montreal, Toronto-Dominion, the Westdeutsche Landesbank (WestLB), Christiana Bank, General Re, and Swiss Re, among others.

Every one of them had rushed to join Enron's leveraged game, and got burned. As is practically always the case, the early figures on the losses these credit institutions had incurred because of Enron were major underestimates, but there were some overestimates as well. With time, exposure figures were revised:

- Up, because the banks (and others) also had a major derivatives exposure with Enron, and credit risk counts (see Chapter 10)
- Down, because increasingly banks that originated big loans sold pieces of those loans to other banks, spreading their exposure (see Chapter 11).

The footprint of major loans losses did not escape the attention of independent rating agencies, and with good reason. Typically, it led to downgrading the bank. In the wake of bankruptcies like Enron, Global Crossing, and WorldCom, among others, on July 25, 2002, Moody's changed its outlook for J.P. Morgan Chase from positive to negative because of:

- Deteriorating asset quality in the portfolio
- Concentration in telecoms, media, and technology lending, and
- Damage to the bank's image, and reputational risk.

In mid-2002, US Senate Committee hearings revealed that J.P. Morgan Chase and Citigroup had set up complex financial transactions for Enron; offshore shell companies hid Enron's true P&L and loans diverted through prepays had resurfaced as "profits." These were not minor items; they amounted to a respectable $8.5 billion (there is more on this below).

There were other energy companies on the list of unsecured creditors, including major oil companies: ExxonMobile, BP, Shell, and ChevronTexaco. The energy firms were: Dynegy, Duke, Williams, El Paso, Mirant, Reliant, along with a number of electric utilities: Southern, American Electric Power, Consolidated Edison, San Diego Gas & Electric. Law firms involved with these entities included Vinson & Elkins, Sullivan & Cromwell, Bracewell & Patterson, and LeBouef Lamb. The most prominent of the accountants was

Arthur Andersen. A number of states were also slated to lose a small fortune: California, Colorado, Georgia, Florida, Nevada, and Massachusetts; as well as cities like Dallas, San Antonio, and Austin, in Texas; Glendale and Pasadena, in California; De Funiak Springs and Lakeland in Florida. States like Massachusetts went to court to recover pension money due from Enron.

Also not to be forgotten are the institutional investors. Examples of funds taken to the cleaners included: Fidelity, Alliance Capital, Janus, and Putnam. Credit institutions like Barclays and Citigroup booked significant losses, not just as lenders but also as investors. All these are very interesting case studies on of the "domino effect" of Enron's collapse.

In the wake of all these losses, well-managed institutional investors got active. In the aftershock of Enron's collapse, TIAA-CREF, the $275 billion US teachers' pension fund and the second-largest US pension fund, stepped up its proactive international corporate governance program. The focus of its effort was to abolish unequal voting structures, and to implement an equitable system of "one share, one vote." The campaign also targeted companies in continental Europe in which it invested as part of its international portfolio – for instance, entities in Sweden, the Netherlands, and France, where voting rights restrictions are commonplace. The pressure for change in European corporate governance has been growing; the TIAA-CREF commitment to "one share, one vote" concerns all of its 500 largest holdings worldwide, spelling out the fund's opposition to:

- Voting caps
- Double voting rights
- Golden shares, and
- Pyramid structures.

TIAA-CREF also animated four main corporate governance initiatives for US companies in the wake of Enron's collapse. They are worth mentioning because they are the spearhead of demands for better corporate governance by other major institutional investors:

- Stock option accounting
- Auditor independence
- Misuse of poison pills, and
- Board independence.

TIAA-CREF is a member of a loose nine-institution alliance known as the Global Institutional Governance Network (GIGN) which issued a common statement on auditor independence. Investors and regulators understandably became more active than ever in the aftermath of Enron because of what was revealed about secretive partnerships and other questionable deals. This created a tremendous discussion about management's *accountability*.

Next to the big banks and institutional investors, in terms of losses from Enron's and related companies' collapse, came the insurance industry.

Some estimates put the cost to insurance companies at between $2 billion and $3 billion, mainly through:

- Directors' and officers' liability insurance provided to Enron
- Professional liability coverage to Enron's auditor, Arthur Andersen, and
- Financial guarantees on Enron's projects.

The insurers which held Enron stock or debt had to write down the values of those assets. This and similar write-offs due to stock market blues came at the most inopportune moment, two months after the dramatic events of September 11, 2001 (9/11) and continuing litigation in other sectors like asbestos and tobacco. In asbestos alone, for example, the estimated burden of claims on US and non-US insurers was of the order of $35 billion.

Outside the US, one of the financial markets most affected by Enron was Japan's. Information which came to public attention indicated that four money management funds, holding some $850 million in Enron bonds, were severely hit. Enron's bankruptcy triggered customer redemptions of an order of magnitude larger than the funds' holdings of Enron bonds, slashing the value of these institutional investors below face value.

Not to be outdone, three Japanese banks revealed an exposure to Enron in excess of $485 million, adding to the tremors hitting the Japanese banking industry since 1991. To stem liquidity problems connected to the Enron collapse, the Bank of Japan pumped $200 billion into its banking system, a multiple of Enron's estimated debt. This is another example of the fact that, as in the aftermath of 9/11, central banks have to apply capital and logistics in a timely fashion to stem off systemic risk.

3   The aftershocks at Enron's banks

Bankruptcy analysts quite quickly came to the conclusion that the Enron débâcle would have far-reaching consequences for the profit reports of many other companies. In meetings I held in the US and the UK, experts suggested that the entities most at risk included all those that built into their balance sheet quite substantial goodwill through acquisitions:

- Companies which loaded up on debt during the 1990s
- Large-cap stocks, likely to be hit harder than small and medium-sized firms.

In the fast-growing companies of the 1990s senior executives increased their income, but many of them left business morals behind: they multiplied their possessions, but reduced their company's real value. The late 1990s were a time for more freedom in wheeling and dealing, but also for less sound business principles.

Analysts were increasingly concerned about the economic impact of class actions. Four months after the fall of Enron, on April 8, 2002, nine big banks and two law firms were added to a class-action lawsuit against Enron that alleged that they had helped Enron defraud shareholders. The 485-page amended complaint named J.P. Morgan Chase, Citigroup, Merrill Lynch, CSFB, the Canadian Imperial Bank of Commerce (CIBC), Bank of America, Barclays Bank, Deutsche Bank, and Lehman Brothers as key players. The target of this class action was a series of allegedly fraudulent transactions, creating a "mythical picture" of Enron's profitability. Information from Congressional hearings and press reports established that a number of the banks, J.P. Morgan Chase, CSFB, CIBC, Deutsche Bank, and Merrill Lynch, were involved in funding Enron's controversial LJM2 partnership (see section 5). The class action claimed that the banks:

- Took stakes in off-balance sheet partnerships created by the energy company's CFO, that helped Enron to hide debt, and
- Produced underwriting filings on debt issues sold to the public showing that Enron's finances were sound while they seemed to know otherwise.[2]

The lead plaintiff for the Enron shareholders was the University of California. Its general counsel, James Holst, said: "These prestigious banks and laws firms used their skills and their professional reputation to help Enron's executives shore up the company's stock price and create a false appearance of financial strength and profitability which fooled the public into investing billions of dollars ... In return, these firms received multimillion-dollar fees, and some of their top executives exploited the situation to cash in personally."[3]

Prosecutors and regulators started to fine-comb conflicts of interest. Eliot Spitzer, the New York State Attorney General, widened the investigation into the independence of Wall Street analysts, ordering several investment banks including CSFB, J.P. Morgan Stanley, Salomon Smith Barney, Goldman Sachs, Lehman Brothers, Lazard Brothers, and UBS Warburg to hand over documents. Wall Street watchers correctly surmised that these disclosed documents could reveal possible conflicts of interest between analysts and investment bankers.

The Wall Street settlement of April 28, 2003, included findings of fraud with associated penalties and disgorgements to the tune of nearly $1.4 billion, as shown in Table 9.2. Announcing the settlement in Washington, DC, William Donaldson, chairman of the Securities and Exchange Commission said: "I am profoundly saddened – and angry – about the conduct that's alleged in our complaints. There is absolutely no place for it in our markets, and it cannot be tolerated."[4] But it was tolerated during the boom years of the late 1990s and beyond, and tolerance allowed the banks to behave as if they were unaware of legal risk involved in their acts.

The $1.4 billion might well just be the beginning. After having settled with the Attorney General and the regulators, Wall Street firms can now expect plaintiff layers to start filing civil suits. Eliot Spitzer remarked during the

Table 9.2   The April 28, 2003 settlement with Wall Street firms ($ million, in order of importance)

	Penalty	Disgorgement	Independent research	Inventor education	Total
Citigroup	150	150	75	25	400
CSFB	75	75	50	0	200
Merrill Lynch	100*	0	75	25	200
Morgan Stanley	25	25	75	0	125
Goldman Sachs	25	25	50	10	110
Bear Stearns	25	25	25	5	80
J.P. Morgan	25	25	25	5	80
Lehman Brothers	25	25	25	5	80
UBS Warburg	25	25	25	5	80
Piper Jaffray	12.5	12.5	7.5	0	32.5
Total	487.5	387.5	432.5	80	1,387.5

* Payment made prior to the April 28, 2003 settlement.

settlement that malfeasance went way up the corporate food chain.[5] While the CEOs of the financial institutions which reached the settlement have been spared personal indictment, future class actions might cover aspects of malfeasance.

To appreciate how legal risk can creep up and become a flood, the reader should recall that when this issue first came to the public attention, Spitzer left open the possibility that criminal charges could be laid against banks and analysts, but confirmed that his office had sent subpoenas to several Wall Street banks in the search for irrefutable evidence. Like Merrill Lynch, which was the first to settle, many institutions were accused by the Attorney General of privately disparaging companies while publicly telling investors to buy the shares. (As we saw in Part I, the broker settled for a fine of $100 million, without admitting guilt.)

Investment banks came under fire from regulators and investors for giving positive stock recommendations in the hope of securing fees for helping these companies sell stock to the public. More than 30,000 emails were subpoenaed by the Attorney General's office and they revealed the extent of the conflict of interest – including references to companies such as InfoSpace, which syndicates internet and wireless content, as being a "piece of junk."[6]

The mission stated by the Attorney General was to craft a settlement that would eradicate the conflicts of interest that he believed were endemic. This is easier said than done, because conflicts of interest are part of human nature, even if their existence came under the microscope when the collapse of Enron raised major questions about corporate governance and financial disclosure.

The débâcle of Enron, as well as of the telecoms firms, has thrown the spotlight on to investigators. Investors, and the public at large, expected them to identify and punish those parties who had been unloading billions of dollars in shares before accounting problems came to light, and showering themselves with all sorts of "loans" and options at shareholders' expense. It is the job of regulators, investigators, and prosecutors to bring to public knowledge cases of financial fraud, and make sure that senior management malfeasance, of all sorts, cannot happen again.

The events of 2001 and 2002 showed that this problem of ethics is much more widespread than it might seem at first sight. Classical fraud has morphed into high-tech-based attacks. In early 2002, a survey by PricewaterhouseCoopers found that 42.5 percent of large European companies who responded had been the victims of economic crime in the past two years, at a total cost of Euro 6 billion ($3.17 billion) – equivalent to an average of Euro 6.7 million ($3.32 million) per organization. This is of course a drop in the ocean compared to the billions of dollars lost by investors. In the US, the Securities and Exchange Commission (SEC) would like to demand that investment banks have a lawyer present whenever contact is made between corporate financiers and equity research analysts. The pressure to do so has increased as the debate over the independence of analysts has intensified. The SEC is also considering a rule that bans any contact between research analysts and investment bankers working on the same deal, by creating a "Chinese Wall." The actions taken by the Attorney General and by the SEC do not necessarily overlap:

- The New York State prosecutors mainly concentrate on lower-impact but high-frequency stock frauds, such as the "boiler rooms" of high-pressure selling operations and fallacious analysts' comments
- The SEC targets policies and practices by large investment banks which come under its jurisdiction – high-impact cases whose frequency tends to be somewhat lower.

In the UK, the Financial Services Authority (FSA) has put in motion a process of closing another loophole which permitted investors to be misled. Its target is tightening up on the advertising of financial products by their designers and vendors, to ensure that headline figures about past performance do not dominate the message. Past performance has finally come to be seen as an increasingly unreliable indicator of how well a fund will do in the future:

- Star fund managers move frequently
- Management groups merge or are taken over, and
- While past risks may have been rewarding, future ones may turn out to be catastrophic.

Greater transparency and dependability are so much more important when, as the FSA aptly suggests, vendors of financial products are increasingly structuring them using complex underlying investments and financial derivatives. The risks associated with these products are unfamiliar to most investors – particularly to retail investors to whom they are increasingly addressed – and even experts can find it difficult to untangle complex structured deals. Investment managers can lure clients by highlighting double-digit yields, while they are burying risk warnings about potential capital loss altogether, or confining a warning to the fine print. The FSA seems inclined to promote as a metric "gross redemption yield," which will show the effect of capital loss. Analysts say that the aftermath of implementing it will baffle most investors.[7]

The tightening of regulation and a greater depth in the investigation of fraud did not necessarily need to follow a major business failure, but Enron's bust acted as a trigger. It also revealed that parties thought to be above suspicion were not, which led investors to make a beeline for the court house. As section 4 shows, we are still quite a long way away from having experienced all of Enron's aftershocks.

4   Prepays, J.P. Morgan Chase, and surety bonds

Citing evidence that the company might have engaged in shell contracts with Enron, a Federal Judge in New York on March 5, 2002 thwarted J.P. Morgan Chase's efforts to collect $1 billion in insurance cover. This was supposed to represent compensation on trading losses with the bankrupt energy company. The judge's ruling was a legal setback for one of Enron's leading creditors. That decision:

- Created a precedent affecting how Enron's financial débâcle (and that of other companies) might spread to Wall Street's investment banks
- Opened a gaping hole to the argument that operational risks and some trade risks could be insured rather than being covered through capital reserves,[8] and
- Threw cold water on the novel legal argument by J.P. Morgan Chase that insurance firms were liable whether or not fraud was present.

Behind J.P. Morgan's court action was the argument that the insurers' obligation in their contract was described as "absolute and unconditional." That does not mean that fraud is a protected business practice, wrote US District Judge Jed S. Rakoff, who called J.P. Morgan Chase's demand that insurance companies should pay the losses an "extraordinary proposition."[9] The eleven insurers listed as defendants included Chubb, CAN Financial, Fireman's Fund, Liberty Mutual, Travellers, and Safeco. The cover in question was provided through a financial instrument known as *surety bonds*, intended to cover J.P. Morgan Chase's potential losses on energy trading with Enron. The surety bonds dealt with trades of natural gas and oil trades conducted through a non-transparent organization called Mahonia Natural Gas, based in a tax haven in the English offshore Channel Islands. The financial plan called for Enron to sell the commodities to Mahonia.

Chase Manhattan Bank, the predecessor institution to J.P. Morgan Chase, set up the transactions between June 1998 and December 2000, and financed them. In this way, by means of a complex deal, the money for the commodities would:

- Come from Chase
- Go to Mahonia, and
- Be relayed to Enron.

In his preliminary opinion, Judge Rakoff wrote: "Taken together, these arrangements now appear to be nothing but a disguised loan." At the very least, he said, the case merited further investigation, particularly because the insurers had uncovered a striking series of coincidences. The insurance companies could obtain evidence from Enron and J.P. Morgan Chase which brought the legal issues of this particular case a long way from the English Channel Islands and into the US.

At the end of July 2002, in their defense before a US Senate Committee on another matter, Citigroup and J.P. Morgan executives argued that the banks were, in fact, little more than Enron's victims. If further blame were needed, they suggested, it should be directed at Arthur Andersen, Enron's auditor, which had signed off all transactions. The Senate Committee had in its possession, however, emails which proved that bank executives were aware of what was going on, and these emails surfaced in the jury trial (there is more on this below).

As defendants, the insurance companies said they were not providing cover for bad loans: in fact, it was illegal for them to do so. The defendants pressed the point that they did not know Enron was contracting to repurchase natural gas and oil from a company called Stoneville Aegean, with Enron allowed to pay for its purchases in the future – an unorthodox setup. The insurers argued in court that:

- Enron was simply keeping Chase's money and getting its commodities back
- Chase was making a disguised loan – the famous *prepays* to which reference was briefly made in Part I.

"Prepay" transactions are a financial instrument of the late 1990s. Banks put money upfront roughly equal to what specific trades might realize some time in the future. This seems to have been tried first at Enron – and on a big scale. J.P. Morgan Chase structured twelve of these deals, providing $3.7 billion. Citigroup structured fourteen, providing Enron with $4.8 billion. This was a total of $8.5 billion in Enron's accounts, money channeled through shell companies registered offshore, particularly in Jersey.

The crucial accounting question with prepays is whether such money should have been counted as a loan, or as something closer to a payment for a future profit. If they were loans, which is the more reasonable interpretation, then the impact on Enron's balance sheet should have been negative and profound:

- Enron's debt would have risen by 40 percent, and
- Its cash flow would have fallen by 50 percent.

Such significant balance sheet changes would have had a harsh impact on Enron's creditworthiness and on the company's stock value. This was not the only financial invention of a creative accounting nature. The Yosemite transactions which transferred Enron risk to investors were another example. The problem here was that the actual Enron risk was different from that portrayed by Enron's incomplete and misleading financial disclosures. Citigroup allegedly used the money from the Yosemite offerings to fund the prepaid transactions, creating what could appear to be a vicious circle of financial engineering, potentially disastrous to investors. "Citi promised investors that the credit-linked notes would perform similarly to straight Enron bonds – and they have," Rick Caplan, a Citigroup executive said.[10] But this should be interpreted in the most negative sense possible – including their legal after effects. One of the legally unwanted consequences – from the bank's viewpoint – was that on December 23, 2002, Judge Rakoff ruled that the jury could see emails in which a senior J.P. Morgan Chase executive, vice chairman Donald Layton, described the prepay contracts as "disguised loans, usually buried in commodities or equities derivatives," adding "I am queasy about the process."

"Mr. Layton's comments are a red herring," J.P. Morgan spokesperson Kristin Lemkau said. "They do not in the least support the theory being argued by the insurance companies." But Judge Rakoff said that the emails were "explosive," and might be "highly probative," meaning they could influence the jury against the bank.[11] On January 2, 2003, ten days after these comments had been made J.P. Morgan Chase and the eleven insurance companies reached an out-of-court compromise. The insurers agreed to pay 60 percent of the disputed $1.1 billion surety bond triggered by the Enron bankruptcy, while the bank absorbed the other 40 percent in its P&L statement. Experts said that though the prepays were an unorthodox sort of deal, and J.P. Morgan Chase had shot itself in the foot with the emails, two things weighed against the insurers. One was the "absolute and unconditional" clause the jury might have interpreted either way in connection with the hidden loan to Enron. The other, was evidence that the insurers' agent in Houston knew that the Enron contracts were in effect loans, and had probably informed the insurance companies who had underwritten this major operational risk.

J.P. Morgan Chase had another fairly similar claim against the Westdeutsche Landesbank (WestLB), which had led a syndicate of banks into another contract guaranteeing Enron performance for $165 million. This is one more example of the "casino society" in which credit institutions were involved.

On Wall Street, that sort of gamble led many analysts to question whether Bill Harrison, J.P. Morgan's CEO, can manage risks in its loan book and trading portfolio.[12]

J.P. Morgan Chase's Mahonia transactions with Enron are being investigated by the US Justice Department, Securities and Exchange Commission (SEC), and Federal Reserve Bank of New York. The Manhattan District Attorney Robert Morgenthau has also begun a grand jury investigation in connection with the billions of dollars of gas and oil trades J.P. Morgan Chase and Mahonia handled with Enron.

By structuring the whole business of prepays and other doubtful deals as trading transactions, with the assistance of its banks, Enron could report the cash infusion as sales revenue rather than debt. The colorful aspect of these different creative accounting inventions is increased by the fact that the trading organizations of Mahonia and Stoneville Aegean were set up by the same person; they had the same director and the same shareholders. It is not possible to regulate human ingenuity.

5   Merrill Lynch, LJM2, and the Nigerian barges

According to published reports, Merrill Lynch's dealings with Andrew S. Fastow, Enron's CFO, were complex and questionable. Complex because Merrill's drive to win underwriting fees conflicted all the way with its obligation fully to inform investors of all possible problems with the securities it sold to them. Questionable because there were several corners cut in the multiple business relationships Merrill Lynch had with Enron, where it acted as:

- Lender
- Underwriter
- Investment advisor, and
- Counterparty in energy derivatives deals.

Merrill Lynch was not alone in funding Enron's highly controversial LJM2 partnership; the list includes an array of investment bankers: J.P. Morgan Chase, Crédit Suisse, Lehman Brothers, the Canadian Imperial Bank, and Deutsche Bank.[13]

At the center of this corporate culture, and of the management risk associated with it, was not only the lure of perceived profits but also the bending of rules to avoid being cut out of Enron's lucrative other deals, as long as they lasted. In its defense, Merrill Lynch said that its employees had done nothing improper and that its management knew no more than the public did. But this response pleased neither regulators nor investors. "I didn't know" is the personalization of management risk. It is also a defense that regulators and law enforcement officers are increasingly unwilling to accept, with good reason. A banker is supposed to know the people and entities he is dealing with, particularly so when he engages with them in big, complex trades. If he doesn't, either the banker is totally incapable, or he is somebody destined to fade away in the market's rear view mirror.

The most picturesque of all deals concerning Enron and its bankers, even more so than Mahonia, is the relationship involving Merrill Lynch, Fastow, and LJM2. It started in 1999, a little over two years before the crash, when Fastow hired Merrill Lynch to raise money for LJM2 Co-Investment L.P., one of his "companies." Reportedly, Fastow informed the brokerage that he hoped to use his limited partnership, LJM2, to launch his own investment operation. Acting under two hats – as Enron's CFO and an independent investor – Fastow was in a conflict of interest. His dual role as Enron finance chief and LJM2 general partner made him at the same time an employee of and competitor to Enron.

It will never be known unequivocally if this raised eyebrows at Merrill Lynch. Merrill's private equity sales team nevertheless raised $265 million of the partnership's $387 million capital, by appealing to its best clients:

- Pension funds
- Family trust funds, and
- High net worth individuals.

This was money that eventually went down the drain and Merrill's clients lost their assets. But Fastow also took Merrill's own managers and investment advisors for a ride. The brokerage itself invested $5 million and agreed to loan the LJM2 partnership $10 million, while ninety-seven Merrill executives personally contributed another $17.6 million to a total of $32.6 million. Was this money just thrown out of the window? Not quite, the experts say, because its special relationship with Fastow's shell company gave Merrill Lynch a close insight into Enron's finances. It also provided some lucrative business, and therefore profits, for the broker. The Merrill–Enron deals were polyvalent since they included:

- Underwriting of stocks and bonds
- Lending to the energy company
- Assisting as lead fund raiser, and
- Acting as counterparty in energy derivatives deals.

In spite of such a complex relationship which, according to sound management principles, should have profited from thorough scrutiny by Merrill's top executives, the broker says: "I didn't know." Post-mortem, on Wall Street, experts suggest that some people at Merrill Lynch must have felt uneasy about the Fastow relationship.

Two of the broker's Texas-based investment bankers who had day-to-day contact with Enron questioned the then company's President Jeffrey K. Skilling about the LJM2 issue and (presumably) its risks. He reassured them that Enron would put internal controls in place to oversee Fastow.[14] Nothing of that sort was done. Instead, Fastow promised to set up an advisory committee to review conflicts of interest. The caveat was that he himself decided what constituted a "conflict," and whether to refer it to the committee. Many experts are now of the opinion that Merrill Lynch knew a great deal about these deals, as well as the foggy bottom of Enron's finances. Merrill must have gained insight as lead broker, from its investments in the LJM2 affair, and as counterparty in Enron's Nigerian barge deal (see below), as well as the electricity swaps. The risk and return associated with this business could not have escaped senior management's attention.

Senior management must also have known that in 1998 Enron had pressured the investment side of the firm for positive analyst reports. There are stories about information which should have been subject to careful screening, but was not. In October 2000, for instance, LJM2 reported that it had had a 69 percent rate of return. Nobody bothered to check the figures, and when Enron went bust, LJM2 went down with the other "assets." For Merrill Lynch, all there is left of its involvement is lawsuits, regulators' investigations, and reputational risk.

Reputational risk is high, not only because of the $100 million settlement with the Attorney General's office, but also because it is reminiscent of the SEC's 1998 case concerning its role in the Orange County bankruptcy. Without admitting or denying guilt, the broker paid dearly to settle civil charges that it had sold collateralized mortgage obligations to Orange County, and Orange County notes to the investing public – omitting to mention in its securities offering documents what it knew about the county's risky investment strategy.

People and companies never learn from past mistakes. The SEC has begun a formal investigation of several Merrill–Enron deals, say sources close to the inquiry, including a series of power swaps that allowed Enron to claim millions in profit in 1999. One of the outstanding issues under the regulators' microscope is that of Enron, Merrill Lynch, LJM2, and the Nigerian barges. The Nigerian barges is an interesting deal that came to light as the dealings between investment banks and some of the highly leveraged companies they dealt with unrolled. Merrill seems to have been helping Enron to fabricate profits by acquiring some of its assets as far away as Nigeria, so that Enron could beef up its year-end earnings. The SEC, the Justice Department, and LJM2 investors who were taken to the cleaners now ask whether Merrill Lynch had access to Enron's financial and other documents, and direct access to the company's top brass and should have been able to see the deception which lay behind the Nigerian deal. According to published reports, James Brown, a Merrill Lynch banker who specialized in structuring complex financial transactions, was one of the first to fret over a deal in which the broker agreed to pay Enron $28 million for an interest in three power-generating barges off the coast of Nigeria. On December 21, 1999, he wrote: "Reputational risk i.e. aid/abet Enron income [statement] manipulation."[15]

The sale of barges in Nigeria allowed Enron to book a $12 million profit. Post-mortem, however, documents released by the Senate's Permanent Subcommittee on Investigations show that this was not a straightforward sale because, according to the terms of the agreement, Enron was promising to find a buyer for the barges in six months, and it also guaranteed Merrill Lynch a total return of 22.5 percent.

In fact, it kept its promise. The buyer was none other than LJM2, the shell company in which Merrill Lynch had some of its own money as well as $265 million of its clients' assets. Merrill money was recycled by LJM2 and Enron as Merrill's profit. Under SEC rules, a company cannot recognize revenue from a sale:

- If it is obliged to take the product off the buyer's hands in the future, or
- If the risk of ownership does not pass from seller to buyer.

In this particular case, it did not. The Nigerian barges deal and the involvement of LJM2 put Merrill Lynch and some of its top executives in conflict of interest. Post-mortem it transpires that investment in LJM2 biased the judgment of some senior people in connection to the company's evolving relation with Enron.

According to released reports, the conflicts of interest went further. At about the same time as the Nigerian barges deal, Merrill Lynch was asked to kick in $10 million of a $65 million syndicated loan to LJM2. When a Merrill Credit Committee rejected the request, the executives who had originally contributed their own money to LJM2 saw to it that the Credit Committee was bypassed. Merrill ultimately lent Fastow the $10 million, in violation of any credit risk standard. The investment bank's shareholders were given plenty of opportunity to appreciate what is meant by management risk.

6 Enron and the weather derivatives market

Enron had made a good name for itself in promoting new talent, but also for giving free rein to people who did not yet have the experience to calculate risk and return at a reasonable level of confidence. This was bad, and it became even worse when the company lacked a system of internal controls that allowed senior management's attention to be focused on extreme events, unwanted commitments, and poorly managed risks.

An example of the precipice to which the combination of these factors can lead was Enron's foray into weather derivatives. These lie at the interface of the insurance industry and capital markets. Enron was not an insurer and weather derivatives were way beyond its core business. This was a foray which violated good business sense.

Weather derivatives were invented by insurance companies which, instead of classical reinsurance, used the capital markets as intermediary for risk transfer.[16] Institutional investors were attracted to weather derivatives because of risk diversification reasons, but they could be a dangerous instrument if sellers, buyers, or both, did not pay real and immediate attention to the exposure involved, and to its evolution over time.

"At Enron, you had a bunch of kids running loose, without adult supervision," said James O'Toole, Professor at the Center for Effective Organizations at the University of Southern California, quoted in a feature article on Enron in *BusinessWeek*.[17] In 1997, Lynda R. Clemmons, a 27-year-old gas and power trader, launched Enron's weather derivatives deals. The enterprise seemed to be successful, at least in the number of contracts being signed. By 1999, she had written $1 billion in weather hedges:

- The object was to protect companies against short-term spikes in the price of power during heat waves and cold snaps
- The product was novel, and Enron profited from the fact that weather derivatives was a high-potential deregulated market.

But, as with other Enron initiatives, the party did not last long. "It was such a flaky business," John Olson, an analyst at Sanders Harris Morris in Houston suggested in the same *BusinessWeek* article. "They got more mileage out of the public relations than they actually made in earnings." As long as business is good and the cash flow continues to be strong, public relations and earnings tend to correlate. They both feed into, and are fed by, the unrelenting emphasis on earnings growth, individual initiative, and a certain absence of corporate checks and balances. In the long run, however, this absence of internal control which at the start helps to promote new initiatives like weather derivatives, tips the culture from one that rewards aggressive market moves to one that increasingly relies on corner-cutting. Post-mortem, analysts and investors discovered that at Enron – and many of the other companies that failed in 2000–3 – the necessary management controls to minimize failures were absent.

As a result of management risk, a lot of bad debts were placed on businesses that were unpromising to begin with, and became a drag as time went on, and when they turned sour nobody exercised damage control. In this culture, success and failure come remarkably fast. On the positive side, Enron managers and professionals were inventive and they tended to move relatively quickly, the downside was that:

- The necessary checks were rare
- The balances were badly kept, and
- In the last analysis nobody was in charge.

As the losses mounted, billions in off-balance sheet debts hidden in different partnerships and other special purpose vehicles melted like ice. Enron's CFO seems to have been more busy in deal making than in identifying and controlling the losses. The puzzle, however, is that Enron's bankers did not notice, and the CEOs of the big banks financing Enron, and trading with it, did not ring any alarm bells. The alarm bell rang only after Enron's sinking fortunes came to the fore and it was the market, not the bank's CEOs or Enron's own CEO, who pressed the button. This led to a spreading contagion of enterprise-wide dimensions, as the bottom line of questionable partnerships, assets disinvestment, weather derivatives, and many other non-core business deals, rapidly unraveled.

While there were many losers, some people profited from Enron's downfall. The best placed among them were those careful enough to pick up the few remaining real assets. Warren Buffett's purchased a former Enron natural gas pipeline from Dynegy for $600 million *less* than Dynegy had bought it from Enron.

7 Banks and bad debts

In December 2001, the bankruptcy of Enron and of Argentina followed by other tremors like the bankruptcies of Global Crossing, Adelphia Communications, and WorldCom, brought major concern to regulators. Investors were worried over the impact of large amounts of bad debt in the financial system. These concerns weighed on both the stock and corporate bond markets, with investors cutting back on their exposure wherever they could.

Many experts have suggested that the fall-out from Enron reshaped US institutions; some, however, added that it was doing so in non-predictable and possibly negative ways. Analysts suddenly discovered that there might be many collateral casualties, while worries mounted that the credit problems could hurt bank earnings and the financial system at large, damaging consumer confidence and swamping economic growth.

Banks have not unreasonably been at the heart of analysts' attention. At the end of December 2002, Citigroup announced that it had set aside $1.5 billion in the fourth quarter of 2002 to settle claims that it had misled customers with biased stock research, an operational risk. To cover different loans losses, which represented credit risk, Citigroup's provisions included a $400 million payment to settle regulatory probes into Wall Street's conflicts of interest in stock research, as well as funds for related lawsuits. *Bloomberg Professional* suggested that Citigroup faced at least sixty-two lawsuits tied to its research practices, according to regulatory filings.[18] The charge which it took was expected to reduce its fourth-quarter 2002 earnings by 29 cents a share. On the upside, it created a legal reserve which gave investors some confidence that the credit institution was taking care of its management risks and other exposures.

Some analysts commented that all these extra reserves might not ultimately be enough to cover the entire cost of settling private litigation – which is part of the financial industry's operational risk. In the 1990s, for instance, Prudential Securities ended up paying 300 percent over its originally estimated liability to settle regulatory charges and investor lawsuits to the tune of $8 billion. Citi was the first of several banks taking action after the December 20, 2002 announcement of a $1.4 billion settlement over research conflicts between state and federal securities firms. Bank of America also announced that it was setting aside $1.2 billion in reserves for the fourth quarter of 2002, mainly for loans losses. Other big banks followed a similar path.

Classically, credit institutions are particularly vulnerable to counterparty risk.[19] In the first years of the twenty-first century, because of major bankruptcies, both corporate and sovereign, nobody was immune to the downgrading of credit. By January 2002, for instance, the motor sector of the economy had a grim time with company-specific stories driving Ford, DaimlerChrysler, and Fiat sharply lower:

- DaimlerChrysler was hard hit as it disappointed the market with a bigger cut in its dividend than expected, because of sharply lower 2001 profits
- Ford suffered more in the longer term, as its sales slumped, its credit rating deteriorated, and this carried over into 2003.

The energy sector of the economy also became suspect as an investment, not only in the US but also in other G-10 countries. Reports in financial dailies said that Italy's central bank did not want San Paolo IMI and Banca di Roma to help finance Edipower, a consortium partly owned by Fiat, which was bidding for a power-generating company owned by the large Italian utility Enel. Fiat's dire financial conditions influenced the decision. Other reports suggested the Bank of Italy objected to the possibility of such financing because the banks involved already had a major exposure to Fiat, whose Italenergia power group was also participating in the bidding consortium. In Milan, traders said that the central bank's reaction underlined Fiat's liquidity problems. The auto company had just closed a Euro 1 billion capital increase, but this did not seem to have resolved its financial problems.

The central bank of Italy was very careful, and rightly so, but commercial bankers around the world don't seem to have taken this long, hard look. Yet credit risk is on the increase. Bankers should appreciate that in their line of business one can be at the top of the heap one moment, and out of cash the next. One of the manifestations of management risk is the inability to take hold of exposures in the bank's loans book and trading portfolio.

Yet, many valuable lessons have been learned at both the corporate and national economic levels since the 1980s. In 1983, the US was the largest creditor nation in the world; in 1985, it became a debtor nation for the first time since 1914. By 1987, US foreign debt was greater than that of Mexico, Brazil, Peru, and Argentina put together – and it continues to grow. The same happens with enterprises (and, eventually, with people), in terms of liabilities not kept under lock and key. When the going is strong, many companies tend to overload themselves with debt, and banks are only too happy to lend them money. Or, they use their "rising sun" syndrome to tap the vast resources of the capital market, as happened with Enron's debentures.

Enron issued large amounts of debentures based in practice on very little. They sold well because money market funds and other investors trusted Arthur Andersen, the auditors. According to some reports, Citibank, through its partner Nikko Securities, sold many Enron debentures to Japanese investors.[20] At the end of 2001, Tokyo money market funds, which held most of the Enron and Argentina paper in Japan, had reportedly lost $25 billion–$35 billion. According to some estimates, the situation was so dangerous that the Bank of Japan had to conduct direct money market operations, purchasing large amounts of commercial paper from money market funds and banks to avoid a crash, at a time when the Japanese market was itself in a deflationary spiral, and the banking system was effectively not functioning.

With Enron and many others of the high fliers of the 1990s there was also operational risk on the financial analysts' side. Chapter 8 noted the case of Chung Wu, a UBS Painwebber stock advisor, who told clients they should sell their Enron shares and was fired. Chung Wu contended that UBS Painwebber gave in because it had lucrative business with Enron.[21] The rest is history: in mid-November 2001, three months after Wu's warning, Enron acknowledged that results for the previous three years had been overstated by more than half a billion dollars:

- A billion-dollar error "several years earlier," had inflated the company's net worth, and
- A questionable decision had been taken by senior management to exclude the results of three partnerships from its financial statements.

Enron's performance fell far short of the cozy picture painted by management in its earnings releases, and believed by bankers and investors. Wu had seen that, but Enron was not alone. In 2001, corporate America charged off a record $125 billion, a big chunk of it for assets, investments, and inventory that were not worth as much as management had reported – if they were worth anything at all.

On June 26, 2002, the SEC said that it would require Wall Street analysts to certify that their stock picks were not influenced by investment banking relationships. This is a start on the road to improving investor confidence, as it makes the analysts personally accountable for the ratings they give in interviews, public appearances, and published reports. Ratings must now be accompanied by statements pledging that the analysis has not been influenced by any type of relationships with companies. The National Association of Securities Dealers (NASD) also notified Jack Grubman that it was meditating possible punishment for making recommendations to investors without a "reasonable basis." The NASD investigation concerned Grubman's coverage of Winstar, which he continued to recommend to investors even as it unraveled; it should be recalled that Grubman played a role in promoting WorldCom and its business prospects, as well as other firms including AT&T. Winstar, a client of Citigroup's Salomon Smith Barney investment banking units, sought bankruptcy protection in April 2001. In the biggest US bankruptcy to date, WorldCom filed under Chapter 11 a few months later.

10
Trading and the Risks of Derivatives Exposure

1 Introduction

In testimony before the Senate Committee on Governmental Affairs, on January 24, 2002, Frank Partnoy of the University of San Diego and formerly of Morgan Stanley, described Enron as, "at its core, a derivatives trading firm," whose activity "makes Long-Term Capital Management look like a lemonade stand." At its zenith, LTCM was not "a lemonade stand" but the Rolls-Royce of hedge funds. What Enron, LTCM, Bank of New England, and so many other financial institutions have in common is that they have been ill-fated derivatives' speculators. As a former investment banker, Partnoy detailed how Enron had used derivatives dealings with its 3,000-plus off-balance sheet subsidiaries and partnerships to shield volatile assets from quarterly financial reporting and artificially inflate the value of many of its assets. As the preceding chapters have documented, Enron used these manipulations to:

- Hide repeated speculative losses
- Hide huge debts incurred in financing unprofitable new ventures, and
- Inflate the value of its stock in spite of economic downturn and of non-performing business units. According to Frank Partnoy's Congressional testimony, most of what Enron represented as its core business divisions were not making money and it also appears that the same was true of the profits and losses of Enron's derivatives operations, as we saw in Chapter 9. More cases of losses concerning derivative financial instruments are presented in this chapter.

Andrew S. Fastow, Enron's CFO, used shell companies and dummy accounts, rigging its valuation methodology to create false profit entries and cover the losses from the derivatives which it traded in increasingly large amounts. The similarities between the Bankers Trust case in 1994 and Enron's case in 2001 illustrate how derivatives can be used to inflate the value of assets and help companies seem solvent, when in reality they are not.

In many respects, Enron reflects the aftermath of a fatal convergence between financial and energy deregulation. In its Securities and Exchange Commission (SEC) filings, Enron described itself as an investment bank. Testimony before the US Congress detailed the extent to which it was a derivatives trader rather than an energy company. At the same time, however, it was free of any supervision by the Federal Reserve, Office of the Comptroller of the Currency, and Federal Deposit Insurance Corporation (FDIC). Enron's reported $200 billion derivatives portfolio paled by comparison with the holdings of big banks, but then in several of the markets where it gambled, like telecom bandwidth (see Chapter 8), Enron was just getting started as a major player in derivatives instruments. But Enron was not the only supposedly industrial company to speculate in finance:

- GM with GMAC and GE with GE Capital are two more examples among many
- Figure 10.1 documents that, while manufacturing output fell, derivatives exposure boomed.

In a leveraged economy, losses can come from many sides. The $105 billion drop in assets at J.P. Morgan Chase during the fourth quarter of 2001 (see section 4) suggested that the bank's derivatives losses were mounting. Hidden in complex off-balance sheet structures and shell partnerships of the Enron type, derivatives exposure can eat the flesh of companies which think they are immune from failure – when in reality they are digging their own grave.

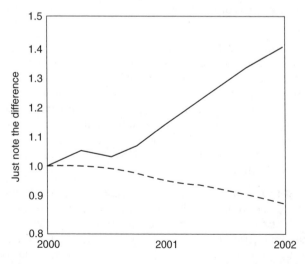

Figure 10.1 While US manufacturing falls, derivatives soar, US, 2000–2

2 The leverage obtainable with derivative financial instruments

The Basel Committee on Banking Supervision advises that when banks oper-
ate with very high leverage they increase their vulnerability to adverse economic events, and therefore enhance the risk of failure. The Bank for
International Settlements (BIS) defines "leverage" as "a low ratio of capital
to total assets."[1] Figure 10.2 gives a snapshot of the allocation of leveraged
capital among different investment channels.

All banks are leveraged, but some are much more leveraged than others.
Other things equal, the most leveraged of all financial institutions are the
hedge funds, as well as those companies which emulate hedge funds'
behavior – Enron being an example. Few institutions truly appreciate that
leverage is a two-edged sword. Its undisciplined use is the single most important reason why modern companies go bust at unexpected moments and a
surprisingly large amount of traders lose money in the futures market.

The *futures market* offers a great deal of leverage, because of the way in
which it works. Initial good faith deposits, known as a *margin* (not to be con-
fused with a margin for stocks) is usually at 3 percent–10 percent of contractual value. On average, this makes leveraging 20 or more times up
feasible – and much more than that if one works on borrowed capital. The
high leverage made possible through modern financial instruments sees to

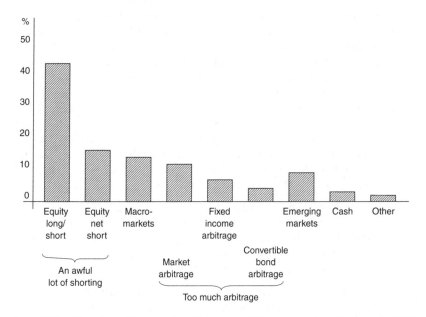

Figure 10.2 Allocation of leveraged capital among different investment channels, 2002

it that among its other functions the futures market functions as a supply of capital of last resort. It provides *virtual money* to players who cannot get cash elsewhere in the market, for whatever reason. At the same time, however, leverage makes futures and forwards a fragile business prone to accidents.

The lack of prudential supervision makes these conditions worse. This is most visible with hedge funds and the *alternative investments* they offer to institutional investors and consumers.[2] Big hedge funds, some 400 of them out of a total population of nearly 6,000, are watched by regulators for the threat they might pose in terms of systemic risk, but regulators should also take such risks under real control. Only a series of debacles in 2001–2 prompted the SEC to launch an investigation in May 2002 regarding the representation to investors and bad valuation of hedge funds assets.

High leverage and low ethics are at the roots of these ills, and both were demonstrated in Enron, WorldCom, and many others. The lack of accountability increases the magnitude of the problems: the high risk of futures and other geared deals is largely a consequence of failing to exercise control over one's business activities, as well as of being careless about their aftermath. One of the ironies of over-high leverage is that:

- People and entities are doing financial transactions which they don't understand, and
- They equally fail to appreciate that they are sitting on a time bomb.

One of the best examples of the toxic effects of overleverage, and of the consequences of big egos, was the virtual bankruptcy of Long-Term Capital Management (LTCM) in September 1998. Financial institutions and many other companies failed to appreciate that high gearing through both complex instruments and overvalued equity in the stock market would lead to bubbles. The Japanese authorities in the late 1980s, and the American regulators ten years later, allowed a speculative bubble to grow. Both cases ended badly because they defied the lessons taught by economic history. At no time in the past have assets bubbles of such magnitude been deflated in an orderly way, because it is not possible to hit four birds – curbing fraud, ensuring greater transparency, protecting unsophisticated investors, and leading the economy back to a safe harbor with one well-placed stone. The readjustment is always painful, as evidenced by:

- The crash of the French Banque Royale
- The Mississippi bubble
- The South Seas bubble
- The Nikkei Index/real estate bubble, and
- The NASDAQ and European tech bubbles of the late 1990s.

Augmented by creative accounting, which inflates earnings figures and hides losses through derivatives, excesses in assets valuations led to major collapses with equities going down 80 percent, 90 percent or more. Investors are practically never forewarned. In the case of the Nikkei and NASDAQ bubbles, for instance, nobody wrote bearish reports in Tokyo or on Wall Street, when there was still time to prick the ballooning prices and let the hot air out.

Neither, as has been shown in retrospect, have people learned anything from adversity. In the mid-to-late 1980s, the Japanese attributed the very high price/earnings (P/E) ratios of their companies to "local accounting rules" that permitted entities to understate earnings to keep their taxes low. They also argued that cross-holding of stock was instrumental in propping prices up, because fewer shares were available for trading. In fact, the opposite was true:

- When the Tokyo stock market caved in, cross-holding became a millstone for Japanese companies, magnifying the amplitude of their fall
- But creative accounting prospered, particularly among Japanese banks which used it in the 1990s to develop a new generation of balance sheet cosmetics.

Technology, media and telecommunications (TMT) provide another example of the fatal aftermath of the high-leverage factor. The beating the market eventually gave to TMT stocks in 2000–2 is characteristic of *disorderly deleveraging*. Of course, this is not an unheard-of phenomenon; the difference is that in the first years of the twenty-first century it happened on a grand scale.

In recent financial history, one of the first technology equities to rise then go down was Memorex. The value of this stock rose and rose to $96, then went straight down to $2 and Memorex fell off the trader's radar screen. In 2002, WorldCom and many other TMT companies repeated the experience; either they asked for protection from bankruptcy, or they ran into much deeper trouble than they had ever expected.

Superleveraging combined with creative accounting is widely practiced in developing markets. In the past, this combination was synonymous with lack of sophistication. In 1980 and thereafter it was possible to buy equities in Kuwait with postdated checks – up to millions worth of equities. Nearly everybody was doing it. Then, as the bubble burst, the pyramiding of postdated checks crashed:

- Today, financial trickery has become synonymous with sophistication, rather than the lack of it
- But this, too, however, is reaching its limits. In 2003 there were blacklists circulating in the global derivatives market, enumerating institutions too shaky to trade with.

For a few years, Enron gave respectability to this practice. Stocks going higher and higher then busting, and trades whose underlay is hollow, which teach that anything can happen in a leveraged market – with terrible consequences. Lack of rigorous risk control makes matters worse, because there are a lot of people who do not understand what is going on, and who do not appreciate the wisdom of applying the brakes.

3   Enron's use of energy swaps

Swaps are transactions in which two parties exchange cash flow for a predetermined period on a specified notional principal amount. This notional principal is never exchanged, but it constitutes the contract's legal reference. Interest rate swap contracts, for instance, usually represent the contractual exchange of fixed and floating rate payments of a single currency, based on a notional amount and an interest reference rate.

Foreign currency swaps generally involve the exchange of two different currency principal balances at inception, re-exchanged at a specified future date at an agreed-upon rate. Foreign currency interest rate swaps also include the exchange of interest payments based on the two different currencies:

- Notional balances, and
- interest reference rates.

Credit default swaps (CDS) are instruments where the seller promises to pay the buyer an amount equal to the loss that would be incurred on holding an underlying reference asset as a result of a defined credit event. The buyer is not required to hold the underlying reference asset but pays the seller a credit protection fee expressed in basis points. The amount of this fee is dependent on the credit spread of the reference asset.

Energy swaps, in which Enron specialized, follow these rules. The term refers to the widespread practice of energy and telecom companies, particularly the newer ones, selling each other capacity on their networks, booking the sales as revenues and the costs as capital expenditures. This unethical creative accounting helps them to overstate their revenue, thereby misinforming investors. Enron improved on this, counting its gross sales of energy as revenues without deducting the amount it had paid for that energy. This made Enron seventh on the *Fortune* 500 revenue list in 2000, and fifth in 2001, despite its bankruptcy.[3]

A similar case can be made about booking and reporting business connected to energy forwards and futures (the former are traded over the counter, the latter in established exchanges). Superficially, energy forwards and futures look like any other energy trade. In reality, however, there is a major difference. While with all other futures and forwards contracts there is a *lead time* between the deal and the delivery of the commodity, with energy forwards and futures delivery must take place in real time. This provided a golden opportunity for creative accounting practices, misrepresentation of profit and loss, and misinformation of investors.

Nothing seems to have been learned from the late 1990s, specifically from the failure of Bankers Trust because of such derivatives deals. Yet this is a first-class example of how fast a bank, or any other company, can sink because of the toxic waste and associated legal risk from derivatives exposure. At the beginning of the 1990s, Bankers Trust was a merchant bank selling its derivatives expertise to a growing number of clients, supported by its state-of-the-art information technology (IT) and mathematical models. Yet, even the best game plan can turn belly up. Bankers Trust's derivatives holdings had exploded by 1993–4 after a series of six successive Federal Reserve interest rate hikes which followed a string of interest rate cuts. The aftermath was chaos in the overall derivatives markets, and most particularly in the mortgage-backed securities (MBS) market. Rumors that Bankers Trust was insolvent began to circulate. In March 1994 the Granite hedge fund collapsed and by April Kidder Peabody, a leader in mortgage-backed securities, was first destabilized and then failed.

As the market focused its attention to the huge exposure assumed with derivatives, investors lost millions, some went to court. Gibson Greetings filed suit against Bankers Trust, accusing it of fraud. Investigations by the SEC and Commodities Futures Trading Commission (CFTC) revealed that derivatives traders at Bankers Trust had misinformed Gibson about the value of the instrument the bank had sold them.

Unfortunately for Bankers Trust, the Gibson Greetings case was followed by other derivatives-related court action by Procter & Gamble, Sinopec, Unipec, and Air Products. Eventually, the Fed and Treasury effectively took control of Bankers Trust and sold it off. But, as in the case of Enron, what remained after Deutsche Bank's acquisition of the bank was just a shadow of the once-proud institution.

Theoretically, the 1991–4 timeframe was the ideal environment for new financial instruments to provide protection to investors and to help the bank itself safeguard its assets. In practice, as in so many other cases, the real goal of using derivatives was not hedging but gambling and profits. Enron and many other companies demonstrated that nothing had been learned from the failure of Bankers Trust and the Bank of New England.

Like Bankers Trust, Enron thought that a novel derivatives instrument (energy swaps) would be its way to decream the market. As we saw in Chapter 8, Enron was able to escape the prudential supervision of CFTC, but creative accounting can turn crisis into opportunity only in the very short term. Bad debts have the nasty habit of blowing up at the most inopportune moment.

4 J.P. Morgan Chase's derivatives exposure

Credit institutions are always subject to the unexpected consequences of bad deals. On January 1, 2002, J.P. Morgan Chase was America's second-largest bank with $694 billion in assets, behind Citigroup with $1.05 trillion in assets but ahead of Bank of America with $622 billion. The three, which easily outdistanced the rest of US financial institutions, were followed by Wachovia ($330 billion), Wells Fargo ($308 billion), Bank One ($269 billion), FleetBoston ($204 billion), US Bancorp ($171 billion), National City ($106 billion), and SunTrust ($105 billion).

No cracks were visible to the naked eye in this constellation, except the fact that at the end of the third quarter of 2001, J.P. Morgan Chase had reported $799 billion in assets, which meant that in the third quarter of 2001 the bank had lost $105 billion in assets. J.P. Morgan Chase's explanation for this drop was that the majority of the reduction reflected the resolution of the industry-wide clearing and settlement problems experienced in September of that year. The existence of major industry-wide derivatives problems was denied before and after the September 11, 2001 (9/11) events.

On Wall Street, analysts were not happy with this explanation of a sudden drop in assets of more than 13 percent, with the result that the bank's market capitalization dropped sharply. On December 31, 2000, when the acquisition of J.P. Morgan by Chase Manhattan was completed, the newly christened J.P. Morgan Chase & Co had a market capitalization of $86 billion, of which $26.5 billion came from Morgan and $59.5 billion from Chase Manhattan.

Fourteen months later, on February 22, 2002, the combined institution had a market capitalization of $57 billion, less than Chase Manhattan's alone at the time of the merger. Some Wall Street bank watchers attributed this huge loss in capitalization to the staggering amount of derivatives, well beyond other banks' levels, amounting to roughly half of all US commercial bank derivatives portfolio. Others suggested the troubles were much deeper because:

- A loss equivalent to just under 0.2 percent of its derivatives portfolio would be sufficient to wipe out every penny of the bank's $42.7 billion in equity capital
- The loss of $105 billion in assets corresponded to less than a 0.5 percent drop in the derivatives portfolio, which is a drop in the ocean, and
- There was also J.P. Morgan Chase's exposure to the failed Enron, Kmart, and Global Crossing, and also the troubled Tyco, in addition to its losses on loans to Argentina (WorldCom had not yet gone bust).

J.P. Morgan Chase had a polyvalent exposure to bankrupt Enron: beyond loans to the company, it was an investor in some of the Enron partnerships, bought Enron stock for investment funds it managed, and entered into derivatives deals with it – being a major player in the credit derivatives market, and selling credit derivatives with guarantees if Enron defaulted on its bond payments (see Chapter 9). These complex connections to a failed company amounted to an extraordinary toxic waste.

In early December 2001, after Enron's bankruptcy, J.P. Morgan Chase put its loan exposure to the company at $900 million, but a few weeks later was revealed that it had also incurred $1 billion in losses on deals it had done with Enron through Mahonia, the offshore Morgan affiliate in Jersey (the court case discussed in Chapter 9). Analysts became nervous when a news item in *Wall Street Journal* revealed that:

- The Federal Reserve Bank of New York was investigating these Mahonia transactions, and
- Its examiners were focusing on the fact that what were effectively loans to Enron seem to have been disguised as energy trades.

As Chapter 9 has explained, these prepays meant that Enron got the money, but kept the debt off its books. Theoretically J.P. Morgan Chase protected itself against a possible Enron default on the Mahonia transactions by buying credit guarantees from insurance companies. In practice, when Enron filed for bankruptcy and Morgan tried to collect, the insurance companies refused to pay, claiming the deals were not legitimate transactions. This case went to court and the reader is by now aware of the after-effects – and the reputational risk that went with it.

A bank lives on its reputation and the court travails with eleven insurance companies and with WestLB was bad news for J.P. Morgan. Some experts suggested that the extent to which the *Wall Street Journal, New York Times, Financial Times,* and other major financial newspapers were reporting the problems was an indication of how serious the troubles were. Holders of the bank's equity and debt were trying to protect themselves from a potential Morgan default. On Wall Street and in the City of London, financial analysts looked at the market's response as the price a credit institution paid for extracurricular activities. Their benchmark became a credit derivative which would pay off, in the event of a default on a $10 million Morgan bond. That particular option went from $35,000 at the end of January 2002, to $80,000 in late February 2002, a clear sign that institutional investors were growing increasingly nervous about the survivability of the credit institution. The bank's stock suffered, going under $20 in mid-September 2002, then hitting a low of $115.45 a share on October 9:

- In mid-April 2002, at $35, the bank stock had lost a third of its value since the merger
- By October 9, even this meager $35 was cut by another 56 percent.

Several analysts attributed the problems faced by J.P. Morgan Chase to a series of big-bank mergers that had culminated in the $30 billion merger of two of America's greatest financial icons, J.P. Morgan and Chase Manhattan (the three other banks in the megamerger were Chemical Banking, Manufacturers Hanover, and New York Trust). This led to an institution crippled by bad loans, an astronomical derivatives exposure, venture capital losses, and failing markets. Critics charged that the September 2000 megadeal was too expensive, poorly timed, and badly executed.

As the largest corporate lender in America, J.P. Morgan Chase turned up in almost every bad loan on Wall Street – Enron and WorldCom were only two examples. Beyond non-performing loans, losses of $1.3 billion in private equity caused the bank to miss earnings forecasts for four of the five quarters to March 31, 2002. Nor was globalization a great help, despite the fact that both Chase Manhattan and J.P. Morgan were very active internationally.

J.P. Morgan Chase faced an exposure of $10 billion to Japanese banks, a lot of money in potential private equity write-downs, and a $140 billion portfolio of standby credit lines which could be activated by financially shaky companies. The bank's greatest risk came from its derivatives portfolio which, in notional principal amount, stood at an unheard off $24 trillion on March 31, 2001, and zoomed to $26.5 a year later (the latest available information when this book was written). The irony is that this 10 percent:

- Was relatively small by derivatives trading standards, where year-to-year increases in toxic waste typically stand at the 25 percent–30 percent level
- On Wall Street, some expert saw this deceleration in J.P. Morgan Chase's derivatives portfolio growth as an indication that other banks had become more careful in trading with the institution, rather than as evidence of greater caution by its own management.

As Dr. Alan Greenspan, the Fed chairman, stated in his November 19, 2002, address to the Council of Foreign Relations (CFR), in Washington: "Derivatives, by construction, are highly leveraged... [their] Achilles heel is excess speculation."[4] This is made worse by the fact that, as we have just seen, a derivatives portfolio has the nasty habit of growing by 25 percent–30 percent per year.

While banks and their regulators talk of diversification of risk, mergers see to it that in terms of loans, derivatives financial instruments, and other products, the result is *concentration* of exposure. This is another reason why, in retrospect, the whole concept of megamergers is flawed. "It was a bit like stacking doughnuts," said a rival bank's chief executive. "The holes are all in the same place."

And there was also legal risk "I don't own J.P. Morgan because I think there is a lot of headline risk," said Anton V. Schutz, fund manager for Burnham Financial Services Fund, quoted in *BusinessWeek*.[5] The roster of investment banks legally exposed to the Enron débâcle included two of the merged bank's components, Chase Manhattan and J.P. Morgan, as well as Citigroup, Merrill Lynch, Crédit Suisse First Boston (CSFB), the Canadian Imperial Bank of Commerce, Bank of America, Barclays Bank, Deutsche Bank, and Lehman Brothers.

5   Derivatives, Fannie Mae, AIG, and Enron

Among the potential derivatives busts commanding attention in early 2002, in the aftershock of Enron's bankruptcy, was what, on February 20, 2002, the *Wall Street Journal* called "Fannie Mae Enron." Even the US Federal budget had a section on the increased risk at Fannie Mae and Freddie Mac, the two huge Federally backed real estate mortgage agencies which securitized their holdings quite aggressively. (Established in 1936 by the Roosevelt Administration. Fannie Mae stands for Federal National Mortgage Association. The Federal Home Mortgage Loan Corp., or Freddie Mac, was established in 1970 to perform functions similar to those of Fannie Mae – i.e. the discounting of mortgage loans made by credit institutions).

There were reasons for the concern expressed in the opening paragraph of this section. In 2001, the two agencies wrote down $7.4 billion due to derivatives losses.[6] Since then, their dependence on derivatives significantly increased. Others, fearing a derivatives implosion, pointed to the huge American Insurance Group (AIG), and J.P. Morgan Chase, the financial institution most exposed in derivatives, as we saw in section 4.

On January 1, 2002, the exposure of US commercial banks to the notional value of off-balance sheet derivatives stood at an estimated $55 trillion–$70 trillion, an increase of 33 percent over January 1, 2001. This gave the banks $93 in derivatives contracts for every dollar of equity capital, a most perilous condition. A year later, on January 1, 2003, there was a split in the experts' estimates regarding derivatives exposure in notional amounts:

- The more conservative guesstimates put the US banks exposure at the level of $70 trillion–$90 trillion, itself a scary figure
- But pessimistic guesstimates placed the global derivatives exposure at $300 trillion–$400 trillion, which would mean about $180 trillion–$240 trillion for US banks.

Even demodulated to the level of toxic waste, both the conservative and the pessimistic estimates are mind-boggling in exposure terms (see also section 6). All sorts of companies, including insurance companies such as the American International Group (AIG), as we shall see below, are hit by the risks they take with derivatives, and those at the tip of the iceberg are most obviously at greatest peril.

This rapid growth in the notional principal amount in inventoried derivatives contracts among US banks and other institutions is shown in Figure 10.3. This exposure is backed by "only" $6.6 trillion in assets and $586 billion in equity capital, according to some estimates I located during my research. A loss equivalent to less than 0.7 percent of the total derivatives portfolio would be sufficient to wipe out the entire capital of the American banking system, while a drop of 7 to 9 percent would zero-out all the deposited and managed assets, which after all belong to the depositors.

Next to J.P. Morgan Chase, Fannie Mae, Freddie Mac and AIG, other big financial companies at risk of a derivatives implosion are Deutsche Bank, Citigroup, Bank of America, Merrill Lynch, and General Electric Capital, in that order. In late November 2002, General Electric announced that it would

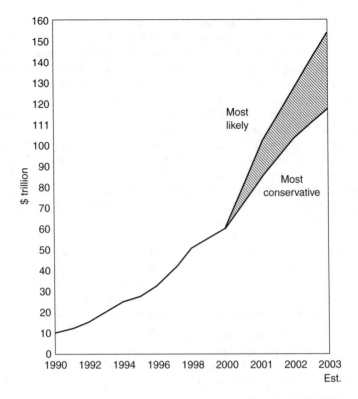

Figure 10.3   Derivatives exposure soars at US commercial banks, 1990–2003

inject $4.5 billion into GE Capital, in addition to adding $1.8 billion to its Employers Reinsurance business unit.

Other parties who in early 2003 were faced with challenging problems were brokers who not only arranged the sale of bonds from defunct companies like Enron to the public, but were also partners with now bankrupt entities in a number of the ventures including special-purpose vehicles (SPVs). Enron's partnerships (see Chapter 9) are an example. The surprise is that in many entities top management was not aware of the risks inherent in a derivatives-based financial system, coming not only from overexposure in derivatives but also from colossal leveraging:

- Markets are manipulated in order to make them very volatile,
- Then derivatives are sold as a measure of protection against volatility.

The extraordinary danger presented by such mega-speculations is aggravated by the fact that derivatives financial instruments can be used to hide a company's true financial condition, as in the case of Enron. Investigations by the Japanese government have brought to light numerous examples where Wall Street firms employed derivatives to help Japanese financial institutions and other companies hide losses.

An example of insurance companies which went for derivatives in a big way is AIG. The market opinion is that AIG has a large and growing participation in complex derivatives trades. AIG management suggests that, on the contrary, derivatives play an important part in reducing the company's overall risks.

The market's opinion, based what I heard in several meetings, was that AIG's credit exposure to derivatives, while below that of banks – was rapidly rising. It was $17 billion in 1999 and it became $33 billion in 2000, according to the company's annual reports – a nearly 100 percent increase in one year. Gross exposure grew from $435 billion to $544 billion[7] and this leads to some very interesting statistics:

- In 1999, with a $435 billion gross derivatives exposure, the toxic waste was $17 billion, corresponding to a demodulator of 25.5 (see section 6)
- Only a year later, in 2000, a gross exposure of $554 billion corresponded to a toxic waste of $33 billion. The demodulator had shrunk to about 16.8.

It is appropriate to recall that 1999 was a good year for business, confirmed by a demodulator of 25.5. Also 2000 was not a particularly bad year for the insurance industry (unlike 2001, because of 9/11). The demodulator shrinks not only in nervous markets, however, but also for other reasons, like poor risk management by companies. In AIG's case, the demodulator between gross and net derivatives exposure lost 30 percent in just one year. Part of the fall in AIG's share price in early 2002 could be explained by the market's suspicions about sophisticated but opaque forms of financial engineering. Apart from the toxic waste in its portfolio, the insurer was at the center of a dispute over off-balance sheet partnerships held by PNC Financial, a regional American bank, and some other deals. In a way reminiscent of certain Enron SIVs, some 800 AIG managers now own Starr International, a private company named after Cornelius Vander Starr, who in 1919 founded the group in Shanghai. Starr International is an SIV.

Off-shore residence is still another problem. AIG's proxy gives as its home a Bermuda PO box, yet according to the company's file in Bermuda's registry, its true home is in Panama. This makes the ownership structure of America's second-largest financial institution, for all practical purposes, immune to many aspects of American law and taxation.[8]

In January 2003, Wall Street became nervous about big companies registered in tax havens, because of after effects of President Bush's plan to eliminate the taxes investors pay on stock dividends. Buried in the fine print of the proposal to Congress was a condition which would strike a blow against corporate tax shelters by forcing companies to choose between slashing their own tax bills and ensuring dividend relief for their investors. For instance, a company that did not pay corporate income taxes thanks to different sorts of credits, offshore tax shelters, and the like, would find that the eligibility of its shareholders for dividend tax relief was very limited:

- Theoretically, this could push CEOs and CFOs to trim their reliance on tax breaks and tax havens
- In practice, it will quite likely make investors move away from equities of companies which persist in patronizing "tax optimization" policies.

"This is a big deal," said one congressional tax expert. "You are dramatically changing the economics of these tax preferences." Such a move will undermine the will of boards to condone corporate tax avoidance. How much the difference in terms of tax dollars might be is shown by one estimate which says that, among large companies, book earnings in 1998 exceeded taxable income by $287 billion.[9]

There is another reason why both regulators and analysts are nervous. Though AIG boasts of its dominance in various business lines and countries, it discloses only the broadest loss ratios. A source of its resilience is its policy of reinsuring about one-quarter of its underwriting. However, while this helps in spreading risk, no outsider really knows what business the company keeps and what business it cedes to third parties.

Analysts say that plenty of opportunities thus exist for creative accounting, as the example of Enron and so many other companies documents. September 11 also means that the insurer has some hefty losses. The destruction of the World Trade Center cost AIG more than $800 million in claims – and less than three months down the line, on December 2, 2002, the insurer was hit with a $69 million loss linked to Enron.

Practically every major company suffered from September 11, 2001, but not from Enron. Berkshire lost $2.4 billion from 9/11, and 2001 was its first non-profitable year. Swiss Re, the world's second-biggest reinsurer, put its cost from September 11 at nearly CHF 3 billion ($1.8 billion), but took heart from the fact reinsurance rates were rising while risk coverage was being cut.

6   Derivatives and the deregulation of financial institutions

Financial institutions in America and other G-10 countries won deregulation by convincing law makers and bank supervisors that they could manage their risks and put a cap on their complex new instruments as well as their conflicts of interest. The fact that some conflicts of interest can arise when investment banks and commercial banks are under the same roof was at the origin of the Glass–Steagall Act of the early 1930s, which divided investment banking from commercial banking. In their drive to kill the Glass–Steagall act, credit institutions argued that both investors and depositors would benefit from the resulting synergies between commercial and investment banking. But as the events of 2001–2 demonstrated, these assurances ring hollow. Big institutions have used deregulation to enrich themselves and they have favored big clients at the expense of other investors who have been uninformed, or even misinformed, about developments.

A growing number of investors now complain that they were absolutely in the dark about what has been going on in deals like those made by Enron and WorldCom – many of which were on the edge of the letter of the law, if not over it. Nor did they appreciate finding out that the banks in which they were investing were loaded with a gross and net derivatives exposure, making their equity even more fragile.

Lack of transparency and the accumulation of toxic waste work in synergy. As far as lack of transparency is concerned, the "see-no-evil" approach adopted by many companies who made billions in the 1990s is undetermined by the fact that many of these deals were flawed in terms of risk and return.

The bottom line is that if financial institutions do not take seriously the need to manage conflicts of interest, they risk a rollback of the market liberalization that characterized the 1990s. Many voices are being raised in this direction, making a new wave of re-regulation unavoidable in the longer run. Equally unavoidable is the salvaging of big banks through taxpayers' money, as reserve banks find themselves obliged to pull them out from the hecatomb in which they have fallen, because of their poorly studied loans and mammoth derivatives exposure.

This message was delivered by Federal Reserve Governor Ben Bernanke to a November 21, 2002, meeting of the Washington-based National Economics Club – where he promised the Fed would do whatever necessary "as many US dollars as it wishes, at essentially no cost."[10] This is of course misleading because "no cost" can turn into huge cost, as shown by the history of hyperinflation in Germany in the mid-1920s, which led to political upheaval and brought Adolf Hitler to power.

The reader will appreciate the rapid increase in risk-exposed assets which in most companies we have considered escaped top management's attention, by keeping in mind the fact that in their first incarnation derivatives were regarded as *hedges*. A hedge tends to be seen as effective if, at inception and throughout its life, the holder entity can expect:

- Changes in the fair value of cash flows of the *hedge item*
- Almost fully offset by the changes in the fair value or cash flows of the *hedging instrument*.

With derivatives, such equality of cash flows is largely theoretical and in practice is very rarely, if ever, the case. Banks therefore tend to regard a hedge as more or less effective if actual results are within a range of 80 percent–125 percent from its targeted fair value or cash flow. Entities adopt hedge accounting when they determine that a derivative is not so highly effective as a hedge, or if the derivative expires, is sold, terminates, or is exercised.

An effective hedging relationship is one in which the entity achieves more or less offsetting changes in fair value or cash flows for the risk being hedged. The opposite condition is that of *hedge ineffectiveness*, which represents the amount by which change(s) in fair value of the derivative differ from changes in the fair value of the hedged item by a certain margin. A similar statement is valid in terms of cash flows or other designated variables.

Fair value hedges primarily consist of interest rate swaps used to protect against changes in the fair value of fixed-rate medium- to longer-term debt, due to changes in market interest rates. Foreign currency interest rate swaps are also used as hedging instruments but measuring hedge effectiveness is more difficult because it involves both exchange rate and interest rate risk exposure of the underlying hedged debt instruments.

Cash flow hedges are interest rate swaps designed to protect against changes in cash flows of certain variable-rate debt issues. However, as we have already seen, the energy swaps made by Enron and continued by major money-center banks and other operators involved no hedging. They were pure P&L transactions often used to misrepresent sales and earnings and fudge the books:

- Derivatives lack transparency and "for profits" deals excel on that account
- By far the larger amount of derivatives traded today around the world is not for hedging but "for profits."

Figure 10.4 presents in a nutshell the pattern of distribution of derivatives trades, with North America in the lead. Whether it is or it is not a hedge, the *gross* exposure taken in a derivatives transaction is expressed through the notional principal amount, also called a *face amount*. This is specified by the contract, but it is rarely exchanged. It may be a number of shares, currency units, kilos, bushels, or other metrics specified in the derivatives contract, which establishes the counterparties' obligations based on this notional principal.

Section 5 brought to the reader's attention the difference between gross derivatives exposures expressed through a notional principal and net derivatives exposure. The latter is usually toxic waste derived from the face amount and inventoried in the portfolio. It is also an amount of losses which must be recognized in the entity's financial statement, in the aftermath of Statement of Financial Accounting Standards (SFAS) 133, published in June 1998.

Section 4 made the reference that conversion from gross to net derivatives exposure is done through *demodulation*.[11] The rationale behind this is found in the fact that the best approach to life, and the only one for effective risk management, is to ask what can go wrong and put in place some indicators which predict the red ink to be expected. Demodulation is an inversion. As the mathematician Carlo Jacobi advised: "Invert, always invert." It should be remembered that the notional principal amount is contractually specified;

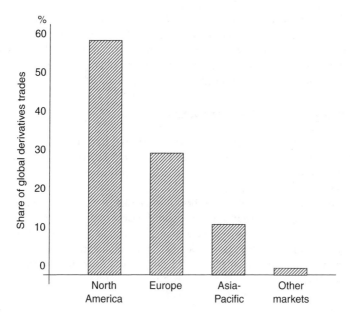

Figure 10.4 The distribution pattern of derivatives trades, with the US in the lead

therefore it is inescapable. The question is how much of the gross derivatives exposure is net exposure and so what should be the notional principal's divisor. This varies with:

- The type of instrument
- The distribution of values of the underlier
- The market's nervousness, and other factors.

While basically net derivatives exposure is market risk, it also has characteristics of credit risk. For instance in the case our bank "wins" but the counterparty is unable or unwilling to pay, then market risk gives way to credit risk. A case where the net derivatives exposure became credit risk is that of J.P. Morgan which "won" $480 million in a gamble, but South Korea's SK Securities, the loser, refused to pay. The case went to court.

Demodulation is becoming more popular and a number of institutions have moved or are currently moving away from the percentage rule of exposure which dominated in the early-to-mid-1990s into an analytical basis of *replacement value* of transactions with counterparties. This accounts for the notional principal reduced to a *credit equivalent* level:

- Using valuation and pricing formulas already employed in trading, and
- Doing worst-case tests of the computed replacement value until maturity of the transaction.

One of the best ways to proceed is to calculate the credit equivalent on the basis of a maximum of an envelope of possible replacement values during the lifetime of the product(s) under consideration. Financial products availing themselves of this procedure are interest rate swaps, interest rate options (caps, floors), swaptions, and other fixed-income options.

7   Ponzi games can have derivatives

Most derivative transactions relate to speculative trading activities and the buying and selling of toxic waste, not to hedging. Legitimate sales activities include product design, both structuring and marketing of derivative products for and to counterparties. The majority of these counterparties to derivatives deals today are correspondent banks. It is as if General Motors (GM) was selling more than half of its production of motor vehicles to Ford. Product design involving derivatives is creative accounting's counterpart. Trading involves market-making, positioning, and arbitrage. Market-making requires a system of quoting bid and offer prices to other market participants, with the intention of generating revenues based on spread and volume. Not everybody truly appreciates that there is an enormous difference between:

- A process whose purpose is equilibrium between supply and demand, and
- Supply *or* demand having a selection function, not one of equilibrium.

An example of the second bullet is credit derivatives and other credit risk transfer instruments, where capital arbitrage is the driver. Other examples include all those financial products where commissions are established on the basis of the volume of deals executed by the trader:

- The goal is to push the selection function in a way which generates more deals
- This is done without appropriate attention to the current and future risks assumed by the trader, the desk, and the bank.

There are also failures of risk control. Effective risk control in practice requires real-time positioning, done in an accurate and documented manner. *Positioning* includes the identification and managing of market risk positions, with the expectation of profiting from favorable movements in prices, rates or indices. This should be an integral part of arbitrage which concerns itself with identifying and taking advantage from price differentials between markets and products.

Relatively, but only relatively, exposure tends to be lower with those financial instruments which are standardized in regard to their notional principal amount and settlement date(s). These products are usually exchange-traded, designed to be bought and sold in active markets. But the majority of derivatives are custom-made for individual counterparties, typically exchanged over the counter at negotiated prices. This is both the strength and the weakness of derivatives:

- It is a strength because it makes feasible the design of flexible instruments adjusted to the counterparty's desires
- It is a weakness because derivatives are like the genie in Pandora's box: when it escapes control it can bring disaster.

This is exactly what hit LTCM and Enron, and not only those two entities. While derivative financial instruments are often marketed as hedges they may also turn into customized confidence games, of which Carlo Ponzi would have been very proud. Here is an example. This Ponzi scheme seems to have been set up by Sam S. Brown Jr., a one-time oil promoter in the US and Leslie W. Chorlton, a British subject.

In Atlanta, Brown formed SBC Chorco Inc. and allegedly solicited funds from investors to finance Chorlton's efforts to free up an $800 billion fortune that Chorlton purportedly had amassed by facilitating the trading of commercial paper among European banks.[12] In a way not dissimilar to what Fastow and Enron did with their partnerships, it seems to not have been difficult to convince people the fortune was being wrongfully held by the banks, as Brown promised $10 million per $1,000 invested. According to the SEC it took three years to discover that none of the Chorlton fortune had turned up, or was likely to do so. In its 1992 suit, the SEC said that Brown had

- Sold unregistered securities and
- Was promising astronomical returns.

The common failure is that of not seeing the risks involved in this kind of foggy deal. All people see is "an opportunity they can not refuse." In Enron's LJM2 and Raptor 1 cases, Merrill Lynch investment bankers put millions of their own money and that of their investors on the block, with:

- No deep analysis of risk and return, and
- No other documentation than the statements of Enron's CFO in an investment conference.

Post-mortem, Enron lawyer Jordan Mintz said he wrote Jeffrey K. Skilling seeking his signature on LJM deal-approval sheets – which he believed policy required. Skilling never responded,[13] but in his Congressional testimony he stated he did not recall seeing the documents or Mintz's memo. Skilling also claimed the approval sheets "provided" for his signature, but did not require it. The question was asked: "Was Skilling involved in restructuring the Raptor vehicles, which let Enron avoid $500 million in pretax charges?" In his testimony, Skilling said, he told the Enron board's investigators that he was informed only generally about the Raptors' problems and had no real involvement. He told Congress that he might have called the accountant, but when asked if he had approved the Raptors' restructuring, he responded: "Not to my recollection."

Others, however, had a different opinion. According to the Enron Board Committee's report, evidence from senior Enron employees showed that Skilling was aware of the problems and was very interested in the resolution of the Raptors' issues. There are some curious parallels in these stories concerning investor misinformation and pyramiding of claims. But since the Enron case is still far from having been tested in court, it is better to look at this matter as an alleged pyramiding, while the Brown/Chorlton affair is the real thing.

As was to be expected, misfortune struck those investors foolish enough to put their money in the Brown/Chorlton deal. A Columbia, MO, real estate developer, for instance, invested $650,000 together with a colleague. The SEC lawsuit estimated that Brown raised more than double that from investors, on the grounds that the capital was needed to make a $75 billion bribe to the Swiss Banking Commission to finally free the Chorlton treasure.

This was not the only deal on record connected to the Chorlton imaginary fortune. In a scheme resembling a derivatives deal, James B. Gilmore, an Atlanta-area promoter, tried to convince many of Brown's original investors that Chorlton and Brown had engineered a secret side deal to cut them out. Gilmore raised more than $2 million to fund a European investigation by selling unregistered securities, dubbed "war chest receipts," to more than 1,000 new and existing investors, the SEC said.

According to the SEC, investors then started to get fearful for their money and their fears intensified when Chorlton and his wife were found strangled near their French home in July, 1991, in what police described as a "mob-style" murder. Gilmore was not discouraged by this turn of events. He told his investors, who were becoming impatient, that:

- He had located the Chorlton fortune, and that it totaled $1.5 trillion, and
- He had obtained a court order requiring the banks holding the funds to disburse them to him.

The SEC said that the Scottish lawyer who conducted the investigation for Gilmore found that the estate was worth no more than $350,000, the ratio between what Gilmore claimed and what the SEC found was 2,800,000 percent. (The Rolls-Royce of hedge funds, LTCM, had a leverage of only 35 percent.)

The lesson to retain is that after the money of the first "investors" was eaten up, another wave of people allowed themselves to be victimized. As Gilmore's promised payout date kept getting postponed, some of the original "investors" were apparently making money on their own by selling sub-interests in their shares to others, who resold them yet again. It sounds like the promises made about alternative investments in the early twenty-first century.[14]

Finally, in August, 1992, a third scheme was unleashed. The SEC contends that Gilmore began selling unregistered shares in International Trading Inc. (ITI), an imaginary company described in Gilmore-produced literature as a Liberian gold and diamond trading firm. Shares were priced at $100 each and were paired with a free warrant said to be redeemable "by next April 1, 1993" (note the date) for $200,000, once the Chorlton proceeds were obtained. According to the SEC, the supposed value of the Chorlton estate was now upped to $10 trillion.

Among those who bought this sales pitch was a Burlington, CO based fertilizer salesman. He headed a syndicate that invested $160,000 in Brown's original deal, and also put some money into ITI. By October the SEC obtained a court order that froze whatever assets remained under the control of Gilmore and ITI and Brown went bankrupt. As with Enron, Global Crossing, Adelphia, WorldCom and so many other cases in 2000–3, investors were left to lick their wounds.

11

Investors, the Securitization of Bad Loans, and the Probability of Default

1 Introduction

As reported in a *New York Times* article, Citibank, a major lender to Enron, apparently protected itself from a significant portion of its Enron's credit risk by passing it on to investors in credit-linked bonds. What the article did not mention, however, was that Citibank accomplished this risk transfer through an innovative transaction that combined credit derivatives and insurance with traditional securitization.[1]

Something comparable can be said about instrument design features, regarding the "Bistro" transactions invented in 1997–8 by J.P. Morgan. As synthetic securitizations, these became the tip of the iceberg of a major new trend in structured finance. Today, the name of the game is an increasing use of securitization to *manage risk* rather than to sell assets or raise funds. J.P. Morgan Chase seemed to have perfected this method with WorldCom. While experts on Wall Street and in the press suggest that its loans exposure to the now bankrupt telecommunications company amounted to $17 billion, the bank itself says that its loans exposure to Enron was only $20 million. Presumably nearly $17 billion was securitized and sold to investors through the channel of the capital markets (see section 7).

Asset-backed securitization (ABS) and credit derivatives correlate. While originally the idea behind securitizing debt instruments was to recover invested capital, improve the credit institution's liquidity, and move forward with new deals, today a factor which is rapidly gaining importance is that of an alternative means for credit risk management. There are two approaches to securitization:

- Issuance *by the bank itself*: In this case, the credit institution stills holds in its balance sheet the loans and associated credit risk/interest rate risk, but it is covered by the securities sold to investors
- Issuance through a *special purpose vehicle* (SPV): With this approach, credit risks are transferred out of the bank's balance sheet. This is where credit risk management comes in. Notice, however, that this transfer can also

be effected through *credit derivatives*, which is the fastest-growing segment of the OTC derivatives market.

From 1998, when it started really moving in connection with corporate loans, to the end of 2002, the credit derivatives market increased nearly tenfold, to about $1 trillion. Over the same period, syndicated loans grew by 70 percent per year, leading many analysts to suggest that several credit institutions had chosen the method of unloading the credit risks in their portfolio to investors.

2   Capital markets defined

Capital markets, as we know them today, are a late nineteenth-century development. They were invented to serve the needs of railroads for vast sums of development capital. The modern capital market was fathered in the US, and with it came investment banking houses which it made relatively easy for industrials and transport firms to tap a wide pool of European and American capital. As the largest US industrial enterprises augmented their resources through equity sold in the capital market, between the 1880s and 1914, the market prospered, though there were also several downturns and some panics. Capital market instruments eventually created a self-feeding cycle for capital needs, and the capital market grew with them.

To appreciate the original self-feeding cycle one has to remember that railroads transported ore to the furnaces, and the mills produced steel for the rails. The construction of railroads and rapid urban growth gave work to unskilled immigrants, and the new workforce not only provided labor for growing industrial enterprises but also increased the demand for their products. This required still more capital. The rest is history.

But during the twentieth century the role of the capital markets was changing. A growing number of people and institutions look at such markets not only as sources of capital but also as risk management instruments. This was the outgrowth of a new trend in loans, investments, and trading which saw:

- The sources of financial losses become more diverse than ever before
- And the possibility for spreading risk simultaneously increasing by leaps and bounds.

This was a post-1945 development, more specifically of the mid-to-late 1990s. An equally modern development is that of using novel ways of insurance, by expanding the classical range of activities of the insurance industry. For instance, following the trade-related losses at Barings, Sumitomo, and other entities, in the 1990s one of Lloyd's syndicates, SVB, began offering "rogue trader" insurance. This reimburses a firm for damages sustained from unauthorized trading that has been concealed from management's attention. Rogue trader insurance is the forerunner of the operational risk insurance promoted by Basel II with its emphasis on capital requirements for operational risk.[2] The first reported buyer of this new type of insurance was Chase Manhattan. It bought $300 million in rogue trader cover for a rumored annual premium of $2 million, or 2/3 of 1 percent. This is one of the best examples regarding insurance cover as an alternative to holding capital for operational risks reasons. But, as we shall see in section 3, there is also credit risk-linked insurance.

Capital requirements, insurance coverage, and capital market action are themselves a self-feeding cycle. The most impressive characteristic of a capital market, particularly of the US capital market, lies in the vast financial resources which it can command, provided business confidence prevails. That is precisely why it is so important to preserve business confidence in capital markets through reliable financial reporting and a rigorous framework of laws, regulation, and supervision.

The second most fundamental characteristic of a capital market is the democratization of credit and investment. The capital market is not an engine in the hands of an oligarchy of "capitalists"; it is open to everyone who has the market's confidence. This is both a result and a precondition of doing business. Market confidence is the reason why disasters like Enron, Adelphia Communications, Global Crossing, WorldCom, Tyco, and so many others are what capital markets do not need: they destroy business confidence well beyond these entities themselves. This process of destruction has come at the worst possible moment as capital markets start to play a third major role: that of *insurer of last resort*. Insurance companies themselves are turning to the capital markets as a sort of "super-insurer."

Financial institutions and industrial organizations see in capital markets a yet further role: a means of transferring away from their balance sheet primarily credit risk, but also some market risk. But there are limits: overdoing risk transfers, and burning the counterparties, can have the potentially disastrous result of killing business confidence. Prior to examining this issue of risk transfer by means of capital markets, it is therefore appropriate to take a closer look at the evolution of credit insurance, as well as its current status. This is the theme of section 3.

3   The evolution of credit insurance

Credit risk protection insurance has developed from an original function of providing commercial and industrial firms with cover for outstanding receivables, protecting against risk of buyer insolvency, default, or plain bad will – in short the counterparty's inability or unwillingness to perform. Risk protection insurance may also support financing needs:

- Reducing the risk of non-payment of trade receivables
- Permitting the company to borrow at lower interest rates, and
- Assisting the operations of the company's trade credit department.

Credit insurers went through significant consolidation during the years since 1988. Today, there are five leading companies in this domain. In order of revenues, these are: Euler, Coface, Gerling, Hermes, and NCM, sharing among themselves some 80 percent of the market. Competition is inducing credit insurers to provide new products as well as to unbundle services like credit information, debt collection, and lines of credit for commercial purchases.

Experts look at credit insurance as a growing business. During the 1990s, premium growth in Europe averaged about 5 percent per year. In the US, premium growth was more rapid – about 10 percent per year, but from a smaller base, because in the post-Second World War years credit insurance was more popular in Europe than elsewhere.

Technology and globalization, too, affected credit insurance. The internet is having an impact on credit insurance, particularly in conjunction with the credit insurers themselves. It helps sharpen their expertise in credit risk management, and promotes their ability to use their proprietary databases worldwide.

Mining information on trade receivables makes underwriting credit much more efficient. Credit information is also being used to provide new services in credit control, in addition to credit insurance proper – for instance, continuous monitoring of creditworthiness of different insured customers, better servicing of account receivables, and the optimizing of payment and settlement procedures.

Figure 11.1 shows in a snapshot the three-party agreement between insurer, seller, and buyer. This process capitalizes on the fact that buying on credit from suppliers is the single largest source of short-term company debt. Trade credit accounts for up to half the total assets of a typical non-financial company, but when goods are sold on credit, there is a risk to sellers that

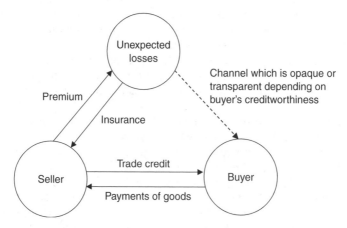

Figure 11.1 The credit insurer as a meta-layer in the seller–buyer nexus

their customers will pay late, or that they will default. Credit insurers aim to enhance the quality of their services, by improving communication with clients and speeding the claims process. Reliable information is key to effective credit insurance. Among the data needed from the credit insurance client are company identification, the value of the trade, and the date and place of sale. Efficient handholding is very important because while technological developments have improved the exchange of information between insurer and insured, there remain frequent personal interactions, particularly in sorting out claims that have gone or might go sour. Policyholders like to be in personal contact with insurance providers.

The concept underpinning this discussion serves to clarify how credit insurance works for banks. The concept is that by buying credit insurance and paying a premium for it, sellers *transfer to the insurance company* the risk associated with default by their buyers:

- Credit insurers manage this risk by holding a diversified portfolio
- They back it up with equity, and use their expertise in assessment of creditworthiness – and therefore – of the probability of default.

In the early stage of this process, the insurer served foreign clients, but dealt with domestic risks. In the next stage, the credit insurer sold its services in countries which required local expertise to monitor trade credit risk. Now, most credit insurers offer both export and domestic credit insurance, as with globalization the boundaries between the two are becoming blurred. A further distinction to keep in mind is between:

- Insuring a standalone, specific account or deal in a credit sense, and
- Offering whole turnover insurance, which covers the entire portfolio of receivables of a client company, not selected or sorted by risk.

Credit insurance coverage may be whole-amount (proportional) or non-proportional. In a proportional insurance contract, the insured receives indemnification for every insured loss. Its amount depends on the retention, that is the non-insured percentage. In a non-proportional insurance contract, of the excess of loss or catastrophe type, the contract provides a layer of cover for losses beyond a certain level. This is the right approach for firms that want to insure themselves against the risk of single large losses, by paying a commensurate premium.

Premiums for credit insurance can be high, and to keep costs in control, there are deductible alternatives. Under a whole turnover for a proportional contract, the deductible is usually between 5 percent and 20 percent, and it largely depends on the quality of receivable accounts the client companies trade.

The safeguarding of accounts receivable is essentially a trading decision which, however, has a financial corollary. Typically the creditworthiness of only the most regular clients is known in advance to the seller, but even this information may not be available to the bank financing the seller organization.

Therefore, companies with credit insurance are able to get better credit terms from banks.

Some banks also require credit insurance before they provide financing, because credit insurers can provide value to the seller by supplying the services needed at each stage of the settlement chain. To benefit from this value differentiation, seller companies must decide on the proper ratio between self-retention and credit risk transfer.

Another basic decision regards exceptions. All of the above factors are milestones when the seller comes to evaluate the creditworthiness of a prospective client. Information has a cost, and internal information costs increase with the heterogeneity of the insurer's client base as well as with its globality. On the other hand, without reliable information credit insurance becomes very risky. A similar statement is valid in connection with buying securitized financial products.

4   The role played by securitization

The securitization of all types of loans – from mortgages to auto loans, credit card receivables, and corporates – is itself a sort of credit insurance – with the capital market as an intermediary between the issuer and the investors. For all the talk about return on assets (ROA) and return on equity (ROE), banks care less about profitability and more about staying in business. Securitization provides them with an opportunity for doing so:

• To survive, credit institutions need both to earn revenues and to be in charge of their risks
• If they securitize some of their assets in the banking book, they recover loaned out capital and at the same time discharge part of their credit risk.

The process of securitization is based on the packaging of pools of loans and other financial receivables, with an appropriate level of credit enhancement. This is followed by the distribution of securities to investors based on these packages. Securitization permits banks and corporates to have an alternative to on-balance sheet lending. It also:

• Permits improved use of capital at a time of balance sheet constraints, and
• Provides investors with a broader range of opportunities.

Ultimately, securitization conveys more of a sense of credit risk transfer than anything else, particularly if what is securitized is non-performing loans or debt of companies which may be approaching default in the foreseeable future (see section 6). While the process of securitization itself was invented in the mid-1920s, the practice really took off in the mid-1970s with mortgage-backed securities (MBS), in the mid-1980s with auto loans and other instruments, as shown in Figure 11.2, and in the mid- to late-1990s with corporate loans (there is more on this below).

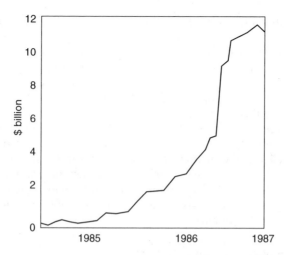

Figure 11.2 US cumulative offering of securities backed by auto loans, credit-card receivables, and computer leases, 1985–7

Asset-backed securities (ABS), which include auto loans, card receivables, and several other products, are sold to institutional investors and the public. According to the Bond Market Association, by the end of 2002 there were more than $1.5 trillion in ABS outstanding. Of this total amount in US securitized consumer credit:

- 28 percent were backed by credit-card payments
- 17 percent were backed by home equity payments
- 14 percent were backed by auto-loan payments, and
- The other 41 percent were diverse instruments, among them factoring of receivables.

Yet, while $1.5 trillion in securitized consumer credit is an impressive amount, as 2002 came to a close asset-backed securities accounted for only 7 percent or so of the $20 trillion + US bond market. What's more, ABS was falling well short of the $4.5 trillion in MBS, and the $4 trillion in corporate bonds (there is more on this below). On the other hand, ABS did play an important role in the capital market.

The careful reader will bear in mind that the effect – and, indeed primary goal – of MBS, ABS, and credit derivatives is to take the loans off the banks' books, transferring them to the owners of these securitized products. Because of deteriorating credit rating, shifting losses from banks to pension funds and other institutional investors, as well as private individuals, has been a rewarding strategy for the securitizers – which cannot be said about the buyers of these securitized instruments.

The story of securitized corporates is that of *credit derivatives*,[3] a fast-growing market (see also section 5). Credit derivatives are sold as hedges and portfolio diversification instruments, but they don't really qualify for this label. This statement is not intended to throw doubt on the usefulness of credit derivatives as financial instruments, particularly on their underwriter, but rather to make the reader aware that:

- Credit derivatives can involve significant exposure
- This becomes most significant in a market where credit risk is on the rise.

There are strategic and financial objectives relating to securitization of all sorts, from MBS to ABS to credit derivatives. The crucial variables are potential market, the types of assets that will be securitized, and their relevant structures. An integral part of the process is the calculation of possible credit losses, and the basis risk relating to the parties and their roles.

It is the details of assets included in the pool which determine whether it is worth doing securitization. Surprisingly, this question is not always asked by the issuers or the investors of securitized instruments. Nor is the probability of default of the loans in the pool properly analyzed in all cases.

In spite of these shortcomings, as shown in Figure 11.3, the market for asset-backed securities both in the US and in Europe continues to grow – in

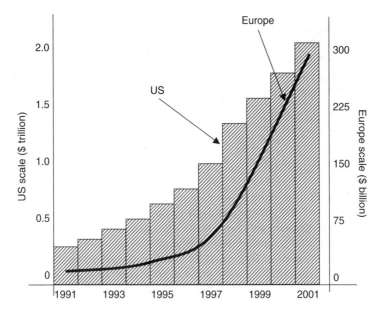

Figure 11.3 Asset-backed securities, US and Europe, 1991–2001

Source: BIS, *72nd Annual Report,* Basel, 2002.

Europe much faster than in the US, but starting from a smaller base. The advice the reader should remember from this discussion relates to the need for rigorous analytics to properly identify risk and return. Unless assumed credit risk is clearly defined ABS may be an investment the holders may come to regret.

One of the aspects of securitization that is worth examining is the evolution of the process of *disintermediation* which affects the banking system. Because major companies can tap the capital market directly, banks now perform less lending to industrial borrowers than was the case in the past. On the one hand, the money flow between investors and borrowers is still funneled through the banking system, but on the other the capital markets play the most crucial role because they influence the process of securitization in a dual sense:

- They give scope to the packaging and sale of conventional loans receivables and other assets, and
- They make feasible the direct issuance and sale of securities to institutional and other investors; and hence to the market at large.

Investment banks act as advisors and agents in the issuance of these securities, including issues connected to financial structures as well as legal and tax aspects influencing the risks and opportunities associated to securitization. The same is true about the triggers associated with investor motives. As with all debt instruments, *credit rating* is necessary. The ability of independent rating agencies to assess credit risks is key to the eventual investors' profits or losses. It also influences another critical matter: how to price a securitized issue correctly, and how to keep a real-time pattern of critical P&L evaluation which follows established accounting norms, rather than using creative accounting (see Chapter 3):

- Defining the quality of the asset pool
- Evaluating the security of cash flow
- Estimating how a rating agency looks at credit enhancements, and
- Establishing other risk factors, such as reinvestment, currency risk, and interest rate risk.

A critical question in connection to credit enhancement is how much of it is required, and who will provide it. Also what are the costs of credit enhancement (since it will shave some basis points from the offered interest rate), how pool insurance works, and how dependable it is. This question is always important – much more so with distressed assets whose volume traded in the secondary market continues to grow, as shown in Figure 11.4.

There is also the case of *event risk*. Since the downgrading of R.J.R. Nabisco debt, because of leveraged buyout (LBO), an increasing number of bond buyers are getting issuers to include safeguards. The most popular is an implied

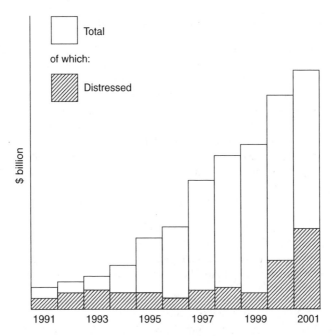

Figure 11.4 Global turnover data on secondary loan trading, 1991–2001

Source: BIS, *72nd Annual Report*, Basel, 2001.

covenant compensating the buyer if, due to a takeover or any type of buy-out, the bonds drop to junk level (BB rating or less). Event risk covenants are also known on Wall Street as *poison puts* aimed to enable investors to get back their principal, and sometimes a few points more. Some poison puts kick in if a large chunk of a company's stock is bought by one buyer. But there is also a silver lining in the deal. Because they ease buyers' fears, covenants lower the issuers' costs:

- They give the potential bond buyer some form of insurance, and s/he will be willing to give up a little in rate
- A company may save one-third of a point in annual interest by means of well-devised covenants.

In conclusion, securitization is a derivatives instrument. Other types of derivatives can be, and are, used to enhance a securitized offer or simply to attract the potential buyers' attention. Such enhancements are also used for inventoried loans. An example is credit default swaps (CDS) which account for credit risk exposure in the loan portfolio. Gains on CDS are used as economic hedges, hopefully to offset credit losses.

5   Securitization of doubtful loans and moral hazard

In the 1990s, by securitizing first consumer receivables then corporate loans, banks have moved aggressively to get credit risk off their balance sheets. This is a totally different practice from the first forty or fifty years after 1945, when loans were the focal point of interest. Some estimates indicate that, today, banks retain only about 10 percent of the stocks, loans, or bond issues they underwrite. The new policy is based on the concept that a deal may be good enough to underwrite, but not good enough to keep in the books. This shift by credit institutions made it much easier for companies to raise money, and it also helped to bankroll the economic boom of the 1990s. At the same time it put institutional investors and retail customers on the front line of credit risk. It is not difficult to understand the motives:

- Credit institutions are feeling vulnerable, as outstanding corporate credit doubled in the 1990s, to beyond $5 trillion in 2002
- The downside is that this financial liquidity relies on the willingness of institutional investors to buy loans, bonds, and commercial paper from banks.

Since 2001, however, huge loans losses connected with Enron, Global Crossing, WorldCom, and other bankruptcies are changing the nature and dependability of assets in the bondholder's portfolio. Credit institutions have been quick to securitize their loans, and bondholders now argue that banks, which enjoy the cheapest source of funding, need to take on more credit risk.

Institutional investors burned by instruments with poor credit risks they assumed by buying securitized corporates, and by other deals, are going to the courts. We have seen in Chapter 9 the legal battle in 2002 by a group of eleven insurers who won a legal battle against J.P. Morgan Chase over Mahonia, an Enron off-balance sheet partnership the bank helped to create. Reference has also been made to problems facing Citigroup, including a Congressional investigation. Both banks were big lenders to Enron, underwrote its bonds, and recommended its stock. Enron pension funds are also suing the company's bankers and the roster of entities going to the court because of unwarranted risk increases. In mid-2002, WorldCom's meltdown angered institutional investors even more than that of Enron and of Global Crossing or Adelphia. The banks had issued a record $11.8 billion in WorldCom bonds in May, 2001, with about half the amount raised going to pay back short-term bank loans:

- When WorldCom admitted to accounting fraud and restated five quarters of earnings in June 2002, banks were left with about $2.7 billion in exposure
- The bondholders were stuck with an estimated $30 billion in debt instruments that started trading at huge discounts.

Both J.P. Morgan Chase and Citigroup, the lead underwriters on WorldCom bonds, responded by saying they had relied on WorldCom numbers and could not have foreseen the fraud. The bonds, they said, were underwritten based on the company's 2000 audited accounts (by Arthur Andersen). But Congress uncovered evidence that senior bank executives were well aware of what was going on. Since much of this evidence was in emails, by early August 2002 it had raised the issues of mail fraud and wire fraud, both of which are punishable in the US.

Among the justifications credit institutions find for going wholesale with securitized loans is that bad loans at big commercial banks had jumped nearly 30 percent to more than $25 billion at the end of 2001. This is confirmed by the Federal Deposit Insurance Corporation (FDIC), but it is all the banks' own fault. Throughout the fourth quarter of 2001, lenders warned that they were:

- Slashing their earnings estimates to write off bad loans, and
- Taking reserves against bad debt, a process projected to last through 2003, and probably beyond.

Nor did the bad loans securitization strategy get the banks off the hook. As we have already seen, post-Enron's bankruptcy the stock of J.P. Morgan Chase fell sharply as it revealed new risks from Enron off-balance sheet vehicles.[4] In mid-December 2001 it said that its unsecured exposure to Enron was triple the original estimates, in part because of credit derivatives. In writedown for bad loans:

- J.P. Morgan Chase lopped off $807 million
- FleetBoston Financial topped that with $1.2 billion, and
- PNC Financial Services Group first counted a cost of $615 million, then added $155 million more after the SEC advised it to change its accounting practices.

This is by no means the end. Ironically, the problems have come at a time of decline in bank lending, as it can be seen in the statistics in Table 11.1. Experts say that much of the slack in fulfilling financial requirements has been taken up by debt securities.

At the same time as commercial loans went down, their mix also changed – for the worse. In the first half of 2002, commercial loans which went sour jumped by about 20 percent; preparing themselves for a worst-case scenario, commercial banks nearly tripled their off-balance sheet credit lines after the last recession of 1990, to about $5 trillion outstanding, as Prudential Securities' analyst Michael Mayo notes.[5]

Even this does not seem to be enough, because credit institutions have on their books a major off-balance sheet risk through credit derivatives. As we saw in preceding sections, these act as insurance for a company that invests in a corporate bond or loan. Enron, and many other companies, have used

Table 11.1   The decline of bank lending, 1980s–1990s

	1980s	1990s
Economies in which bank lending declined		
US	34.5	18.0
France	44.0	21.5
UK	84.0	73.0
Japan	94.5	90.5
Economies in which bank lending increased		
Germany	51.0	57.0

them a great deal. If the debt goes bad, the company that issued the derivative pays the debtholder.

Credit derivatives may act as an insurance cover but there are, of course, limitations to any insurance cover. One is the unknowns involved, which can make pricing haphazard. Another is *moral hazard*. As with all rescue plans, *ex ante* moral hazard relates to the fact that when the risk is fully insured the insured party has less incentive to prevent its occurrence. As a result, the probability of higher credit risk-taking starts to rise, so that the premiums become too low:

- If the moral hazard cannot be properly contained, credit risk becomes uninsurable
- Any insurance coverage would be disastrous because the risk of accident would rise as a result of the availability of insurance.

In the last analysis, the fact that liability insurance was banned in many western European countries up until the nineteenth century is a consequence of this problem. Much more rigorous approaches than those available today are needed to permit insurers and underwriters to fight against moral hazard. An example is partial insurance, that keeps the insured exposed to risk as an inducement to develop prevention activities.

There is also *ex post* moral hazard, exemplified by the increase in claims against an insurance policy beyond the services the claimant would purchase if s/he were not insured. In the case of medical cover, for instance, *ex post* moral hazard includes excessive visits to doctors, too many medicines bought, longer than absolutely necessary hospital stays, and so on. Similar examples exist in finance, but they have not yet been properly studied in terms of aftermath, cost, and prevention.

6   Studying the probability of default

The average American company, says Tim Kasta of Moody's KMV, now has a 4.4 percent chance of default, more than four times the average in the

1990s.[6] A major concern is that even as the market value of their businesses falls, companies continue to add debt. It is therefore absolutely necessary to track the probability of default of every company and every correspondent bank dealt with – anywhere in the world, in any instrument:

- Loans,
- Investments, or
- Derivatives.

Management should be keen to establish *criteria for default* which are observed throughout the organization. The best policy is to adopt the criteria elaborated by the regulators. The Basel Committee's criteria for default are as follows:

- It is determined that the obligor is unlikely to pay its debt obligations (principal, interest, or fees) in full
- The obligor is past more than 90 days on any credit obligation
- The obligor has filed for bankruptcy or similar protection from creditors
- There is a charge-off, specific provision, or distressed restructuring involving the forgiveness, or postponement, of principal, interest, or fees.

Both financial and non-financial companies which are, or which will be, our counterparties should be thoroughly combed for the probability of default. While in several countries the share of bank loans continues to fall, as we saw in section 6, loans still hover around 50 percent of capital provision to the non-financial sector of the economy. Figure 11.5 presents some interesting statistics in this connection, from the European Central Bank (ECB).

The general thinking is that credit risk is usually associated with loans and debt instruments (bonds). This is correct, but incomplete. The probability of default is important not only for loans but also for investment and for derivatives trades. There is a common background of analytics for all lines of business where the counterparty matters – whether it goes out of existence or its behavior is characterized by unwillingness to pay. The four pillars on which this common ground rests are:

- Study of the past to detect strengths, weaknesses, and trends on counterparty's side
- Projection on the future, including discounted cash flow (DCF), cost structure, new products, assumed risks and their distribution
- Examination of management's action to establish the counterparty's efficiency and dependability
- Monetization of risk and computation of the *misery index* which helps in estimating an entity's probability of default.

The misery index which I am using is composed of the sum of two elements: (a) administrative costs and (b) monetization of assumed risks. All costs count, but other things equal, high overhead (and hence administrative

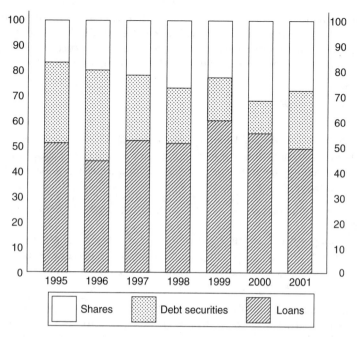

Figure 11.5 Financing of the non-financial sectors, excluding financial derivatives and other accounts payable (as a percentage of total financing), 1995–2001
Source: European Central Bank.

cost) can be fatal. It is advisable to use three thresholds in connection with banking overhead:

- Less than 50 percent of non-interest budget, which is very good
- Between 50 percent and 60 percent, which is rather poor, and
- Over 60 percent, which can become catastrophic.

The monetization of risks embedded in the portfolio should follow the statement of recognized but not yet realized gains and losses (STRGL), which is the law in terms of financial reporting by British banks. The model which I am using is somewhat more extensive, as it includes derivatives, equities, bonds, loans, and all other instruments inventoried in the financial institution's trading book and banking book.

If the lenders to Enron, Global Crossing, WorldCom, and other recently defunct companies had followed the principles guiding the probability of default, and had paid steady attention to customer credit risk surveillance, they would not have suffered their multibillion dollar losses. It is much more difficult for investors of securitized corporate loans to do this, because they don't have the necessary information:

- Between them and the indebted company lies the screen of the bank issuing the securities, and
- Some securitization plans for corporates look as if they might be unsound.

Yet, institutional investors throw good money at them. In the rush to diversify, and for other ill-defined reasons, pension funds, mutual funds, insurance companies, and private high net worth individuals are too careless with their wealth. If they were not, the so-called "alternative investments" would not have had any clients.[7] Bear this in mind next time you are offered alternative investments.

This being said, it is still surprising how many people and companies take credit risk lightly. They don't heed the experts' advice. "With the euro, interest rate risk and currency exchange risk are no more the big criteria," said Samuel Theodore of Moody's Investors Service in a personal interview. "Credit risk is now the key element. Ratings are at the center of capital allocation in the US and they are becoming so in Europe." Theodore added that:

- The beauty of the market is that it crystallizes all information into one price
- The same is true with rating: it distills credit information into one symbol.

This credit rating symbol is closely associated with default probability, as shown in Table 11.2. As in the cases of Enron and WorldCom, concentrations of credit risk exist when changes in economic conditions, industry sectors, geographic area, and other factors affect debtors. The same is true of groups of counterparties, whose aggregate credit exposure is material in relation to a bank's or other entity's total credit exposure.

Risk management is weakened through supposedly miracle solutions. An example is diversification. Although an institution's portfolio of financial instruments may be diversified along industry, product, and geographic lines, ongoing transactions as well as market changes can turn this diversification on its head. If to this is added a concentration of exposure in equity investments and derivative financial instruments, even a bank or other financial institution which until then looked rock-solid can turn belly up.

Table 11.2 Likelihood of failure for rated companies

	1 year	5 years	10 years	15 years
AAA	0.00	0.24	1.40	1.40
AA	0.003	0.43	1.25	1.48
A	0.007	0.65	2.17	3.11
BBB	0.18	1.78	4.34	4.70
BB	1.06	10.97	17.73	19.91

This has happened many times in the past, but it is overlooked by boards and CEOs, as if their institution could defy the laws of gravity. Usually, it cannot.

Notice that both "concentration" and "diversification" are very relative terms based on management's estimates reflected in a range of valuation assumptions, but subject to the law of unintended consequences. For instance, the carrying value of short-term financial instruments, receivables, and payables arising in the ordinary course of business, and their approximate fair value, is subject to market volatility which can hit a portfolio – even if it is theoretically diversified. Furthermore, credit risk policies are most often guided by the overall risk appetite and portfolio targets set by senior management. These tend to lead towards concentrations. Line management initiates and approves all extensions of credit, but does not always treat *credit quality* as a dynamic issue:

- Establishing supplementary credit policies specific to each counterparty and business line, and
- Monitoring portfolio and process quality in a way which is fully updated, factual, and documented.

In order to improve risk management, all executives should be required continuously to identify problem credits, or programs and processes quality, as well as to report their finding. This helps to flush out weak credits, or problem programs, as they develop. It also assists in expeditiously correcting deficiencies, as necessary. At headquarters, the credit policy office, or committee, must conduct independent periodic scrutiny of every individual business channel.

Credit standards and credit programs must be reviewed as frequently as the market's tempo demands – not just annually or at some other arbitrary interface. Credit approvals should reflect projected events, not only historical maturity and the performance of a given counterparty and/or instrument. Studying the probability of default is an ongoing business. Like volatility this probability changes all the time.

7   What is meant by an "asset-light strategy"?

Taking a leaf out of Enron's book, which started as a gas pipeline but disinvested itself of real assets and grew through creative trading, many manufacturing companies have chosen a strategy known as *asset-light*. Olivetti is an example from the late 1990s; another example from the early twenty-first century is Alcatel. Under the so-called "asset-light" strategy, the concept underpinning assets is no longer what it used to be. Creative accounting sees to it that assets are no longer conceived in a solid, tangible way. They become dematerialized electronic book entries which can be manipulated at will:

- Asset-light is essentially financial leveraging by means of loans and the disinvestment of assets, but theoretically the balance sheet still shows these assets as company's property.

- Light assets are *virtual assets*. While the real ones disappear through dis-investments, the virtual ones find their way into geared deals, with institutions advancing the loans rushing to securitize them.

This way, banks become creative arbitrageurs, with a short-term horizon, making their money through commissions and as investment advisors or brokers. Gone is the time of loans having a longer-term horizon and with hard assets backing the collateral. The banks' clients also enter into creative trading through superleveraging and derivatives. But having disinvested themselves of real resources, they are deprived of reserves for a rainy day. That's exactly what has happened with Enron and the other fallen angels.

In the background of this switch towards virtual assets in business orientation is securitized credit, converting loans – including bad loans – into marketable instruments. On paper, securitization's potential is great because it replenishes the capital and removes the balance sheet as a constraint to leveraging. In practice, securitization, particularly of receivables and of virtual assets, is extensive gearing. Companies which parted ways with sound accounting principles loved it because it provides elbow room, allowing executives nearly unlimited possibility of maneuver, and head room to make decisions without seeking constant approval from above. An unwanted consequence, however, is that it disconnects the links between daily activities and business results, as reflected in the balance sheet, cash flow, and income statement. In the medium to longer term, financial reports become unreliable because too many unfounded claims can be made with virtual assets that are not controllable and are not possible with real assets.

The irony is that banks which chose not to securitize their bad loans because they respected their clients as investors were penalized. In April 2002, for instance, Commerzbank (Germany's third-biggest credit institution), said that it would set aside more than Euro 1 billion ($1 billion) against the bad debts expected that year amid a rising tide of insolvencies among its corporate clients. To the credit of Commerzbank is the fact that, unlike the J.P. Morgan Chase loans to WorldCom, the lion's share of which was securitized, Commerzbank itself chose to pay for its mistakes in credit risk. To ease the pressure on its liquidity position it sought a buyer for Jupiter, its UK asset management business (analysts reckoned the bank would be lucky to recoup the money it paid for Jupiter in the mid-1990s). Commerzbank also planned either to sell or find a partner for Montgomery, its American fund management business. To cut costs, it merged its domestic asset management operations into a single group called Cominvest.

In the early years of the twenty-first century, the New Economy is based on financial services, as opposed to the old economy in which manufactured real goods were top for wealth creation. The very concept of value has changed. Between 50 percent and 80 percent of the revenue of many "manufacturing" companies comes from research, distribution, after-sales services, and non-bank financial services. A prime example of the latter is GE Capital.

But the switch to virtual assets does not come cost-free. Look at the global financial crises, such as the East Asian meltdown of 1997; economic and financial shocks arising from the collapse of major actors such as Enron in the US and Barings in the UK; inadequacies in national regulatory and market supervision mechanisms, as evidenced by concerns about accounting and auditing practices; weaknesses and shortcomings, including the role of the IMF and of a new international financial architecture.[8]

- If light assets had been counterbalanced by light liabilities, then the problems would have been easier to solve
- The problem, however, is that light assets correspond to heavy real liabilities, at the level of each entity, and that of the economy as a whole.

This greatly increases the challenges. It also underlines the longer-term aftermath of the asset-light policy followed by many companies, of which few investors are really aware – or they simply accept huge asset leverage and trading leverage as the modern way of doing business. The examples presented in this chapter aim to show the reader the thinking of those who preach the merits of light assets in disregard of the associated liabilities. The author does not believe that the concept of such assets has been properly studied, and doubts if it rests on firm ground in the longer term.

8   SPVs and overleveraging

SPVs of different sorts organized and financed by a credit institution or other company are another way of escaping legal and financial responsibilities. Dissatisfied with some of the answers the Senate Committee received from representatives of J.P. Morgan Chase and Citigroup on July 25, 2002, Senator Carl Levin demanded that the banks' CEOs tell him if they owned any of the special purpose entities used to disguise loans to Enron. Prior to this request, at a Senate hearing on July 23, 2002, representatives of the two banks could not describe the exact nature of the relationship between the banks and the offshore entities that funneled money to Enron.[9] Only later did it become clear that one of the products of these SPVs was the prepays (see Chapter 9). Levin wanted to hear precise answers from the two banks' CEOs. J.P. Morgan Chase's Richard Harrison and Citigroup's Sanford Weill did not appear at the Senate hearings:

- US law makers allege that both Citigroup and J.P. Morgan Chase helped Enron hide debt
- The two credit institutions denied the allegations, but the denial did not convince the market.

"The financial institutions [J.P. Morgan Chase and Citigroup] were aware that Enron was using questionable accounting," said Robert Roach, chief investigator for the Senate Permanent Subcommittee on Investigations, which scrutinized the role of Wall Street firms in the Enron scandal. "They actively aided Enron in other business dealings."[10] The law makers called their behavior "a charade" and "a cancer" on the financial markets. During the ten-hour hearing, the Senate Committee revealed documents showing the banks and their overseas operations, including some law firms, had set up and run offshore shell companies that had funneled billions of dollars in financing to Enron in the 1990s:

- The Senate hearings focused on twenty-six transactions designed to look like legitimate energy-contract trades, these were accounting schemes that served no business purpose, the senators said
- Heavier debt on Enron's balance sheet would have seriously hurt its credit ratings and hastened its meltdown, as executives from Standard & Poor's and Moody's Investors Service testified.

On July 25, 2002, Moody's changed its outlook on J.P. Morgan Chase from Positive to Negative, for three reasons:

- Deteriorating asset quality in the portfolio
- Concentration in telecoms, media, and technology lending
- Damage to the bank's image and reputational risk.

The reader is already familiar with the new alchemy of turning liabilities into assets through *prepays*. J.P. Morgan Chase and Citigroup executives denied any questionable or illegal behavior in financial transactions with Enron from 1992–2001. But a long trail of emails, letters, and other documents disclosed by Congressional investigators seemed to show that the banks had worked closely with Enron to help it hide more than $8 billion in debt.

In its own words, the Senate Permanent Subcommittee on Investigations had evidence indicating that through overseas shell companies the banks had knowingly engaged in deals with Enron. A November 1998 email from a J.P. Morgan Chase executive to another bank executive read: "Enron loves these deals as they are able to hide funded debt from their equity analysts because they [at the very least] book it as deferred revenue or [better yet] bury it in their trading liabilities." Senator Carl Levin, D-Mich., the Subcommittee's chairman, said the documents clearly showed that Enron saw the deals as a way to get cash without reporting liabilities.

Senior people on Wall Street had a very negative reaction to these revelations, because in their judgment they killed market confidence and turned investors off. One of the analysts suggested that while the booms and busts of the nineteenth and twentieth centuries are poorly understood, even today their common background shares certain characteristics:

- Overexpansion in some sectors followed by financial panic, and
- Deals which make investors both cynical and skeptical about how business is done.

Overleveraging is also a common characteristic of the nineteenth-century busts and those we experience now. In the 1830s, with an annual budget of only $50,000, the State of Indiana floated $10 million in bonds. A building boom followed and land values soared. By the early 1840s eight states and the territory of Florida had defaulted on their debts. Construction land prices and the US economy collapsed. The crisis of 1873 was caused by a period of catch-up and overexpansion in railroad construction following the American Civil War. Periodic banking panics occurred because overexpansion caused busts and failing banks meant lost savings and less credit.

The busts of the 1890s and the early twentieth century had many of the characteristics of the internet bubble of 2000–2. In the 1900s, the day was saved by initiatives of J.P. Morgan. Then, in 1913, Congress created the Federal Reserve to prevent banking panics. Deposit insurance protection against lost savings was enacted in the 1930s. There are parallels with the past like the overexpansion in the dot.com and telecom sectors, as well as in creative accounting schemes and unreliable financial reporting practices.

Part III

Problems don't Disappear because they are Ignored

12
Case Studies of Banks which are Finding the Going Tough

1 Introduction

This chapter provides the reader with a pattern of mismanagement, a sample of what is currently happening in the financial industry. Appreciating this pattern is most important at a time when the markets are wondering just how bad things can get, and are questioning how and why we have come to the point where unwarranted greed and poor management are working in synergy to make a bad situation even worse.

The stories the reader will find come from a variety of financial institutions and other high-stakes players. Some have to do with basic mismanagement and the absence of internal control. This is the case of the American subsidiary of Allied Irish Bank (AIB), Ireland's largest credit institution known as Allfirst.

In the first week of February 2002, a loss of $750 million threatened AIB's independence. The bank stunned investors and customers when it disclosed that it had called in agents from the FBI after one of its traders, John Rusnak, failed to report to work at his office in Baltimore, MD, on Monday February 4:

- Allegedly, the forex trader went missing after racking up huge foreign exchange losses at its US subsidiary, Allfirst
- $750 million lost from the books provided every evidence that management was not in charge (see sections 2 and 3 for details).

The other case studies in this chapter are different, but all have to do with the fact that the bottleneck has been at the top of the bottle. This is the case with the $1 billion lost by American Express in dubious investment instruments which should not have been used in the first place (section 4).

Section 5 concentrates on the problems Merrill Lynch had with the Unilever pension fund and other of its clients to whom it promised, in terms of asset management, more than it could deliver. Section 6 describes the problems Crédit Lyonnais created for itself with Executive Life Insurance and section 7 explains some of the reasons why some of the largest credit institution in continental Europe may also be an accident waiting to happen.

The banks who gambled and lost with Enron, WorldCom, and others are not isolated cases, but part of a pattern. There is a saying in Chicago: "If you are shot at once, it may be an accident. If twice, it might be a coincidence. If three times, you have a friend." Investors have many friends, and most of them are part of the bottleneck – sitting pretty at the top of the bottle.

2   Who was to blame for the losses at Allied Irish Bank?

According to available reports, the $750 million losses arose at Allfirst after a series of unauthorized over the counter transactions, involving a number of foreign currency contracts. An individual dealer allegedly entered into a variety of spot and forward foreign exchange trades, which were apparently offsetting foreign currency option positions also entered into by the same dealer. Allegedly, also:

- The senior management of the institution was "unaware" of these deals
- The bank's internal control did not see any warning signals and risk management was absent.

Theoretically, but only theoretically, the profits and losses arising from the foreign exchange deals would have been offset against profits and losses arising on the options transactions. This unwise "netting" is an activity undertaken by experienced traders, within approved risk limits, in many banks. In practice, even if foreign exchange deals are transacted in the normal manner, the offsetting currency option contracts might be fictitious, or the market might turn against the bets.

On Wall Street, experts in this sort of deal said that a loss of $750 million would probably have resulted from positions that were many billions of dollars in size. Allfirst's internal control should surely have got wind of them. Others noted that from October 2001 to late January 2002 the yen had weakened against the dollar by about 25 percent – meaning a trader would have had to have a $3 billion open position over this timeframe to suffer a $750 million loss. Still other experts pointed out that this kind of loss generally occurs either when there is inadequate separation between the trader and the bank's settlement staff (the backoffice), or when a trader is dealing with exotic options whose price is difficult to determine. Not only AIB but also many other banks – indeed, the majority – pay only lip service to the importance of separating a trader and his backoffice. Yet this is one of the crucial lessons that should have been learned time after time from earlier débâcles. In my judgment, AIB:

- Was negligent in operational risk management, and
- Had a substandard internal control and compliance system.

Both bullets point to senior management responsibility – allowing its traders free rein in a far-flung operation, while bosses and superiors fondly believe that they are engaged in risk-free arbitrage. Management which is in charge sees to it that no trader can do what s/he pleases (remember Baring's Nick Leeson). AIB's top management in Ireland, and in the US, has only itself to blame.

A $750 million black hole is not created overnight, it builds up over time, and during its early time of development it should be caught. Long before the losses risked bringing down the bank, its president, COO, CFO, internal and external auditors should have hunted down the malpractice by analyzing the institution's trading books.

Barings fell in February 1995 when presented with the £860 million ($1.32 billion) bill from Nick Leeson's unauthorized trading in Japanese equity derivatives executed in Osaka from the bank's Singapore office. Allied Irish Bank did not turn belly up, but it had to absorb a loss which eventually exceeded the $750 million and it suffered severe reputational risk.

The news of such large-scale asset depletion for a medium-sized bank alarmed investors, who two months earlier had been destabilized by the Enron bankruptcy, and then the Global Crossing fall from a cliff. Investors were already in a state of deep anxiety about corporate financial reporting and missing internal controls. Officially, AIB said that John Rusnak had accumulated large losses in the spot and forward foreign exchange markets trading the US dollar against the Japanese yen. The options contracts which usually offset such losses were bogus. In January 2002, executives at Allfirst belatedly became aware of a potential problem because of cash being sought by the trader to support his trading "strategy."

That forwards trades are real but hedging through options is bogus is nothing new. It may well happen if the options contracts are real but the market turns against the hedger. Serious questions were raised among analysts and investors about the quality of AIB's risk management and of the seriousness of its senior management as a whole:

- The board, CEO, COO, CFO, and auditors at Allied Irish Banks in Dublin
- All of the senior executives at Allfirst, AIB's American subsidiary
- The backoffice and treasury managers in Baltimore and Dublin, and
- All the compliance and risk officers at both sites.

It is the board's, CEO's, CFO's, and the other managers' *duty* to know what happens in the bank. External auditors, too, in this case PricewaterhouseCoopers, should not get off scot-free from the débâcle (see also Chapter 6).

What took place at AIB/Allfirst, Barings, and so many others, documents that senior management and the auditors are simply not up to speed on their duties. In 1997, a trader concealed the mispricing of interest rate options, which cost National Westminster Bank officially said to be £100 million ($162 million) but unofficially rumored to be three times that much. NatWest Markets was dismantled and sold, and National Westminster Bank, the parent company, fell to the Royal Bank of Scotland.

Each time such a top management failure happens, there are painful inquests and earnest resolutions to do better – but in the end nothing is done. If management had been vigilant there would not have been such cases. Why do managers of banks take so long to discover long-running problems at the heart of their financial operations? The answer is widespread *mismanagement*. An obvious motive for traders to conceal activities from their employers is an inclination to gamble in the market, with healthy commissions as the reward if they win. It may be hard for outsiders to understand why anyone would hide losses on his trading book with false options contracts for a year, unless there was simultaneously a big financial reward and management failure. A rogue trader can gain in two ways from dealing with a counterparty at off-market prices:

- By selling financial instruments more cheaply, or
- By buying them more expensively than market rates.

That sort of dealing takes money out of the pocket of the dealer's bank, in a sort of external collusion which is very difficult to perceive when there also exists some sort of internal collusion – or when management is asleep at the wheel.

Another way is to sell options for cash and find a way to keep the cash hidden. In AIB's case this appears unlikely, because as the bank said: "The fraud that has been perpetrated actually did generate cash," but senior management also suggested that the cash was used to cover other losses.[1] The object, in all likelihood, was commissions, but they still defraud the investor.

3   Commissions have damaged Allied Irish Bank

Commissions, even large ones, are legal. What is irrational – and should not have been permitted by top management at AIB or any other institution – is the generation of trades at any cost, and any level of risk, in order to get commissions. For a bank to miss the distinction between "commission as reward" and "commission for greed" is to drive nails into its own coffin. The challenge presented by king-size commissions is not yesterday's problem. Over the years, the boards, CEOs, and senior managers of financial institutions have been both unwilling and unable to solve the problem because they compete for traders in the skills market and try to poach the best trader from other banks:

- Traders are rewarded at an irrational level for the deals that they make
- Commissions are computed in the short term, but the financial institution assumes all the risks in the longer term.

It finally comes to senior management's attention and the public eye that traders have been deceiving the bank by fostering an illusion that they were making large profits, helping to boost the traders' and the bosses' annual bonuses, while hiding the losses. When Warren Buffett became the CEO of Salomon Brothers, after the treasury bonds case, he tried to act on the subject of irrational commissions. He did not succeed because there were huge vested interests behind the traders' commissions.

One of the basic reasons for hiding losses while emphasizing profits is the belief that a trader will be able to trade their way out of trouble, by capitalizing on the fact that markets turn around. Having made an initial loss, a trader or desk prefers to cover it up rather than confess it to senior management:

- The longer the deception goes on, the harder it becomes to cover it up, and the bigger the loss grows
- Losses grow by leaps and bounds because risk management is substandard and the bank's internal control system has broken down.

As far as Allfirst and AIB are concerned, most of the rogue transactions seem to have been in East Asia, with dollar–yen the main contract. A series of spot and forward transactions resulted in losses that were supposedly offset by options contracts (there is more on this below), but then – as already mentioned – it was revealed that these contracts had never actually been entered into.

It is a misconception fairly widespread in the financial industry that arbitrage trading is a rather low-risk deal, which takes advantage of tiny price discrepancies between different markets resulting from superior market knowledge. This hypothesis was one of LTCM's capital sins.[2] Because there are no longer discrepancies between the prices of currencies in different trading zones:

- Pure arbitrage has more or less disappeared from the spot currency market
- But there are still limited arbitrage opportunities in trading forward and futures currency contracts.

Some analysts suggested that instead of pursuing the relatively lower-risk strategy suggested in the second bullet, John Rusnak was using it as a cover for higher-risk currency dealing. But how did a trader manage to create fictional options contracts without management getting wind of it. Was Allfirst's *and* AIB's senior management complacent about the risks being taken?

The board, CEO, CFO, treasurer, and the auditors should have been alerted to rogue transactions since premiums would have to be paid on the contracts. On the other hand, when internal controls are wanting, and the level of management illiteracy about derivative instruments is significant, it may not be impossible to convince directors that contracts did not need to be paid for immediately.

This is more true in recent years as traders have made increasing use of exotic currency options. These have the characteristic of offering a more flexible way of hedging currency risk, but they also help to hide losses and fictitious transactions. With some exotic options it is not always necessary to pay a premium on purchase; instead, the contract may allow the premium to be paid on the expiry date.

As the preceding paragraphs have documented, there are plenty of serious issues to be addressed by both internal and external auditing – as well as, most evidently, by top management. Apparently at AIB they were not; otherwise it is difficult to explain how Allfirst, a relatively small bank not known as a major player in derivatives or in forex markets, could have racked up such losses:

- Either AIB's senior management was running much larger gross positions in the bank's American treasury than would appear sensible
- Or the losses were piling up over a long period, in which case regular controls and cash reconciliations ought to have caught them.

While no institution can really claim to be completely invulnerable to skillful and determined fraudulent trading and reporting, losses skyrocket when top management becomes negligent about reviewing and strengthening the controls. The breakdown of internal control was by all likelihood one of proportion and more than a handful of persons were responsible for it. According to what became public information there was a dual reporting line to the top management at Allfirst and ultimately to AIB in Dublin. Neither functioned properly. If it had, John Rusnak's trading position should have been monitored at the end of each day. Under AIB's internal controls, the capital markets division in Dublin was supposed to keep monthly tabs on the treasury operations of subsidiaries (in the US and Poland). There is no evidence this was done effectively.

Both the Barings and AIB cases are a reminder that a key question top management must address is why such traders, who conceal trades for more than two years, are not caught sooner. Is the bank's organization so deficient? John Rusnak, for example, had engaged in arbitrage which is, by definition, a form of proprietary trading. Who was responsible for controlling this trader's exposure?

Weak internal controls and retrograde risk management is often matched by Paleolithic information technology (IT).[3] This is another reason why losses remain concealed. Matters become worse when the trades involve derivative transactions that are poorly understood by senior managers. This was the case with NatWest Markets: the trader did not conceal his trades; he mispriced them in full view of his managers by using the so-called "volatility smile."

For starters, the effect of low volatility estimates is to lower the price of an option, or other financial instruments, because the amount of risk being projected is so much lower. It is *as if* volatility "smiles" to the trader and to the salesman. Lower price makes it easier to sell the product. On the other hand, if these estimates are biased, the bank assumes a very significant risk, because the products which it sells are underpriced.

These machinations can be caught only through *stress testing*, which many banks do not do because they lack both the stress testing culture and the tools.[4] The wholly owned US subsidiary of Allied Irish Bank had a reputation as a sleepy, conservative regional bank that served the local community for more than 200 years. Allfirst started life in 1806 as the Mechanics Bank of Baltimore, one of only thirty banks established in the US at the time. More than fifty years and several names changes later, the Mechanics Bank merged with First National Bank in 1864 and settled on the name First Maryland Bancorp. It was in this name that Allfirst:

- Established its reputation as a solid community bank, and
- Continuously paid dividends to shareholders throughout the Depression.

AIB became involved with First Maryland in 1983 when it agreed to acquire a 49.7 percent stake in the bank for $150 million over five years. When this happened, Allfirst was a very small bank in the context of the US banking system, and was always viewed as a solid but unexciting business. Yet, it operated about 250 bank branches in Maryland, Pennsylvania, Washington DC, northern Virginia, and Delaware.

Still another irony is that foreign exchange dealing was not a core activity for AIB or for Allfirst. Indeed, one of the main AIB attractions for investors was its relatively limited exposure to investment banking. The institution depended on retail and commercial banking for 97 percent of its profits.

What about the parent company? AIB was itself the product of a merger of the Munster and Leinster Bank, the Provincial, and the Royal banks in the 1960s. It also had an insurance subsidiary, ICI, which had been bailed out by the Irish government in the early 1980s at a cost of £I100 million.

Finally, in terms of banking culture, a negative factor was that AIB had been found by a parliamentary committee to have been the main facilitator of some bogus non-resident bank accounts set up in the 1990s, forcing it to make a Euro 114 million ($114 million) settlement with the tax authorities.[5] Some analysts suggested that the fact that the same person was the AIB Group's finance director and top risk manager did not help matters in making rigorous risk control function.

4 Red ink at American Express

The Minneapolis-based money manager American Express Financial Advisors (AEFA) represented nearly 20 percent of its parent company's revenues. AEFA markets financial advice, mutual funds, insurance, and annuities through a salesforce of 11,000 agents called "financial planners." It managed assets of about $250 billion and had $4.2 billion in revenues in 2000 and a respectable $1.0 billion in earnings. What happened in 2001, however, adds to the inventory of mismanagement of financial institutions.

The cause was AEFA's investments in high-yield junk bonds, which led to more than $1 billion in write-offs in the first half of 2001 alone. On Wall Street, analysts were expecting more bad news from the company's $34 billion pool of proprietary investments.

On the evening of July 26, 2001 the financial networks carried the news that after years of turning out powerful earnings, quarter after quarter, and maintaining a share price that was the envy of the industry, American Express had suddenly hit the skids. Senior management had invested in risky junk bonds and collateralized mortgage obligations (CMO), the result being $1 billion in losses – the AEFA affair. This was both sad and ironic for a financial services firm whose 11,000 investment counselors advised some 2.5 million clients on how to place their money in a profitable but secure way. As the company's own investments began to turn sour, Kenneth Chenault, the then new CEO of American Express said: "I'm going to do everything in my power to assure that something like this doesn't happen again. If it does, it will be a big, big problem." He then added that he had also launched a search for a "risk specialist," a newly created position[6] – a statement which repeated that:

- American Express, and with it AEFA, lacked risk management expertise
- Yet the institution engaged in risky trades and had accumulated toxic waste from junk bonds and CMOs in its portfolio.

Not just a "risk specialist" but a chief risk management officer with plenty of risk specialists should have been working at American Express, and all other financial institutions, for a long time. Analysts noted that, as of mid-July 2001, the pretax charges of more than $1 billion American Express had taken were 35 percent higher than its 2000 net income – while risk management and with it internal control appeared to be in a shambles.

Through AEFA, the parent company had made disastrous bond investments. The stream of bad news started in April 2001 when American Express revealed write-offs of $182 million from, among other things, defaulted junk bonds issued by struggling movie-theater chains and companies hit by asbestos liability. At the time, Kenneth Chenault reassured investors that the worst was over. But as we just saw, at the end of July 2001, three months after those assurances, the company added a further $826 million to the red ink. These investments were made under Harvey Golub, Chenault's predecessor as CEO. The origin of the débâcle is to be found in 1997, at the AEFA unit. The underlying bad judgment seems to have been caused by the then CEO's drum-beating for higher earnings growth. He demanded that the Minneapolis unit meet a return in equity growth target of 20 percent, an aggressive level for the industry even in the Clinton years.

The market was not enthusiastic about the new CEO when the billion dollar loss occurred. Asked why his company had put its money into risky junk bonds, Chenault answered, "I don't know. This is a strategy that was embarked upon seven or eight years ago. I don't know all the rationale and philosophy." "He didn't say, 'I made a mistake,'" said Lewis Rabinowitz, who heads up R. Lewis Securities, a money management firm and American Express investor. "He basically said, 'I didn't understand the risk.' I feel that is something that is – unacceptable for a CEO."[7]

What Chenault did not say was that since AEFA's main business of financial advice, money management, and insurance was not growing fast enough to meet this target, the company tempered with its own portfolio through collateral mortgage obligations (CMOs), as a way to get incremental income and beef up return on investment. The good news is that, allegedly, only the company's own assets became damaged goods – not those of its clients:

- The junk bond and CMOs' strategy did not seem to affect the $262 billion in assets American Express managed for wealthy private individuals and institutional clients
- American Express did, however, repackage and sell some high-risk securitized instruments to its client base.

A CMO mitigates prepayment risk by redirecting cash flows from underlying collateral pools to bond classes known as *tranches*. The result is securities with different risk and return profiles designed to please different investors because – at least theoretically – they take care of prepayment risk and increase the amount of leverage, although in reality they widen the assumed exposure – something many financial entities and investors prefer to forget.

CMOs also expand the reach of the mortgage market by creating tranches whose timing of cash flows is taken care of through algorithms. Besides this, under the US 1986 tax reforms, the Real Estate Mortgage Investment Conduit provision allowed CMOs to be tax exempt if certain conditions were met. On the other hand, however, CMOs are very risky instruments if the market turns against the investor, and the hypotheses s/he has made about trends in the economy fall to materialize.

Leveraging itself through CMOs, Orange County lost $2.1 billion and went bankrupt in 1994. Even the pros can go wrong with CMOs, and they often do. In 2001, not only did American Express announce losses of over $1.0 billion but J.P. Morgan Chase lost $1.1 billion. This is the irony in modern leveraged finance:

- The stream of popular highly risky instruments seems to be uninterrupted
- Few people truly appreciate that heavy losses can hide beneath this growth curve.

It should therefore come as no surprise that by late 2001 American Express still had about $2.7 billion in junk bonds, and more of its top-shelf investments were poised to slip into the red zone. Another billion dollars of the

AEFA's portfolio was tied up in travel and insurance debt, where defaults were inevitable. Analysts said that still more write-off would be necessary to cover junk bond losses, and to some extent they were right.

The law of unexpected consequences can hit a company's bottom line hard. As far as American Express was concerned, the falling price of its stock rekindled intermittent rumors that the company could be acquired by Citigroup or Morgan Stanley because it had become vulnerable to a takeover. It has not happened so far.

5   Unilever and others v. Merrill Lynch Investment Managers

In late 2001 Merrill Lynch Investment Managers (MLIM) allegedly entered into secret discussions with disgruntled pension-fund trustees at Unilever, Sainsbury, Astra Zeneca, Surrey County Council, and South Tyneside Pension. Merrill attempted to dissuade these counterparties from taking legal action against its investment management subsidiary, even though such persuasion would not be cost-free for MLIM. The first talks to come to fruition were with the Unilever Superannuation Fund, which had alleged negligence in MLIM's management of its £1 billion ($1.62 billion) in assets. To settle this issue, the fund manager agreed to pay £70 million ($113 million) plus costs to Unilever. But in spite of paying a great deal of money in an out-of-court settlement, MLIM remained adamant that none of the five pensions funds had a case that would stand up in court.

Some legal experts and analysts in the City of London suggested that had MLIM come to terms before the Unilever trial it could have had to pay considerably less than its final bill, and would have avoided the damaging publicity that came with a long court battle. MLIM had suffered a month of damaging headlines, and its reputation as a fund manager was badly hurt.

It puzzles me that big investment banks and asset management companies are so lacking in terms of screening sales terms, implementing internal controls, and instituting quality assurance (QA) procedures. Both the technology and the methodology have been available for many years.[8] All they need is the will to apply it, and the capacity to do so in an efficient manner.

A first-class example of internal control and QA procedures is provided by the use of normal, tightened, and reduced inspection in connection with customer services. Developed during the Second World War for the Manhattan project, this method is perfectly applicable to credit risk and market risk, including exposure taken in connection to derivative financial instruments:

- *Normal* inspection is used when the estimated process average is inside the applicable upper and lower limits
- *Tightened* inspection is instituted immediately after the estimated process average touches or exceeds limits, no matter what's the reason

- *Reduced* inspection may be used if process average is significantly less than the upper and lower limits.

In banking, the conditions for reduced inspection would signal that volatility was steady. Other criteria, too, may be used focused on the quality of customer service. Volatility and credit risk (or market risk) limits should be mapped in a statistical quality control chart. The same is true concerning a portfolio's performance where the limits constitute the commitments made to the client. If QA is deficient or non-existent, and/or the associated internal control channels are clogged, then it is inevitable that relationship management will reach a breaking point. A similar statement is valid about handholding. As I wrote in October 2002 to Merrill Lynch:

> It is the duty of senior management to crush improper behavior of the company's agents – not to condone it.

Decisions to offer the counterparty a settlement which would guard against reputational damage can be painful in financial terms. In Unilever's case, the problem started with the return on investment (ROI) targets the fund manager offered to get the business. When these were not met, litigation occurred. In the pre-trial mediation the two parties were poles apart:

- MLIM's settlement offer ran to less than £25 million
- Unilever, which had at one stage hinted that it might accept £45 million, stretched its claim to £60 million.

This case centered on the accusations by Unilever's Superannuation Fund that MLIM (formerly Mercury Asset Management) had been negligent in its management of £1 billion of the fund's money. As the settlement discussions dragged on, Unilever claimed £130 million in damages after alleging that MLIM had failed to provide the necessary risk controls to that ensure its money was managed within the framework of its agreement with the fund.

MLIM argued that its risk control measures were perfectly adequate and that the poor performance of Unilever's portfolio was due to unusual market conditions. It is a proof of Merrill Lynch's determination to settle that it agreed to the £70 million, while arguing mainly over the content of the settlement statement to deter other potential litigants:

- Merrill Lynch insisted on a clause pointing out the "unique circumstances" of the Unilever contract, and
- It refrained from any phrases that might suggest that the fund manager accepted liability or negligence on its part.

This Unilever settlement came as one more frustration. Clashing with a client in the courts with the media hot on the case, temporarily at least, made it nearly impossible to win new business in the tough and competitive environment of asset management. It also gave ideas to other MLIM clients that they might have something to gain through litigation. In mid-December 2001, a short time after the Unilever settlement, the Trustees of Sainsbury's pension fund met to consider taking legal action against MLIM. Sainsbury's £1 billion pension fund was thought to have suffered similar underperformance to that experienced by Unilever – its pension fund:

- Was managed by the same team as the Unilever fund, and
- Had a contract with similar tolerance for underperformance.

The trustees at Astra Zeneca, the South Tyneside Pension Fund, Surrey County Council and others, also kept close watch. Penalties paid for under-performance should be a lesson to all fund managers who overstate their case to win customers and fees. Making promises which one knows one cannot keep is not just ethically wrong, it is a policy which boomerangs as this and so many other similar cases demonstrate.

6   Crédit Lyonnais and Executive Life Insurance

In mid-2001, claiming that Crédit Lyonnais had fraudulently gained control of Executive Life, California's Insurance Department launched a civil suit against the French bank. In Washington, the Justice Department was winding up a Grand Jury investigation. Such investigations did result in a criminal indictment as well as reputational risk. Even if Crédit Lyonnais avoided the worst-case scenario, this is still an interesting case study.

The purchase of Executive Life Insurance by Crédit Lyonnais (when the French credit institution was still a nationalized bank), dated back to the early 1990s – the Mitterrand years. It blew up a decade later, and Crédit Lyonnais used both legal and political means to avoid a federal criminal indictment:

- A favorable Justice Department ruling would undercut the California suits
- But if the credit institution was condemned, the US Federal Reserve could levy fines or even revoke its US banking license.

Was this really a criminal case? In mid-July 2001, *Le Nouvel Observateur* reported new details about the affair, based on testimony from Dominique Bazy, formerly the right-hand man of Jean Peyrelevade, the bank's CEO since 1993. This evidence cast light on a seventeen-page internal fax sent on December 10, 1993 to Peyrelevade's office. Bazy said he was the intended recipient of the fax, which contained explicit details of the fronting arrangements entered into by the bank to circumvent American federal and state laws when it took over Executive Life.

Executive Life was a mismanaged insurance company, facing long-standing trouble. After it went bust in 1991, US insurance regulators opted for a rescue package put together by Crédit Lyonnais. The State of California accepted an offer from Altus Finance (then a Crédit Lyonnais unit known for high-risk investments) to buy the insurer's junk bonds for $3.25 billion. (This was money finally paid by the French taxpayer, when the Baladure government decided to salvage Crédit Lyonnais from its own bankruptcy.)

As part of the Executive Life package, the French bank arranged for a new insurance company, Aurora National Life, to take over Executive Life's insurance contracts. The regulators were told that the consortium set up to own and manage Aurora would be independent of Crédit Lyonnais, as American federal and state laws required.

Members of the consortium of "independent" shareholders in Aurora, led by MAAF (a French insurer), were in fact fronts for Crédit Lyonnais. The bank had confidential agreements to buy back shares in Aurora from consortium members and also arranged in principle for Artemis, a company controlled by François Pinault, a French businessmen, to buy shares in Aurora from the consortium of investors.

Peyrelevade claimed that when he learned of the terms of the Executive Life deal, he informed the US Federal Reserve, one month before Crédit Lyonnais was privatized. Immediately afterwards, in February 1999, the California Insurance Department filed suit against Crédit Lyonnais and others and in January 2000, Pinault and his holding company, Artemis, were added to the California lawsuit. In June 2001 the French government allegedly tried diplomatic pressure to halt the US probe of Crédit Lyonnais.

Although the Executive Life case preceded Peyrevelade's tenure at Crédit Lyonnais, what did he know, and when did he know it? His office received the seventeen-page internal fax explaining the deal some days after he arrived at the bank, according to documents that the bank says it gave to the US Justice Department. But Crédit Lyonnais officials insist that Peyrelevade never signed the fax, meaning that he didn't read it – is this an excuse one expects to hear from a CEO?

If such things can happen in commercial banks which are strongly regulated and efficiently supervised, think of what can take place in hedge funds which have nobody to look over their shoulder. It is not just a matter of "casino-type" gambles by hedge funds which risk tearing apart the world's financial system. There are also matters of ethics which have a great need for regulation and supervision which, so far at least, hedge funds have been able to escape.[9]

This case study helps to illustrate one more of the many aspects characterizing investment and financial management in our epoch. Executive Life and its relationship to Crédit Lyonnais is one more thread in the behavioral tapestry which suggests that, so often, management does not precisely know where the brakes are – or, alternatively, is unwilling to apply them. Hence, the after-the-fact excuses.

This case of Crédit Lyonnais and Executive Life has an interesting postmortem. Through a strange coincidence, indeed, the interests of Jeffrey Isaac, the US federal attorney general in California, and Bernard Tapie, a

French high-flying businessman in the years of the Mitterand presidency, have been suddenly converging. Based on documents seized by the FBI, Crédit Lyonnais did not only use the Altus, Aurora and Artemis fronts, but also the Citistar, a shell company registered in the Cayman Islands.

What has brought Isaac and Tapie together is that in 2001, Crédit Lyonnais also seems to have used the same shell company, Citistar, to take possession and sell Tapie's Adidas, the sportswear firm. The way it has been reported in the French press, Tapie says that through manipulation Crédit Lyonnais/Citistar, took away from him assets worth Euro 300 million.[10]

The legal implication is serious because this polyvalent use of a shell company tends to characterize Crédit Lyonnais as following a policy of deception. The French credit institution, which in 2003 has been bought by Crédit Agricole, has an equity of over $130 million on Citistar. A contract which it allegedly signed with Citibank on December 29, 1992, stipulates that Crédit Lyonnais will assume all the consequences of the confidential transaction involving the California insurance company.

The way the French press had it, not only was the Executive Life transaction illegal but it has also permitted Crédit Lyonnais to do creative accounting with its balance sheet – artificially increasing its assets by $500 million in 1992. The *Canard Enchaîné* was to add that, no doubt, in the California civil court where prosecutors demand Euro 5.3 billion in penalties, the twelve jurors would have no reason to let Crédit Lyonnais off the hook, particularly after the French government's attitude in the Iraqi affair. That's one of the cases where high finance, legal risk, and politics work in synergy to one another – and this not necessarily to the best.

On August 27, 2003, a federal grand jury in Los Angeles issued a criminal indictment against Crédit Lyonnais and others related to the bank's acquisition of failed Executive Life Insurance. Crédit Lyonnais and five companies that, prosecutors say, acted as a front for the bank negotiated a settlement. On September 2, it was announced that Crédit Lyonnais and Consortium de Realisation, a French government agency, agreed to plead guilty to fraud charges in settlementt with the U.S. Justice Department (*Wall Street Journal*, September 3, 2003).

7   Deutsche Bank and Bankers Trust

Deutsche Bank is the largest credit institution in Europe in terms of assets, but is saddled with a $13.5 billion portfolio of poorly performing corporate investments, a money-losing network of retail banking, asset management operations which struggle to show a profit, and a great deal of derivatives which stood at over $11 trillion in notional principal amount in 2002. There have also been organizational problems. "Deutsche announces a new structure every six months but has little to show for its efforts," as Mark Hoge of Bank of America Securities suggested.[11]

Very expensive acquisitions, particularly in America, like the 1999 takeover of Bankers Trust, and in Europe the 2002 purchase of Zurich Scudder Investments, have not produced expected returns. (That high returns should not have been expected in the first place, is another issue.) Nor has Deutsche Bank been able to control its costs. In 2001:

- 89 percent of its revenue went to overhead expenses
- Comparing poorly to an average of 60 percent for European banks.

Analysts looking at Deutsche Bank from an investment perspective suggested that the efficiency of its risk control operations was not beyond reproach. In 1994, the near-bankruptcy of Metallgesellschaft from oil trades in derivatives showed that the bank's oversight of traders had certain blind spots. Investment banking, too, has been deficient. When Daimler–Benz needed advice on its merger with Chrysler in 1998, it turned to Goldman Sachs instead of Deutsche, its traditional bank.

The problems confronting Deutsche Bank are not alien to other European credit institutions. Through most of the 1990s, Europe's No. 1 bank searched its soul for a new strategy. By late 1998 it seems to have decided to turn fully to investment banking, but the jury is still out on how wise this move was.

Like other German credit institutions, Deutsche had shares in many companies, from electrical/electronics firms, to carmakers and cakebakers. This was a strategy followed by Deutsche Bank since its inception in the nineteenth century. But on December 16, 1998, it announced that it was to spin off its industrial holdings by forming separate limited partnerships to manage each block of shares, all controlled by a new unit called DB Investor. "This will optimize value creation for our shareholders," said the then CEO Rolf-Ernst Breuer. The implication was that Deutsche Bank would thereafter be able to pursue M&A and other investment banking deals without raising eyebrows about its stake. But many analysts doubted that:

- The bank would have the horsepower it needed for this sort of strategy, or
- It would be able to hold its own against fierce global competition in investment banking.

"They're all right in asset management and commercial banking," a former Deutsche executive suggested. "But I don't see how they can compete in high-margin business like M&A and primary equities." Deutsche Bank tried to fill the gaps but acquisitions and the hiring of highly expensive M&A specialists did not work as planned:

- Instead of diversifying to address the lucrative global retail market in selected countries, as Citibank did in the 1980s and 1990s
- The majority of big commercial banks squeeze themselves into the cutthroat investment banking business where they lack the skills, misjudge the market, and end by losing face.

The behavior of big banks when it comes to strategic planning is not much different from that of the big established telephone companies. The (unwise) strategy of the latter was to rush after a smaller number of big clients and engage in price wars, when the vast number of small and medium enterprises (SMEs) constituted their best business future.

The race to get into investment banking big deals is no different from the great, and very costly, misjudgment of telephone companies regarding third-generation (3G) mobile services. Today, a significant but unexploited demand for telecoms services and applications, across the globe, comes from SMEs. Though at present the SMEs have nothing to do with the telcos' UMTS licenses,[12] they may in the future become 3Gs' best bet, if carriers can provide any-to-any low-cost, flat-rate network services:

- Bypassing the old, malfunctioning telco plant
- Offering exciting broadband services at affordable prices
- Innovating the concept of enterprise architecture, and
- Personalizing the services they offer to the level of each SME.

Like the mammoth banks with their investment banking dreams, the big telephone operators cannot capitalize on this SME market because they are too monolithic and too preoccupied with their own financial reorganization to save themselves from bankruptcy. This is the business for imaginative well-financed startups – like the 3G offering in Europe by Hutchison Whampoa, which can cut costs to the bone and be free from past mistakes.

In a way, the worry expressed by the former Deutsche Bank executive: "But I don't see how they can compete..." boils down to this paradigm. In the late 1990s, Deutsche Bank management bought the nearly bankrupt Bankers Trust (BT) of New York and investors feared that Deutsche's $9 billion takeover would be plagued by the same cultural clashes that haunted its 1989 purchase of Morgan Grenfell – and time has proved them right.

When Bankers Trust came into Deutsche Bank's fold, analysts and investors wondered whether the strategy might backfire. Could Bankers Trust bring Deutsche Bank the strengths it needed to compete with Morgan Stanley or Goldman Sachs? In retrospect, with the advantage of knowing the results several years down the line, the doubters were right. Cultural differences and inflated paychecks proved to be much bigger obstacles than originally thought.

When in the fall of 1998 Dr. Breuer was negotiating the merger with Bankers Trust, he had initially agreed that Frank Newman, the Bankers Trust chairman would be given a seat on the *Vorstand* (board of management), just like Sir John Craven, chairman of Britain's Morgan Grenfell, had done when Deutsche acquired his bank in 1989. But this was not the case. Breuer seems to have changed his mind when several Deutsche Bank *Vorstand* members told him that there were enough foreigners already on the executive board – asset management chief Michael Dobson was British, investment banking head Joseph Ackermann (now Deutsche Bank's CEO) was Swiss, and Ronaldo Schmitz, the other leading investment banker, was Brazilian.

More important may have been the fact that Frank Newman's high salary irked many people – the $15.5 million he had earned in 1988 was almost as much as the $16.4 million split among the German bank's entire *Vorstand*. Senior Deutsche bankers also felt that Newman had done too little to restore Bankers Trust's credibility after the institution was fined $60 million for illegally transferring unclaimed customer funds into its own reserves.

Though the funds' transfer had happened between 1994 and 1996, before Newman joined the bank, he was responsible for investigating it. Three former Bankers Trust executives were criminally indicted,[13] this worsened BT's reputational risk, and Newman provided no counterweight for damage control.

Apart from the BT acquisitions' aftermath being a major "minus," in the 1999–2002 timeframe there were musical chairs at Deutsche. In 1999 Jürgen Krumnow, a long-standing executive board member, who headed auditing, stepped down after a clash with Breuer. In 2002, Thomas Fischer, a former Landesgirokasse Stuttgart CEO and boss of Deutsche's treasury and market risk (a contradiction in position) also stepped down after a clash with Josef Ackermann, Deutsche's new CEO.

All this weakened Europe's No. 1 bank, leading some analysts to think that Deutsche Bank might turn into an acquisition target. In February 2002 Citigroup proposed that the two banks consider merging, a suggestion Deutsche rebuffed, but the risk of being swallowed up has not gone away.

In London and Frankfurt analysts are of the opinion that an acquisition cannot be ruled out. An alternative is streamlining and re-engineering the institution. The new management plans to sell most of the bank's money-losing and low-return units, putting the proceeds to work in investment banking, asset management, and private banking for wealthy customers. But as already stated, analysts and investors are not convinced. They also point out that some of Deutsche's current operations somehow find themselves in two contradictory rosters: those to be sold and those to be pumped up. An example is asset management.

Another Deutsche Bank business line which will probably come under the hammer is the index-tracking money-management unit, which has $153 billion on its books. Some experts say that the $3.37 trillion global securities-custody business may also be on the block – yet custody is altogether a profitable, if highly competitive business.

The reason why Deutsche Bank is so valuable a case study is that the issues confronting its board and senior management are on the table of practically every financial institution, particularly the bigger ones. Continuing to focus on wholesale lending at a time of high competition leads to the temptation to scrutinize borrowers less carefully than in the past. This is a flawed approach because of increasing credit risk. As for moving all the way into investment banking in the 2003 financial climate, a senior banker said that he would be "more scared from such a move, than from the terrorists."

Notes

1 Senior Management Ethics and Personal Accountability

1. Jack D. Schwager, "Market Wizards. Interviews with Top Traders," New York, New York Institute of Finance, 1989.
2. *Operare*, 3, July–September 1990, Rome.
3. *BusinessWeek*, January 13, 2003.
4. *Financial Times*, February 7, 2002.
5. *BusinessWeek*, July 8, 2002.
6. *Financial Times*, June 27, 2002.
7. Merrill Lynch, "US Strategy Update," July 1, 2002.
8. D.N. Chorafas, *Alternative Investments and the Mismanagement of Risk*, London, Macmillan/Palgrave, 2003.
9. D.N. Chorafas, *Managing Risk in the New Economy*, New York, New York Institute of Finance, 2001.
10. Sun Tzu, *The Art of War*, Delacorte Press, New York, 1983.
11. James J. Cramer, *Confessions of a Street Addict*, New York, Simon & Schuster, 2002; Nicholas W. Maier, *Trading with the Enemy*, New York, HarperBusiness, 2002.
12. *BusinessWeek*, April 22, 2002.
13. *BusinessWeek*, April 1, 2002.
14. *Financial Times*, June 11, 2003.
15. *BusinessWeek*, December 30, 2002.
16. *BusinessWeek*, January 13, 2003.

2 Mismanagement and the Firing of a Bad CEO

1. Edward I. Koch, *Mayor. An Autobiography*, New York, Simon & Schuster, 1984.
2. Emil Ludwig, *Lincoln*, New York, Grosset & Dunlap, 1930.
3. *Global Investor*, Credit Suisse Private Banking, Zurich, July 2002.
4. Connie Bruck, *The Predators' Ball*, New York, Penguin, 1988.
5. *CommunicationsWeek International*, July 15, 2002.
6. *Bloomberg Professional*, November 19, 2002.
7. *Wall Street Journal*, November 18, 2002.
8. *International Herald Tribune*, November 18, 2002.
9. *BusinessWeek*, May 20, 2002.
10. *Libération* (Paris), June 27, 2002.
11. *Financial Times*, June 27, 2002.
12. *Financial Mail*, July 21, 2002.
13. *Herald Tribune*, July 31, 1992.
14. *New York Post*, Communications of the ACM, 45(3), March 2002.
15. *BusinessWeek*, November 22, 1993.
16. *BusinessWeek*, April 24, 1995.
17. *Herald Tribune*, December 20–21, 1997.

3   Creative Accounting, EBITDA, and Core Earnings

1. *BusinessWeek*, July 22, 2002.
2. *The Economist*, June 15, 2002.
3. D.N. Chorafas, *Alternative Investments and the Mismanagement of Risk*, London, Euromoney, 2002.
4. *BusinessWeek*, July 8, 2002.
5. Basel Committee on Banking Supervision, "Public Disclosure by Banks: Results of the 2000 Disclosure Survey," Bank for International Settlements, Basel, May 2002.
6. Frank Partnoy, *FIASCO*, London, Profile Books, 1998.
7. *CommunicationsWeek International*, June 3, 2002.
8. Dimitris N. Chorafas, *Stress Testing. Risk Management Strategies for Extreme Events*, London, Euromoney, 2003.
9. *The Economist*, June 8, 2002.
10. *BusinessWeek*, May 27, 2002.
11. *CommunicationsWeek International*, March 18, 2002.

4   The Misleading of Investors

1. *BusinessWeek*, April 22, 2002.
2. *BusinessWeek*, January 20, 2003.
3. *Fortune*, June 24, 2002.
4. *BusinessWeek*, January 20, 2003.
5. D.N. Chorafas, *Alternative Investments and the Mismanagement of Risk*, London, Palgrave Macmillan, 2003.
6. *BusinessWeek*, October 7, 2002.
7. *BusinessWeek*, February 25, 2002.
8. John Cassidy, *DOT.CON – The Greatest Story Ever Sold*, New York, HarperCollins, 2002.
9. *BusinessWeek*, April 22, 2002.
10. *USA Today*, July 27, 2002.
11. *The Economist*, January 11, 2003.
12. *BusinessWeek*, October 23, 1995.
13. D.N. Chorafas, *Liabilities, Liquidity and Cash Management. Balancing Financial Risk*, New York, Wiley, 2002.
14. *BusinessWeek*, May 20, 2002.

5   Top Management Pay and Options

1. *BusinessWeek*, January 13, 2003.
2. *BusinessWeek*, January 20, 2003.
3. *BusinessWeek*, January 13, 2003.
4. *CommunicationsWeek International*, May 20, 2002.
5. *BusinessWeek*, December 30, 2002.
6. *BusinessWeek*, May 6, 2002.
7. *CommunicationsWeek International*, March 4, 2002.
8. *BusinessWeek*, January 13, 2003.
9. *The Economist*, April 6, 2002.

10. *Daily Telegraph*, April 10, 2002.
11. *Financial Times*, August 1, 2002.
12. *The Economist*, July 20, 2002.
13. Arthur Levitt, Jr., *Take On The Street*, New York, Pantheon Books/London House, 2002.
14. D.N. Chorafas, *Alternative Investments and the Mismanagement of Risk*, London, Palgrave Macmillan, 2003.
15. *Herald Tribune*, May 2, 2002.
16. *Newsweek*, August 5, 2002.
17. *The Economist*, April 6, 2002.
18. *Financial Times*, March 25, 2002.
19. *Le Canard Enchâiné*, Paris, June 2001.
20. *Financial Times*, August 1, 2000.

6 Responsibilities of Certified Public Accountants and of the Board

1. *Financial Times*, February 7, 2002.
2. *The Economist*, January 11, 2003.
3. *CommunicationsWeek International*, April 1, 2002.
4. *International Herald Tribune*, May 2, 2002.
5. *BusinessWeek*, July 29, 2002.
6. *BusinessWeek*, January 13, 2003.
7. D.N. Chorafas, *Implementing and Auditing the Internal Control System*, London, Macmillan, 2001.
8. *BusinessWeek*, February 18, 2002.
9. *BusinessWeek*, September 30, 2002.
10. *BusinessWeek*, May 27, 2002.
11. D.N. Chorafas, *Operational Risk Control*, London and Boston, Butterworth-Heinemann 2003.
12. *The Times* (London), January 24, 1996.
13. *Financial Times*, March 23–24, 1996.
14. D.N. Chorafas, *Membership of the Board of Directors*, London, Macmillan, 1988.
15. D.N. Chorafas, *Modelling the Survival of Financial and Industrial Enterprises. Advantages, Challenges, and Problems with the Internal Rating-Based (IRB) Method*, London, Palgrave Macmillan, 2002.
16. *BusinessWeek*, April 1, 2002.

7 Enron: The End of an Empire

1. *The Economist*, January 11, 2003.
2. D.N. Chorafas, *Managing Risk and the New Economy*, New York, New York Institute of Finance, 2001.
3. D.N. Chorafas, *Alternative Investments and the Mismanagement of Risk*, London, Palgrave Macmillan, 2003.
4. *EIR*, November 9, 2001.
5. *BusinessWeek*, January 21, 2002.
6. *BusinessWeek*, January 13, 2003.
7. D.N. Chorafas, *Managing Risk in the New Economy*, New York, New York Institute of Finance, 2001.

8. Brian Toft, "Financial Risks, Decisions and Behaviour," *Risk Management: An International Journal*, Perpetuity Press, 2001.
9. *The Times*, December 11, 2001.
10. *Financial Times*, December 12, 2001.
11. *BusinessWeek*, February 25, 2002.
12. D.N. Chorafas, *Liabilities, Liquidity and Cash Management. Balancing Financial Risk*, New York, Wiley, 2002.
13. *Financial Times*, February 7, 2002.
14. *Financial Times*, September 26, 2002.

8 Assigning the Blame for Enron Débâcle

1. See D.N. Chorafas, *Managing Derivatives Risk*, Burr Ridge, IL, Irwin Professional Publishing, 1996.
2. See D.N. Chorafas, *Managing Derivatives Risk*, Burr Ridge, IL, Irwin Professional Publishing, 1996.
3. *EIR*, May 24, 2002.
4. D.N. Chorafas, *Alternative Investments and the Mismanagement of Risk*, London, Euromoney, 2002.
5. *BusinessWeek*, July 8, 2002.
6. *Bloomberg Markets*, March 2002.
7. D.N. Chorafas, *Alternative Investments and the Mismanagement of Risk*, London, Euromoney, 2002.
8. *BusinessWeek*, January 13, 2003.
9. *Bloomberg Markets*, March 2002.
10. *Financial Times*, February 7, 2002.
11. D.N. Chorafas, *Outsourcing, Insourcing and IT for Enterprise Management*, London, Palgrave Macmillan, 2003.
12. *BusinessWeek*, January 13, 2003.
13. *NewsWeek*, September 11, 1995.

9 The Bankers of Enron

1. *BusinessWeek*, January 13, 2003.
2. *BusinessWeek*, August 22, 2002.
3. *Daily Telegraph*, April 9, 2002.
4. *Financial Times*, April 29, 2003.
5. *The Economist*, May 3, 2003.
6. Financial Times, April 10, 2002. Henry Blodget, Merrill's high-profile internet analyst who left the broker in 2001 had been bullish on InfoSpace even as the stock started to fall from its peak of $132 in March 2000. In early April 2002, the stock was trading at $1.46.
7. *Observer* (London), April 7, 2002.
8. D.N. Chorafas, *Operational Risk Control*, London and Boston, Butterworth-Heinemann, 2003.
9. *USA Today*, March 6, 2002.
10. *The Economist*, July 27, 2002.
11. *Bloomberg Professional*, December 23, 2002.
12. *BusinessWeek*, January 13, 2003.
13. *BusinessWeek*, April 22, 2002.

14. *BusinessWeek*, September 16, 2002.
15. *BusinessWeek*, September 16, 2002.
16. D.N. Chorafas, *Credit Derivatives and the Management of Risk*, New York, New York Institute of Finance, 2000.
17. *BusinessWeek*, February 25, 2002.
18. *Bloomberg Professional*, December 23, 2002.
19. D.N. Chorafas, *Managing Credit Risk, 1, Analyzing, Rating and Pricing the Probability of Default*, London, Euromoney, 2000 and *Managing Credit Risk, 2, The Lessons of VAR Failures and Imprudent Exposure*, London, Euromoney, 2000.
20. *EIR*, January 18, 2002.
21. *USA Today*, March 7, 2002.

10   Trading and the Risks of Derivatives Exposure

1. Basel Committee on Banking Supervision, "The Relationship Between Banking Supervisors and Banks' External Auditors," Basel, BIS, January 2002.
2. D.N. Chorafas, *Alternative Investments and the Mismanagement of Risk*, London, Euromoney, 2002.
3. *BusinessWeek*, May 27, 2002.
4. *EIR*, December 20, 2002.
5. *BusinessWeek*, April 22, 2002.
6. Freddie Mac faced big problems in 2003 with derivatives, with the result of having fired two presidents in a matter of a few months. In June 2003, the board forced CEO Leland Brendsel and some of his senior executives to retire. Then on Friday August 22, 2003, Freddie Mac announced that it would comply with an order from its regulator and remove CEO Gregory Parseghian and general counsel Maud Mater. Both of these events result from an ongoing accounting investigation by the Office of Federal Housing Enterprise Oversight (OFHEO).
7. *The Economist*, March 2, 2002.
8. *The Economist*, March 2, 2002.
9. *BusinessWeek*, January 20, 2003.
10. *EIR*, December 13, 2002.
11. D.N. Chorafas, *Managing Credit Risk, 2, The Lessons of VAR Failures and Imprudent Exposure*, London, Euromoney, 2000.
12. *BusinessWeek*, October 26, 1992.
13. *BusinessWeek*, February 25, 2002.
14. D.N. Chorafas, *Alternative Investments and the Mismanagement of Risk*, London, Euromoney, 2002.

11   Investors, the Securitization of Bad Loans, and the Probability of Default

1. *Journal of Applied Corporate Finance*, 14(4), Winter 2002, 25.
2. D.N. Chorafas, *Operational Risk Control*, London and Boston, Butterworth-Heinemann, 2003.
3. D.N. Chorafas, *Credit Derivatives and the Management of Risk*, New York, New York Institute of Finance, 2000.
4. *BusinessWeek*, February 25, 2002.
5. *BusinessWeek*, February 18, 2002.

6. *The Economist*, July 27, 2002.
7. D.N. Chorafas, *Alternative Investments and the Mismanagement of Risk*, London, Euromoney, 2002.
8. Dimitris N. Chorafas, *New Regulation of the Financial Industry*, London, Macmillan, 2000.
9. *USA Today*, July 26, 2002.
10. *USA Today*, July 24, 2002.

12 Case Studies of Banks which are Finding the Going Tough

1. *Financial Times*, February 7, 2002.
2. D.N. Chorafas, *Managing Risk in the New Economy*, New York, New York Institute of Finance, 2001.
3. D.N. Chorafas, *Enterprise Architecture and New Generation Information Systems*, Boca Raton, FL, Lucie Press/CRC, 2002.
4. D.N. Chorafas, *Stress Testing. Risk Management Strategies for Extreme Events*, London, Euromoney, 2002.
5. *Financial Times*, February 7, 2002.
6. *Wall Street Journal*, July 27, 2001.
7. *Business Week*, October 29, 2001.
8. D.N. Chorafas, *Reliable Financial Reporting and Internal Control: A Global Implementation Guide*, New York, John Wiley, 2000.
9. D.N. Chorafas, *Alternative Investments and the Mismanagement of Risk*, London, Euromoney, 2002.
10. *Le Canard Enchainé*, Paris, April 23, 2003.
11. *BusinessWeek*, May 20, 2002.
12. D.N. Chorafas, *Enterprise Architecture and New Generation Information Systems*, Boca Raton, FL, St. Lucie Press/CRC, 2002.
13. *Institutional Investor*, August 1999.

Index